Hot Rod
Hundley

HOT ROD HUNDLEY

"You Gotta Love It, Baby"

---

by Rod Hundley
with Tom McEachin

SPORTS PUBLISHING INC.
Champaign, IL 61820

Production Director: Susan M. McKinney
Dustjacket design: Joseph Buck

ISBN: 1-57167-243-5
Library of Congress Catalog Card Number: 98-86643

Sports Publishing Inc.
804 N. Neil
Champaign, IL 61820
www.SportsPublishingInc.com

Printed in the United States.

To my three beautiful daughters,
Kimberly, Jacqueline and Jennifer,
for your love and understanding.

———————————————

Contents

Acknowledgments

For all their help on this project, the authors wish to thank David Allred, Kim Turner, Mark Kelly and the entire Utah Jazz organization, West Virginia University, the Los Angeles Lakers, the Phoenix Suns, Evan Silverman, Jerry West, John Stockton, Karl Malone, Mary Ann Ellis-Cassell, Sheree Josephson, Suzette Thomas, Elaine Ellis, Craig Bolerjack, Steve Brown, Audrey Piper, Kory Hasegawa, Norm Perdue, Don Grayston, Chuck Wing, Susan McKinney, Derek Miller, and especially Mike Pearson for making this happen.

Rod Hundley would like to extend a personal thanks to Pete White, Buddy Quertinmont, Ike Smith, Ed Pastilong, Gale Catlett, Ann Dinardi, Frank Layden, Jerry Sloan, Sam Battistone, Larry H. Miller, Jerry Colangelo, Chick Hearn, Al McCoy, Elgin Baylor, Jim Nantz, Fred Schaus, Brian Douglas, Ron Boone, everyone at KJZZ television and KFNZ radio, and basketball fans across Utah and West Virginia.

Tom McEachin gives a personal thanks to Judith Burns, Jim Wojcik, Kelly Kolhagen, Chris Haft, Carole Leigh Hutton, Randy Hollis, Eric Dieterle, Chris Miller, Ron Matthews, Marilyn Messenger, Suzanne Jenkins, Brian Jones, Jim Stasiowski, and to my family; you've all helped more than you'll ever know.

Introduction

by Tom McEachin

Six hours before Game 1 of the 1998 NBA Finals tipped off, I was speaking about sportswriting to a journalism class at Weber State University in Ogden, Utah. The Utah Jazz were the hot topic of conversation that day, but there also was a great deal of interest both in this book and in Hot Rod Hundley. When asked to share my favorite story about the Jazz broadcaster, it was hard to come up with just one. There was the prank on Howard Cosell to consider, anecdotes about colorful characters like "Baby Ray" Felix, and the yarns about working for Jack Kent Cooke. (Former employees would say, "I refuse to work for a man who talks to me that way." What did he say? "You're fired.") You can't narrow it to just one story.

When someone in the classroom asked what surprised me the most about Hot Rod, though, that was an easy one to answer. I was surprised by how smart he is.

As the words rolled off my tongue, that struck me as something of a back-handed compliment, that I was surprised the guy was intelligent. I was being sincere, though. For the past seven years I've sat behind Hot Rod at every Jazz game played in the Delta Center, watching the games unfold through my eyes while sometimes eavesdropping as he described the games through his. His insights, the enthusiasm he brings to the game and the personable wit he shares with his audience were obvious. But after spending countless hours with him at his dining room table, I developed a much deeper appreciation for what a true craftsman he is.

Rodney Clark Hundley is a natural both in front of a camera and behind a microphone, displaying the same flair and showmanship as a broadcaster that he displayed as a basketball player at West Virginia University, where he earned the nickname "Hot Rod." But when he broke into broadcasting he was smart enough to know you don't just grab a microphone and start talking. He put in the work to learn the craft, just like he put in the work to be a basketball player. Hot Rod has studied the game ever since junior high school in Charleston, West Virginia.

vii

He went on to reach All-America status in both high school and college, and he earned several national awards as a broadcaster as well.

That's quite a feat, really, to excel in two different fields. In fact, he is the only radio play-by-play man in the entire NBA who actually played the game. And he was an All-Star player at that.

There's depth to the knowledge he brings to his broadcasts. Hot Rod doesn't simply know the history of the NBA, he lived it. And when it comes to the Utah Jazz, he is a walking encyclopedia, a courtside witness to both the birth and the rise of the franchise. Ask him about any player in NBA history—Oscar Robertson, say, and Hot Rod can tell you how the guy could put three different arcs on his jump shot, flat, medium and high, depending on the shot needed to get past the defense. And then Hot Rod will tell you a funny story about the first time he had to guard Oscar. And then he will tell you about the only weakness to Oscar's game (he was too harsh on his teammates).

Ask him about any player in Jazz history—Adrian Dantley, say, and Hot Rod can tell you Dantley was great in the low post because instead of stepping away from defenders like most people tended to do, Adrian leaned into them to clear out room. And then he will tell you a funny story about the way Dantley ran the fast break. And then he will tell you ...

Well, you get the picture. There's no doubt in my mind that with his knowledge of the game, Hot Rod could have made a very good NBA coach. That's a path he came close to choosing once. A few years after retiring as a player for the Los Angeles Lakers, he came to a fork in the road. There was a coaching career in one direction and a broadcasting career in the other. He chose broadcasting and never looked back. Ask him why and he gives you an intelligent answer: "Coaches get fired," he says. "Broadcasters don't."

He showed that same savvy as a player, like the time WVU coach Fred Schaus sent him into a game but didn't tell him who to replace. When Hot Rod got to the scorer's table to check in, he asked who the leading scorer was. "You are, with 28 points," he was told. Then he asked who was next and was told Clayce Kishbaugh had 27 points.

"Then I'm in for Kishbaugh," he said.

Hot Rod has always been a student of the game yet he wasn't always a great student. It wasn't that school work was too difficult, he just never had the patience to sit in a classroom. He was too restless and much more interested in reading basketball books than textbooks. When he left WVU in 1957, he was 23 credits short of his degree, and that was something he has always regretted. That's why last summer, at age 63, Hot Rod returned to Morgantown to begin the work needed to graduate.

"It's dumb to go to college for four years and not get a degree," he says today, 41 years after withdrawing from school without one. He put his three daughters through college but until now, he never had a college diploma himself. It's something he believes is worth having, something worth doing whatever it takes to get. He realizes it's never too late. And that's a message he'd like to share with every college athlete who ever left school without a degree.

See, I told you this guy is smart.

Chapter One

CHASING THE RING

I t was Game 7 of the NBA Finals. Tie score. Five seconds left. I had a Lakers jersey on my back and the basketball in my hands, living the dream of every kid who has ever played the game. I had an open look at the basket from about 20 feet away with the game, and the championship, on the line. There was an uneasy hush over the crowd as I studied my move. Two points and we beat the Boston Celtics. Two points to win the NBA title. What kid hasn't played out a fantasy like that? I did it many times myself growing up on the playgrounds of West Virginia, but this time it was real. I had one shot at glory. One shot at a championship ring.

And I passed it up.

It was 1962 and I was standing on the parquet floor of Boston Garden in Game 7 of the world championship series, as the Finals were called then. It was a moment to last a lifetime. I thought about shooting, about trying to be the hero, but Frank Selvy, my team-mate, was wide open from 10 feet away. I had to give him the ball.

I've been chasing a championship ring ever since.

I made it to the NBA Finals seven times in my career as a player and team broadcaster, and I lost every time. In six seasons playing for the Minneapolis and Los Angeles Lakers, from 1957 to 1963, we reached the Finals three times. And the Celtics sent us home all three times. The Lakers made the Finals twice more in the late '60s when I was Chick Hearn's color analyst, and Boston beat them both times then, too. After that, it was a long wait before I made it back with the Utah Jazz in 1997 and 1998. I worked a few championship series for CBS along the way but that wasn't the same. With the networks you're on the outside looking in. You're not really a part of it unless you're a part of a team like I was with the Lakers and the Jazz. I spent five seasons broadcasting for the Phoenix Suns when they were a young franchise and not really legitimate contenders, and I spent five years with the New Orleans Jazz when they were an expansion team. The Jazz got better when they moved to Utah, but it took 18 more years before they finally arrived in 1997.

There was so much talk then of winning a ring for Karl Malone and John Stockton, but I wanted one too. I've been affiliated with NBA teams for 37 years and I've been chasing the ring the whole time. The Jazz fell short, their trip to the Finals. When they made it back in 1998, it was the year I thought Karl, John, and I would win our rings together. For the first time they seemed to really believe they were going to beat the Chicago Bulls. Everything seemed to be going their way. While they waited for the Chicago-Indiana winner to see who they would meet in the Finals, I think privately they were cheering for Chicago. Even though the Bulls were the most dominating team of the decade and they were led by a guy named Michael Jordan, I think they wanted a rematch. Their attitude was, let's beat the best to win it and if we get beat, then we got beat by the best.

It was quite an accomplishment, really, just to get back to the Finals. After coming off the great season we had in 1997, winning 64 games to set a franchise record, I never dreamed we could repeat a record like that even if everyone was healthy. Then John Stockton went down with a knee injury before the season even started. He was 35 years old when he had surgery and he came back as only he could because his work ethic is so unbelievable. They predicted he would be out eight to 12 weeks at the minimum, maybe longer. He was back on the court eight weeks to the day after the operation. He worked out twice a day to rehabilitate the knee but he was working to get himself in game shape, too, so the day he was cleared medically to play, he was ready to go. For a lot of players, once their injury heals it still takes several weeks for them to get back in shape, but not John. He ended up missing just 18 games, coming back a lot quicker than anyone thought. And he hasn't missed a game since.

The team struggled early in the year with Stockton out of the lineup but his injury was only part of it. Howard Eisley did a nice job stepping up at point guard and Jacque Vaughn, a rookie, gave them some minutes, too. But forward Bryon Russell struggled early on and center Greg Ostertag struggled all year. We played the Lakers the first game of the season and at shoot-around that morning, Shaquille O'Neal, L.A.'s 325-pound center, confronted Ostertag and slapped him to the floor. O'Neal was bent out of shape over some harmless comments Ostertag made at the end of the previous season and had been stewing about them all summer. It wasn't much of an incident, but it surprised Greg. He just sat on the floor and never retaliated, and I wonder if he didn't carry that with him into the season. After six games he and Russell were both taken out of the starting lineup. Along with Stockton's injury, that was three starters who weren't giving the Jazz what they got the year before. Still, the Jazz were a respectable 11-7 when John returned on December 8, and they ended up winning 62 games, just two off their record pace of a year earlier.

In addition to injuries and other distractions, the competition the Jazz faced was a lot tougher too. The Lakers had a nice team when everybody was happy and getting along. Shaq O'Neal and Eddie Jones were both coming into their own, and Kobe Bryant was much more seasoned. The Seattle SuperSonics traded away Shawn Kemp but they might have been better without him. They got Vin Baker in return and he made them a better team because he was a more versatile player. There was more togetherness, too. There was no dissension there and they seem to be a happier team. It was amazing George Karl got fired at the end of the season because he did a nice job coaching them. The Lakers and Sonics were at the top, challenging the Jazz to the wire in the Western Conference, but there were a lot of other tough teams, too.

San Antonio had David Robinson healthy after missing most of the previous season, and they had Tim Duncan who would win Rookie of the Year. Houston was aging, but with three future Hall of Famers, they were still dangerous. Minnesota was a talented young team that had more experience and confidence. For the first time in franchise history they were going into games thinking they could beat you. Same with Phoenix, because they could cause so many matchup problems for you. And Portland knew they could beat the Jazz because they won three straight in the regular season. They rebound well and big teams gave the Jazz a lot of trouble.

That's where the importance of Ostertag comes in. We're a small team and if he could ever get it in gear he could be the answer. At 7-foot-2 he could really make a difference on this team. He never really got going all season, though, and that's why the Jazz tried to make the deal for Rony Seikaly in February. They actually did make the trade, sending Greg Foster and Chris Morris to Orlando for him, but Seikaly never showed up, so the Jazz had to cancel the trade.

I think Seikaly might have helped this team because he is so skilled offensively, but it's hard to say if he ever would have fit in. He gets a bad rap and it's probably justified. First he said he had a stress fracture and would be out eight weeks. Then he ended up getting traded to New Jersey and they said it was a bone bruise and he'd miss four weeks. He said he wanted his contract extended, but he also said he wanted to be a free agent at the end of the season. Who knows what happened? But even if he only came in for the end of the season, then said, "Thank you for the world championship, bye," and left, I don't think anyone would have minded.

I like Rony personally. He's a wonderful person away from the game, but he's very temperamental on the court. He's a hard guy to coach and he can disrupt a team. His ego enters the picture because he would have had to accept a secondary role to Stockton and Malone. And there's the question of his work ethic and whether he would have fit in that way. He can shoot, though, and that's where he would have helped us. Teams have to guard him. We could have either put him inside and let Karl go outside, or put him outside and make the defense go out there to guard him, opening things up inside for Karl. We'll never know, of course, but you don't simply add Seikaly to the equation, you subtract what Morris and Foster did for you. They both had huge contributions at times, both late in the regular season and in the playoffs. So I don't know if there would have been a net gain. I find it hard to believe, though, that Seikaly would have gotten us any farther than Game 6 of the NBA Finals against the Chicago Bulls. Maybe it was for the best the trade fell through.

It was right about the time Foster and Morris rejoined the team after spending 48 hours in Orlando that the Jazz took off. Both players were stung by the trade but their teammates rallied around them. They closed out the month of February strong and for the second year in a row they had a phenomenal March. Twelve of the games that month were on the road but they still went 15-2. That set them up for a late run, and they came out of nowhere at the end to catch Seattle, the Lakers and Chicago for the best record in the league. All three of those teams faltered at the end and we got the home court advantage all the way through the playoffs, something we never had before. With a week or 10 days left in the season it looked like we could drop all the way to fourth in the playoff race, but we ended up with the top seed. Everybody else faded a little bit and we just kept on winning our games. The Lakers really went in the tank down the stretch and so did Seattle. So all of the sudden we were in the best position of our 24-year history, the No. 1 seed throughout the playoffs.

Even with the top seed, the road to the Finals was a lot tougher than it was the year before. There was no dodging anybody this time. Instead of getting a first-round opponent like the Los Angeles Clippers, who were 10 games below .500 in 1997, we got the Houston Rockets right off the bat in 1998, and that was the scariest ride of all. We lost the very first game of the series at home and I thought that was the beginning of the end for us. The Jazz and the Bulls are the two best teams in the league at defending their home court, so when we lost the very first game of the playoffs at the Delta Center, I feared it was an omen for us.

We didn't protect our court and it haunted us all the way through the postseason. We rolled into the playoffs feeling good about ourselves and right off the bat we lost at home. Before you know it, we were down two games to one in the series. And the first round is a short series. Because it's only best-of-five while all the others are best-of-seven, you don't have much room for error. So we were in trouble. They even had us down big in Game 4 before we came back to win that game and tie the series.

I think we were a little overconfident as the No. 1 team playing the No. 8 team, but I was always scared of Houston. I know the coaches were, too. The Rockets were the greatest No. 8 seed of all time. They had Charles Barkley, Hakeem Olajuwon and Clyde Drexler, three Hall of Famers, and they were seeded last. I knew we'd have to play like hell to beat them. We finished them off in Game 5 at home, but we showed we were vulnerable at the Delta Center.

In the second round we beat San Antonio twice at home to open the series, but we could have easily lost both of those. Both times, San Antonio had a wide open shot at the buzzer to win the game. It was just a lucky bounce that saved us in both of those games.

Then we went to San Antonio and got smoked in Game 3. We were still up 2-1, but with a couple of lucky bounces for the Spurs, we could have been down 0-3 and on the verge of elimination. Then what? I've always said you need three things to win a championship: You have to be talented, you have to be healthy and you have to be lucky. No doubt we were talented enough to beat San Antonio, but we breezed through that series, four games to one, only because we were lucky, too. That series easily could have been a dogfight to the end.

Once we reached the NBA Finals, Chicago beat us two out of the three games they played at the Delta Center to win it. Counting the regular season, we won two of the four games we played at Chicago, but the Bulls won two out of the four games they played at the Delta Center.

The only series the Jazz dominated at home was the Lakers in the Western Conference finals, and I think the Jazz surprised everybody by sweeping them 4-0. Before the whole thing started, I thought the Lakers might win it all. I thought they were the best team in the NBA, at least the team with the most talent. I was amazed at how easily they took Seattle in their second-round series. L.A. lost the first game but won the next four to take the series 4-1.

The way we were playing, I was afraid they might come in here and get one, and it might be over. But then I saw them play. They were so disorganized it was unbelievable. They have an amazing amount of talent but no idea how to harness it. They just played wild. That's got to be the toughest team to coach in the NBA because you had Kobe Bryant, Shaquille O'Neal, Eddie Jones and a temperamental Nick Van Exel. All four of those guys made the All-Star team in 1998, but they're not disciplined. They're the most talented team in the NBA without question, and we blew them out by 35 points in Game 1. I think that woke up a lot of people.

After we beat them again at home in Game 2 for a 2-0 lead in the series, a reporter from the *Los Angeles Times* asked me what I thought about the Lakers. I said they had no leadership, they were out of control and they had too much emphasis on the Hollywood stuff trying to outdo one another. I played the game and I had been a broadcaster in the NBA for 31 years, so I knew what I was talking about. I told the reporter it didn't look like Del Harris had any control but that I wasn't pointing the finger at him because I didn't think anybody could control that team. I have a lot of respect for Del. I consider him a friend and I think he did as good a job with that group of players as anyone could. I was upset when the paper only printed the first part of my comments. They wrote that I didn't think Del Harris had control of the team but left out the most important part, that I didn't think anyone could coach them. It came across like I was taking a shot at Del and I wasn't. I was taking a shot at the players and the lack of leadership from guys like Shaquille O'Neal.

After the *L.A. Times* article, ESPN interviewed me and did the same thing, only running a part of my comments and making it look like I was critical of Del when my point was that no one could coach this group. It was interesting that Rick Fox of the Lakers admitted I had a valid point, because I had earlier said he was the only player on the team who seemed to know how to play the game.

I will say that Shaq showed me a lot in that series. He finally impressed me as a great center. He's a man-mountain and he really improved into a great player. But when you get ahead of the Lakers that's when they really get wild, and there's not much Shaq can do for them. When they get behind by 10 or 15 points they start firing away from the 3-point line. They try to get the lead back in a minute and just dig themselves a deeper hole.

The Jazz are a lot smarter, usually, and they play with patience. They know they don't have to get it back all at once and they start pecking away at you, two points here, two points there, and they're as much into making defensive stops as they are into scoring points. They don't try to cut the lead all down in one minute, they do it gradually. They don't panic and they stay in the game. When the Lakers fell behind in this series, though, they just played into our hands. They kept taking quick shots and they wanted to be spectacular in everything they did. No doubt they're loaded with talent. They have youth and athleticism on their side, plus Shaquille O'Neal in the middle, but in two years we beat them in eight out of the nine games we played them in the playoffs.

Kobe Bryant might be the greatest talent in the league after Michael Jordan, but he has a lot to learn about basketball. Jordan is a great showman, but his first priority is to make the play. He can do spectacular stuff that dazzles the crowd, but he doesn't feel he has to be spectacular every time he touches the ball. Everything doesn't have to be a show biz move. He's one of the most fundamentally sound players in the game and he knows when it's show time and when it's work time.

Kobe tries to put on a show every time he has the ball and it hurts him and it hurts his team. But he's young. The two years he played the Jazz in the playoffs would have been his freshman and sophomore years in college. If he keeps working and is willing to learn, he could develop into something special. He has yet to prove it, but he certainly has an unbelievable talent. It's frightening to think how good he could be.

I chatted privately with Karl Malone after Game 4 of the Lakers series and told him how amazing it was to beat them four straight after they beat Seattle four straight. "Yeah," Karl said, "but they lost a game to Seattle. We didn't lose one." He was proud of the sweep and rightfully so. You knock off a team with the best personnel in the NBA, and you do it in a sweep, he had a good point. But by getting the sweep, it ended up working against them. They were on top of their game in that series, playing the best basketball they had played all season. They were dominant again at home and equally tough on the road.

But now they had to wait around for the Bulls, who needed seven games to get past Indiana in the East, and it would be 10 days before the Jazz would play again. That's an extremely long time to try to stay sharp. They tried playing simulated games in practice, even bringing in referees and their regular stat crew to work the scrimmages, but there was only so much they could do. It ended up hurting them when the Finals finally started.

It's ironic that of all the games I thought we might lose, Game 1 was the one that worried me most because of the long layoff. And that's the one we won. Before that game I was talking to Chicago's Steve Kerr out on the court and he mentioned the nine-day layoff the Bulls had before the Finals two years earlier. He said it was really tough on them that year.

People don't understand how different that is for a player. From the first day of the preseason to the last game of the playoffs, you play constantly, at least twice a week but usually three or four and sometimes five times in a week. You get so accustomed to that pace, week in and week out, year in and year out, and now you've got nine or 10 days off. That's unheard of. You never have a stretch like that, ever in your career as a professional player. But we won that game—then lost the next three. I thought it would hurt us in Game 1, but maybe it hurt us in the second game instead. It's hard to say because it's so different. We weathered the storm but then we had to come right back and play again with just one day off.

The other problem was that the Jazz were absolutely on top of their game in the Lakers series, helping out on defense and making the extra pass on offense. If they could have gone straight into the Chicago series and continued playing that way, who knows what the outcome might have been.

As much as the layoff hurt us, I still felt our experience would make a difference. I always thought if we could get back to the Finals we would win, I didn't care if we played the Bulls or whoever. This team now had a better idea of what they were in for having been to the Finals once before. The jitters weren't there. I thought this team would be ready to go and could win it. I think a team like the Jazz, the first time there they got caught up in the ballyhoo. Everybody in the world was watching it. There's press from everywhere, the games get broadcast in different languages. You can't even move. There's no room for spectators because it seems like everybody there has a press pass on their chest. Every writer in the world is there and every celebrity is there too.

As worried as I was about that first game, when they ended up winning it in overtime I thought that was it. Even after they lost Game 2 at home, I was confident they could win the series because they proved they could compete with the Bulls. They were evenly matched. Both teams had two superstars, including a dominating player the other team can't stop, and neither team had a dominating center.

The Bulls had no answer for Karl Malone, but while the Jazz knew they weren't going to stop Michael Jordan, I liked the way they could throw Bryon Russell, Shandon Anderson and Jeff Hornacek at him. Bryon and Shandon were both strong enough and quick enough to make him work, and Jeff is a very smart defender who plays great position defense. He stays between his man and the basket better than anyone on the team. If they could make Jordan work enough, I liked our chances in the series.

The Bulls didn't have anyone who could guard Karl. He had a couple of bad games to start the series, but once he got rolling, he proved the Bulls couldn't defend him. Another reason I thought we were going to win was because Brian Williams no longer was with the Bulls. He hurt us the year before, absolutely an unsung hero. I thought that would help us.

Before the series started, Hornacek got good news and bad news from the coaching staff. The good news was that he wasn't going to have to guard Michael Jordan. The bad news was that he drew Scottie Pippen instead. Pippen is a superstar too, another one of the greatest players of all time, and he is so much bigger and stronger than Hornacek. Jordan has to be the most difficult player in the league to defend, but getting Pippen instead is no real break.

I don't know how Jeff went to sleep at night before those games. Jeff did a great job on Pippen and when he wasn't on him, he was on Jordan. He certainly did as well as you could expect, but it wore him down. He had to overextend himself on defense and that affected his offense. Jeff shot just 41 percent for the series and I think all the work he had to put in on defense was a big reason why. Chicago's defense was a factor too. Pippen and Jordan aren't just great offensive players, they're great defenders too. And they're interchangeable. That's tough on anybody. They're both taller than Jeff and they kept in front of him. He didn't get many of those bar-of-soap slip shots driving into the lane in the series because the Bulls did a good job of not letting him get to the basket.

With the series tied 1-1, we shifted to Chicago for the next three games, and the first one there was an absolute disaster. The Jazz got beat 96-54 and the 54 points they scored was the worst of any game in NBA history, playoff or otherwise, since they brought in the shot clock in 1954. The Jazz did a nice job of keeping their composure and their confidence in Game 4 after that horrible loss, but they still lost 86-82 to give the Bulls a 3-1 lead in the series. Up until then Malone hadn't been a huge factor, but that all changed in Game 5.

With their backs to the wall, he proved to be a true superstar in that game, playing what was perhaps his greatest game ever, given what was at stake. It was Karl Malone at his best, scoring 39 points to make sure the series came back to Utah. He was dominating inside as well as outside, and no one the Bulls threw at him could slow him down. The Bulls and their fans were sure they were going to be celebrating a championship that night, but Karl spoiled their party.

Antoine Carr came up huge in that game too, scoring 12 points in the second half, including eight in the fourth quarter. He hit some clutch jump shots down the stretch and sank a couple of crucial free throws with 10 seconds left to preserve the victory. He had four big rebounds in that game too. He also played well in the last game. Looking back, we probably should have gone more to him because Scottie Pippen was on him and Pippen had a bad back.

That was something the Jazz probably could have exploited more. They should have made Pippen work more on defense and when he was on offense they should have gotten up on him more because he couldn't turn on you with the back.

So much of this game comes down to lucky bounces, especially when two teams are so evenly matched. In Game 2, Steve Kerr missed a 3-pointer late in the game but the rebound bounced over Malone and into Kerr's hands. He's the worst rebounder on the Bulls' team but the ball bounced his way. He's 6-foot-2 and can't jump, but he got his own rebound and passed the ball to Jordan who got a three-point play out of it. He got the layup and Hornacek fouled him, and that was the game. The Jazz beat the Bulls both times they faced them in the regular season, but Kerr didn't play in either game.That maybe was overlooked. Kerr gets overlooked most of the time anyway, but this game he made the play that won the game for them, so he did his part.

It wasn't until Game 5 that the Jazz finally got one to bounce their way. The turning point in that game came when Bryon Russell went up for a dunk in the fourth quarter and the ball hit off the rim and bounced high in the air—then dropped in. That gave us an eight-point lead with nine minutes to go. Considering we never led by more than eight points at any time in the series, that play was huge, and we went on to win the game by two points to send the series back to Utah for Game 6.We still trailed 3-2 in the series, but once I saw the ball bounce our way, that was when I thought the series had turned in our favor. I thought we were going to win the whole thing.

At the United Center there's a ramp that the team bus drives down where they actually drive all the way inside the building. Then after the game there's usually several hundred fans lining the top of the ramp to taunt the team as the bus pulls out. After the first two games in Chicago they might have been in the thousands at the end of the ramp, just yelling and screaming at the Jazz.After we won in Game 5, though, John Stockton yells out on the bus, "I don't see too many people out here tonight." That just broke up everybody on the bus. It was a perfect line because it relaxed everyone a bit, but then that was it. Everybody had a good laugh but it didn't turn into any sort of party on the bus because everyone knew there was still a lot more to accomplish. No one lost focus, but it was a nice moment to know they weren't going to let Chicago celebrate that night.

All season long coach Jerry Sloan kept trying to find the right combination at center. He juggled Greg Ostertag, Greg Foster and Antoine Carr continually, with all three of them getting starts at one time or another. By the end of the season Foster was the starter, and he was in the lineup all through the playoffs until Game 3 of the Bulls series. Ostertag got the start that game and got nine rebounds, but he only made one shot in seven tries.

The next game, Sloan decided not to use a center at all, going with three forwards instead by moving Adam Keefe into the starting lineup, and Adam started the final two games. In a sense that's strange to make that many changes that deep into the playoffs but on the other hand, you're playing for a world championship and you're gambling, trying to find a combination that will work. What we had been doing wasn't working, so Sloan looked somewhere else. That took courage and it was the right thing to do. It doesn't really make much difference who starts because you can quickly change things up if you need to. That worked in the second half of Game 5 when Carr, who had played just three minutes in the first half, started the second half and was spectacular.

For the most part, their best lineup all season was small and that's the way it played out in the last game of the year. When the Jazz came home for Game 6, hoping to force a Game 7, Greg Foster only played three minutes and Ostertag didn't play at all. Part of that was because Antoine played so well in the final two games. Sloan either went with a small lineup with Malone at center, or he went with Carr, and that meant Ostertag sat. I think Jerry made the right decision by not playing Ostertag. He hadn't done a thing to merit time to play.

In the end, though, it simply wasn't to be. We won some battles but lost the war. We outscored the Bulls in each of the first three quarters of Game 6, but they outscored us 26-20 in the fourth quarter to win the game by a point—and win the series four games to two. In the two years of playing the Bulls in the Finals, there were 12 games and the Jazz could have won 10 of them. Chicago soundly beat them twice, but the other 10 games were up for grabs in the last minute or two. The Jazz won four of them, losing six times in games they could have and probably should have won. The Bulls just outfoxed us the last two minutes in those close games.

Of course, 90 percent of that is Michael Jordan. He just will not lose. That's when he wants to play, with the game on the line. More than anybody I've ever seen, he wanted the ball and willed his team to victory, just like Larry Bird used to do for the Boston Celtics. Every time it's Jordan who steps up. A year earlier, Jordan stuck the basket at the buzzer to win Game 1, then in Game 6 the Jazz double-teamed him so he passed off to Steve Kerr who hit the clincher. Then in 1998, we had the ball and a one-point lead in Game 2 with 45 seconds to go and lost. In Game 4 at Chicago it was a one-point game in the last two minutes and they killed us down the stretch to win, 86-82. And in Game 6 at Salt Lake City, we led by three with 41 seconds to go and lost. It was Jordan all over again, scoring the last two baskets and getting a steal.

What amazed me most about that Game 6 loss was that we were up by three with 41.9 seconds left and we let Jordan go right in for a layup. He used less than five seconds off the clock to get the basket that cut it to one. We had to put up more of a fight because there were still 37 seconds left and no matter what we did, they were going to get the ball back.

It looked like the sort of play you make if you're up by three with only five seconds left. Then you go ahead and give up the layup because you don't want to foul and give him the three-point play. But we did that with 41 seconds left and that was way too much time on the clock to give up such an easy layup. We just backed off and gave him two points. You shouldn't back off in that situation.

If we could have made him work harder and run even 13 more seconds off the clock, then even if he got the basket there would have been only 24 seconds left. That would have meant Chicago had to intentionally foul or the Jazz would have run out the clock. Then all we had to do is make free throws down the stretch and we would have won. The whole complexion would have changed. But with so much time left, we were in a hole even though we had a one-point lead. We put ourselves in a position where we had to score even though we had a lead, because the clock was in Chicago's favor. If we didn't score, they had a shot to win it, and that's exactly what happened.

In the last two minutes, we always go down the left side of the court with Stockton and Malone. After Hornacek set a screen for Karl along the baseline, Horny cut to the other side. Jordan followed Hornacek for a step or two, then doubled back and snuck up behind Karl and knocked the ball free. It was like Jordan had that move in mind the whole series and saved it for an opportune moment, and he picked that baby off.

Then the Bulls had the ball with about 19 seconds left and a shot to win it. With about seven seconds left, Jordan went to work at the top of the key, making his move on Russell. Jordan gave him such a head-and-shoulder fake he got Bryon off balance, then Jordan gave him a little shove to clear out room and Bryon slipped down. Now Jordan had a wide open jumper from 17 feet out to give the Bulls an 87-86 lead with 5.2 seconds left. We still had the ball with enough time to get a good shot, but we ended up trying a 3-pointer, even though we were only down by one. We couldn't get it inside for a two-point shot. Stockton missed, and the series was over.

Jordan made three great plays in the final 41 seconds to win the game and he got away with fouls on two of them. After he slapped the ball out of Karl's hands, the ball was loose on the floor. Karl had stepped over Jordan to get the ball back but Jordan grabbed Karl's wrist to keep him from getting the ball and Jordan picked it up himself. Then as Jordan went up for the game-winning shot, he gave Russell enough of a shove when he was off-balance to clear out room to shoot. Those sort of plays go on all the time on both sides and rarely get called. If you want to point to the officiating, what really killed the Jazz was Howard Eisley's 3-pointer in the second quarter that was waived off by referee Dick Bavetta.

Howard knew the shot clock was winding down when he got the ball so he turned and fired a long 3-pointer that went in. He launched it in plenty of time to beat the shot clock, but Bavetta waived it off anyway. Bavetta told Howard the ball was still on his fingertips when the clock expired, but replays showed the ball had gone a good 20 feet before the clock went off. It was unbelievable, just a terrible call that took three points off the scoreboard. It was bad enough that Bavetta blew it, but why didn't the other two refs catch such an obvious mistake and overrule it?

The Jazz looked like they had something going at the time and they should have been up by seven points, which would have been their biggest lead of the game. Who knows what might have happened if they had counted the shot. Maybe the Jazz would have pulled away and it wouldn't have come down to those plays by Jordan in the final seconds. That was a heartbreaker.

Personally, I don't like three-person refereeing crews and never have. A lot of times when something happens all three of them are looking at each other. There are a lot of no-calls because one of the refs will see something but he thinks the other two refs will make the call, so no one does anything. They know all three refs can see the same play usually, so a lot of times they wait for one of the other guys to call something. When there were only two refs, they worked their tails off. They hustled to get down the floor and get in position, and if they saw something they called it. There was no waiting for someone else to do it. If there's a no-call with just two referees, the players appreciate the fact the refs probably didn't see it. But when there's a no-call with three refs, the players know they saw it and it aggravates them that the whistle never blew.

A lot of the bickering that goes on out there is because with just 10 players on the court and three officials, how can they miss something? To me there's no excuse when there's three referees and everyone in the building except those three knows what happened. Something's wrong here. It's strange that they let that shot clock call go without even talking about it.

Then the officials made another mistake late in the fourth quarter when they counted Ron Harper's two-pointer even though it came after the shot clock expired. Those five points are huge in a game you lose by one, but it wasn't to be. You can look back and point fingers right and left, but even if the Jazz won that Game 6, they still would have had to beat the Bulls in Game 7. That was the championship game for Chicago but not for us. We still would have had to get them again to win the series.

It was another great year for the Jazz, but once again it ended with a tear in my eye. The fans were wonderful and Michael Jordan even recognized them in his acceptance speech when he was given the Finals MVP award. He mentioned how desperately the Bulls wanted to win in five games so they wouldn't have to come back to Utah. He knew what the fans mean to the Jazz and how hard it is to come into the Delta Center as an opposing player. He also said of his six titles this was the toughest to win and I believe it. Throw out Chicago's 42-point victory, and the other five games were all decided by five points or less. Neither team reached 100 points in the series, so this was really hard-fought, intense play where everyone was just banging away. In my eyes, the Jazz are the greatest team in NBA history not to win a title. And who knows, maybe they have another run left in them.

The big question now is how long Malone and Stockton and Hornacek will play and be effective. John has sure taken a pounding over the years. He is 36, he's played 14 years, he's played hurt and he never quits. It has to all add up against him. He's still one of the better guards, but you can notice he's not the same player he once was. Karl can still go strong because of his body and his size. He takes the same pounding John does, but his body can hold up better. No one's going to embarrass Karl any time soon, but John could start feeling the sting of some of these younger guys.

It would be a sad day to see either one of them step down. What a run they've had. They've got everything in the world. John is the NBA's all-time leader in both assists and steals, and Karl has a Most Valuable Player trophy. They both have All-Star appearances and All-NBA honors, All-Star game MVPs and two Olympic gold medals apiece, everything in the NBA—except championship rings, which is probably the most cherished of all of them if they could get them. That's sad. Two of the greatest players of all time, on their way to the Hall of Fame, to never have the title. This was their best opportunity because of the home court advantage all the way.

Elgin Baylor, one of the greatest players in the history of the game, appeared in 134 NBA playoff games but never won a championship. That was the most in NBA history until Stockton and Malone both passed him in the 1998 playoffs. John has now played in 147 playoff games without winning a ring and Karl has played in 137.

To some, a true superstar career can't be complete without a championship. You have to win a ring in the eyes of some to validate everything else you've accomplished in your career. That's a tenuous and misguided philosophy. Jud Buechler won three championship rings in Chicago. Does that make him a better forward than Elgin Baylor? Sometimes your fate rests in the hands of someone else. If Frank Selvy would have made that shot at Boston Garden in 1962, Elgin Baylor would have had his ring. If I would have taken that shot and made it, Elgin would have had his ring. But it wasn't up to him. He never got the ball.

Chapter Two

ONE SHOT AT GLORY

My professional basketball career never turned out the way I thought it would, but I did have one shot at glory, one chance to make it all mean something. Bill Russell played 13 seasons for the Boston Celtics and won 11 championships. That didn't leave much for the rest of us. From 1957 through 1969, the only teams able to break through were the St. Louis Hawks and Philadelphia 76ers. The Los Angeles Lakers came close, though. In 1962 we won the Western Division by 11 games to earn a bye in the first round of the playoffs. We knocked off Detroit in the second round, four games to two, and that put us in the Finals against the Celtics. We jumped out to a 2-1 lead but Boston tied it 2-2. That's when Elgin Baylor broke out with 61 points, which still stands as the greatest scoring performance in NBA Finals history. Elgin averaged more than 40 points a game in the series and scored at least 30 in all seven games. Both of those marks stand today as records for a seven-game Finals, and that performance in Game 5 put us up 3-2 in the series. Boston beat us pretty good on our home floor in Game 6 to set up the showdown in Boston two days later, a deciding Game 7 with the world championship on the line.

It was a madhouse at the Boston Garden that day and a close game all the way to the wire. The score was tied 100-100 with five seconds to play and we had the ball out of bounds with one shot to win it all. We called a timeout and Fred Schaus, our coach, called my name. I hardly played at all in the series and I was cold and tight from sitting on the bench most of the game. But Schaus put me on the court for the biggest play of my basketball life. I had only played three minutes the entire game and hadn't scored a point. Man, was I scared to death, but this is what it's all about. Some people live a lifetime dreaming of a chance like this. I took a deep breath, put a smile on my face and nodded to my teammates.

We huddled up and Schaus diagramed the play. Jerry West and Elgin Baylor were our best shooters but Schaus didn't want to go straight to them. Boston expected that and would be all over them. I was the best passer on the team so I was to get the inbound pass, then look for the open man off screens. Two other guards came onto the court with me, along with two forwards. The guards, West and Frank Selvy, would break from the wings and cut to the basket while the forwards, Baylor and Rudy LaRusso, set screens for them. It was like running a fast break from half court.

The buzzer blew. The huddle broke and my heart was pounding as I stepped onto the parquet floor. The crowd, in a frenzy the whole game, was suddenly hushed to sweat out the last five seconds. I walked under our basket and scouted out the court. Frank Ramsey was on me, K.C. Jones was on West, Bill Russell took Baylor, Tom Sanders was on LaRusso and Bob Cousy was on Selvy, who was the inbound man. The ref handed Selvy the ball on the sidelines and I broke out to the top of the key. I took the pass from Selvy, spun and took a quick read of the court. My mind was racing as fast as my heart was. Everything was a blur of moving bodies, yet it seemed like it was happening in slow motion.

I knew where the ball needed to go. Jerry West was the greatest clutch shooter in the history of the game and I looked there first on the right side. K.C. Jones was smothering him. There was no way I could get him the ball. What's my next move? A hundred thoughts poured through my head in an instant. I thought about shooting myself. One shot, hero or goat. Every kid's dream. I was looking right down the barrel from the top of the circle, about 20 feet out. It was a straight-away shot, maybe a little out of my range, but it was my shot, the one I loved to take. Sometimes I look back and think I was meant to take that shot, that I could have made it.

But I couldn't do it. I was cold from sitting on the bench and didn't feel right about it. That wasn't how the play was designed. I had to look for Selvy on the left side. If he was covered too, then I'd shoot. But I had to look for Selvy first. And there he was, wide open on the left baseline. After Selvy threw me the inbound pass he faked inside, then cut outside off Baylor's screen and had broken free. I had to go there.

Selvy wasn't 10 feet from the basket, but close to the baseline so the angle was tough. I threw a crisp pass and he handled it cleanly. He went up with two seconds left on the clock. His release was perfect as the ball rolled off his finger tips, but it hit the front of the rim and bounced away. Russell grabbed the rebound and the clock ran out.

That was it, the closest I've ever come to glory. The buzzer blew, the game went to overtime, and the Celtics went on to beat us by three, 110-107. The Boston crowd that had been so quiet watching the final moments of regulation unfold, erupted around us.

There's not a worse feeling in the world, to get that close but get no further. Celtics fans were all over the place, on the court, lining the hallways, cheering their heroes and jeering us as we fought our way to the locker room. It was like a tomb once we got inside. Everyone sat around with their heads in their hands, no one saying a word. Bob Short, the owner, came in to gave us a pep talk, telling us to get our heads up because we played like champions. He said, "The toughest thing you're going to have to do is get dressed and walk out of this building with your chins up." Then as he turned to leave he told us something that made holding our heads up a whole lot easier. "There's an extra thousand in it for each of you," he said on his way out the door.

Wow. With 10 players and a coach he just shelled out 11 grand. That changed our mood in a hurry. We looked at each other and said "A thousand dollars!" My salary was $11,000 for the entire season and some of the guys were making $8,000 or $9,000, so that was a hell of a bonus. The Celtics got $2,000 apiece as the winners' share in the playoffs and we got $1,000 apiece for taking second. Along with the thousand Short had just given us, we got as much money as the Celtics did!

Maybe this wasn't the end of the world. We got dressed and were ready to face the gauntlet of fans telling us how they kicked our butts. It was tempting to say something back to them as we made our way out of the building but I thought instead about that extra grand I just pocketed. I just smiled and kept my chin up.

Poor Selvy. He'll never forget that shot. I made sure of it. Frank and I were old rivals from our college days playing in the Southern Conference. He was an All-American from Furman, averaging 41.7 points a game his senior season to lead the nation in scoring. Everyone on our team knew he averaged 41.7 points a game. We used to kid him about it and he'd play along. We'd say, "Hey, Frank, what did you average in college?" And he would look inside his waistband as if he had it etched in indelible ink and say "Forty-one point seven."

Selvy, West and I all were named to the first team of the Southern Conference's 75th anniversary team, and now we were teammates. Selvy once scored 100 points in a game for Furman, which is still the NCAA Division I record. He had 98 points that day when he threw it in from midcourt at the buzzer to get to 100, yet he couldn't hit a 10-footer from the baseline when a world championship was on the line. He was a good shooter, he just missed it.

I called him up on the phone sometimes and when he answered I'd say, "Nice shot!" and hang up.

For years I went to bed at night wondering what would have happened if I had taken that shot. Even today I think about. If I would have shot the damn thing and made it I could have been the mayor of Los Angeles. Of course if I missed it I would have been the goat. And Frank Selvy would have been the one calling me up years later saying, "Nice shot!"

Chapter Three

I WOULD HAVE MADE A GREAT MILLIONAIRE

Tim Duncan was the NBA's No. 1 draft pick in 1997 and the salary for his first pro contract was set by a rookie salary scale adopted two years earlier. He signed a three-year contract with the San Antonio Spurs worth more than $10 million. Before Duncan, No. 1 picks like Chris Webber were signing $50 million deals. And long before Webber, there was me. The Cincinnati Royals had the first draft pick in the 1957 draft and used it to select me, then they traded those rights to the Minneapolis Lakers. Bob Short, the Lakers' owner, offered me a one-year contract for $8,000. I talked him up to $10,000 and thought I was a shrewd negotiator. A few months earlier I had put together a barnstorming tour in West Virginia, where a bunch of basketball friends of mine traveled the state putting on basketball games. I had $7,000 in the bank from that and with this new contract on top of it, I felt like a rich man.

On the way to Minneapolis, though, I was drafted into the Army. It took them four months but they finally decided my knees were bad enough to discharge me. I had blown out both of them years earlier and had surgery to put them back together. Those are the knees I had to play on my whole NBA career.

The Lakers were struggling before I got there and they counted on me to bring new life to the franchise. George Mikan, the first superstar in the NBA, led them to four championships in five years in the early 1950s. His nickname was "Mr. Basketball" and he was voted the greatest basketball player of the half-century, from 1900 to 1950. Mikan retired after the 1955-56 season, though, and the other guys who helped him win were getting older. The team struggled to draw good crowds when they were winning and now that they were losing the crowds were even worse. They were desperate for a gate attraction and that's where I fit in. I had write-ups in all the national magazines—even the news magazines like *Time*—because of the way I clowned around when I played at West Virginia University. Nobody did the things I did on the court and nobody has done them since. I'd shoot behind my back, sit on the other team's bench and really work the crowd. I was a Globetrotter in college basketball. Because of that—and because I was a legitimate All-American, too—my reputation was bigger than anyone coming out of college that year. The Cincinnati Royals needed a big man and knew they wouldn't find one in the draft, and the Lakers needed a marquee name, so the two teams made a swap. Cincinnati would draft me and trade their rights to Minneapolis for Clyde Lovellette, the Lakers' center.

Bob Short spent the months leading up to the season really building me up, marketing me to market the team. He did a great job selling me, too. He played up that I was the first player taken in the draft, a spectacular ballhandler and passer, a great showman. His work paid off, attracting a really nice crowd to our first game.

And I hardly played.

George Mikan was now coaching the team and he thought I wasn't ready for professional ball. So he kept me on the bench. Bob Short was going around the state promoting me as the savior of the franchise— and Mikan wouldn't even play me.

It was a tough situation for Mikan. He was the most dominating player in the league in his day and success came easy for this 6-foot-10 giant. He was a rough, physical player who overpowered everyone. He would just run over people. And his teams won because of it. He was an enforcer, too. If his teammates were getting manhandled ol' George would tell them, "Throw me the ball and cut. I'll take care of him." So the guy would pass Mikan the ball and cut right past him. As the defender went by, George would greet him with an elbow to the face.

It was easy for George to take control as a player but it was so much different for a coach. He had never coached in his life and now he was coaching a bad team. We couldn't overpower anyone the way he did. There was no one like him on the team he could put on the court. Hell, he was the most famous guy on the team and he didn't even play. When they introduced our team before games, guys would run out to the foul line when their name was called. When they got to George, he would run out to the foul line and pirouette, waving at the crowd. The fans went wild and George loved it. He was the coach and he got five times the applause we got.

Even though he was retired he still loved to play, so he always scrimmaged with us. Our centers never got to practice because George always played. He never coached in practice, he just killed our players. We had to remind him he was the coach. "George, you retired," we'd yell at him. "Get the hell out of there." The Lakers made the trade for me that year but they still had their own first-round draft choice. They used it to get Jim Krebs, a 6-8 All-American center out of Southern Methodist. He'd have to guard Mikan in practice and George would throw elbows into his chest the whole time. George would get the ball and if Krebs was right behind him, George would slam him in the ribs with his right elbow, then spin to his left. That's the way George played his whole career. He couldn't run and he couldn't jump, but he was strong and had a nice little hook shot he would flip in from the shoulders. Usually a guy would beat you up on defense, but George did that on offense. Krebs would take off his shirt after practice and have red welts all over his chest.

Mikan always wanted to tag along with us after games but we didn't want to be seen with him. He was too damn tall. We were 6-3, 6-4, which was taller than most people, but we could still blend into a crowd, sneak around and not get noticed. George was 6-10, though, so he always got recognized. He'd even offer to pick up the tab if we let him tag along.

His personality didn't mesh very well with the guys on the team. He was very straight and conservative and there I was throwing behind-the-back passes. He knew I had a reputation for clowning around on the court and he made up his mind that I wasn't serious about the game. He tried to encourage me, telling me, "You're going to be my Cousy." It never worked out that way, though. I played fancy but I didn't clown around like I did in college. I tried to be serious but he didn't seem to trust me. Mikan would see me throw a behind-the-back pass and think I was goofing around, but I had been throwing those passes since eighth grade. I threw behind my back better than I did straight ahead. So he wouldn't start me. Some nights he wouldn't even play me. It made no sense on that team. He said I wasn't ready, but who was on that team? We were a bad team and we were losing, so why not give me a chance? Short and Mikan got in terrible fights over this.

Playing for the Lakers that first year was the first time in my life I was on a losing team. We lost more games in my first pro season than I did in high school and college combined. It was hard to be serious, even though I wasn't going to clown around and risk costing us a game. It was a bad situation all the way around because in some ways I wasn't ready for the NBA. I dominated in college and expected to do the same in the pros. It was an eye-opener for me. I joke now when the name of Ralph Sampson comes up that he was the most overrated No. 1 draft choice since me. I was never a great shooter but I wasn't bad. People thought I was better than I actually was because in high school and college, I was such a better ball-handler than anyone else it was easy to get layups. I took a lot of crazy shots that hurt my percentage, but they were the type of shots no one thought about when I missed but everyone remembered when they went in. People remembered all the great shots I made in college but forgot how many I missed. Now I was in the NBA where the defenders were better so I couldn't get a layup anytime I wanted. And I wasn't taking those spectacular shots either. I had to shoot jump shots and my shooting was getting exposed. I had to learn a new position, too. I played forward in college but at 6-foot-4 I wasn't big enough to play there in the pros. I had to switch to guard. And I had to learn how to play defense, too. We played zones in college so I didn't have to do much one-on-one defending. Now that's all we did. Suddenly, I was expected to stop Bob Cousy one-on-one. He had 20 points in the first half against me one night and in the locker room at halftime Mikan yelled at me.

"I thought I told you to watch Cousy," he barked.

"I've been watching him, coach," I said. "Isn't he great?"

Because I went straight from the Army to training camp, I was thrown into the fire. I'm having to make all these adjustments while my coach doesn't think I'm serious. The real problem was that no one on the team was serious. After my first practice Bobby "Slick" Leonard said he and Dick Garmaker were going out for a beer and asked if I wanted to join them. That was the first of about 8,000 beers Slick and I had together in our careers. We knew we were a bad team and it was hard to take games seriously when you know you're probably going to get beat. We played two, three, four nights in a row and when you're getting beat it drains you. It's hard to care. We were 1-13 at one point and there was Mikan in the locker room giving fire-and-brimstone pep talks. Players had stopped listening to him.

On a bad team a young player is expected to come in and make a difference right away, but I was way overmatched. If I had gone to a good team, where the pressure wouldn't have been as great, I could have developed gradually and things might have turned out differently. But I was in Minneapolis where the owner thought I was a star and the coach thought I was a bum. Years later I ran into George in Minneapolis when the Jazz were in town to play the Timberwolves. He said, "You know, you really did have a lot of talent back then." We both shook our heads, thinking about what might have been.

Mikan was fired 39 games into the season and John Kundla took over. Kundla had coached the Lakers their first nine years in existence and won five championships, then moved up to the front office when Mikan was hired. Bringing him back to the bench didn't help much. We were 9-30 when Mikan got fired and went 10-23 under Kundla.

That's how much of an impact I made my rookie year—we finished in last place. The good news was that we got the first draft pick after the season and used it to get Elgin Baylor. That changed everything. He restored our pride in playing and brought credibility to us on the court. He averaged 25 points a game as a rookie and led us to the playoffs. We still had a losing record, 33-39, but that was a 14-game improvement from the year before and good enough for second place in the Western Division. Then we got hot at just the right time—in the playoffs—and made it all the way to the 1959 NBA Finals. We beat Detroit two games to one in the first round and upset the St. Louis Hawks, who were led by Bob Pettit and Cliff Hagan, four games to two in the second round. We were down 2-1 in that series but won three straight, one in overtime and the last one by two points.

That's as far as it went, though. The Celtics had Bob Cousy and Bill Russell now and they swept us 4-0 in the Finals. But basketball was fun again for us. Nobody expected us to win the series but Bob Short came into the locker room before Game 4 and told us how much it would mean to him if we could at least win one game and avoid getting swept. And while he was saying this he held up two fingers. He wasn't supposed to be doing this but he was signaling to us he'd give us a couple hundred bucks apiece if we at least won one game. For the series, players on the winning team got $2,000 apiece and the losing team got $1,000 apiece, so an extra $200 would have been nice. But we lost that game by five points and the season was over.

Bob Short was a straight-laced guy who didn't drink, didn't smoke and didn't cuss, but we got along great even though I drank, I smoked and I cussed. Sometimes after games he would offer me a ride so I'd have him drop me off at Buster's, a popular bar in Minneapolis. I'd invite him in for a drink but he never accepted. I think he got a kick out of me.

It was a good season for the team but it also was a good one for me personally. I was getting more playing time, about 24 minutes a game, and learning about the pro game. I averaged nine and a half points and three assists a game that season and in the playoffs I did even better, averaging nearly 12 points and six assists a game.

The next season, my third in the league and our last in Minneapolis, things turned bad again when we brought in John Castellani to coach the team. He was Elgin Baylor's college coach at Seattle and built a reputation off that, but he was inexperienced when it came to the pro game. He wasn't good at game preparations and he wasn't good at game situations. His coaching genius consisted of playing Elgin all the time. Elgin averaged more than 29 points a game, but that wasn't enough. Midway through the season we were 11-25, and Castellani was fired. Jim Pollard finished out the season and we were 14-25 under him. Despite the bad record, we made the playoffs and beat Detroit 2-0 in the first round.

St. Louis whipped us 4-0 in the next round, though, and that was it. Personally, it was my best season as a player. Pollard liked me and let me play. I averaged more than 31 minutes a game for the season and produced career highs across the board: 12.8 points, 5.3 rebounds and 4.6 assists. I was seventh in the league in assists.

Of all the coaches I played for, Pollard was my favorite. He played on the first four championship teams the Lakers had. Arnie Ferrin of the University of Utah played on two of those, then Vern Mikkelsen joined the Lakers to team up with Pollard and George Mikan to make one of the game's all-time great front lines. Pollard was the best forward in basketball in those days, the Kangaroo Kid. He was great to play for as a coach. If I had a bad game he'd tell me to forget about it and keep shooting. He showed confidence in you. I never had a coach say that to me. Usually they scream at you when you miss shots.

I went out that winter and bought a four-door Oldsmobile Super 88 convertible. How many guys do you know who would buy a convertible in Minneapolis in the middle of winter? I loved that car, though, and at the end of the season Bob Short announced he was moving the team to Los Angeles, so buying the convertible was a good move after all. We just didn't draw enough to make it work in Minneapolis so Short decided to move. When it was time to move, Rudy LaRusso and I drove out to L.A. together, but neither one of us was willing to tow the other guy's car. He had a Pontiac Bonneville and didn't want to hitch my car to it, and I didn't want his car hitched to my Oldsmobile, so we drove bumper-to-bumper the whole way, burning up twice as much gas as we needed to.

I was the first player ever to sign a contract with the Los Angeles Lakers. Rudy and I were the first ones to get to town, but he held out signing while I took what they offered me—$10,000— which was the same as I signed for the previous three years. But suddenly I was living in L.A. and the expenses were a lot higher than they were in Minneapolis. That's probably why players have agents these days.

When the team moved to Los Angeles they didn't bring Pollard with them to coach the team. They didn't renew his contract and hired Fred Schaus, my college coach, to take over. Jerry West was our first-round draft choice that year and I'm sure they hired Schaus because of it, just like they hired Elgin Baylor's college coach a couple years earlier. Schaus had a great coaching record at West Virginia, going 146-37 over his six seasons. That still is the best winning percentage in school history, but West and I helped make Schaus a great coach. He had either West or me playing for him in every game he ever coached there. And now he had us again. He did a lot of things well as a coach. He knew the game, he was a good motivator and he prepared his teams well.

Having Schaus and Jerry West there in L.A. made it feel like home. What I didn't realize at the time, though, was that having Fred Schaus there would lead to my downfall as a player. Looking back, I would have been better off with another coach. With or without Schaus, though, I loved playing in L.A. I had known Jerry West since he was in high school and he had followed me to West Virginia University, but this was the first time we were teammates so I was looking forward to that.

Bob Short operated the team on a shoestring budget, playing in small gyms and even an opera house, but I loved being in Southern California. Hollywood, the Sunset Strip, Malibu Beach—this was my kind of place. It was a great city for athletes, too. With the Lakers, the Kings, the Dodgers, the Angels, the Rams, Southern Cal and UCLA all there, this was the sports capital of the world. The ocean was right there and so were the mountains. It's the only city I've ever seen where you could water ski and snow ski in the same day. What more could you ask for? I hated going to practice because I was afraid I might miss something. I couldn't go to bed at night either for the same reason.

That gave us a competitive advantage on the basketball court once the season started. We were the only team on the West Coast that year so when teams came out to play us they usually stayed for two games to cut down on the travel. We always won the second game because those guys on the other team had never been to L.A. in their lives. If we played on Friday and Sunday, they would be out partying on Saturday night and we would whip them on Sunday. Of course, we took to the L.A. lifestyle too.

It took me four years to get a raise from that $10,000 contract I signed with the Lakers my rookie year but I loved life on the Sunset Strip and lived the lifestyle. I had a house I couldn't afford, a car that was too big and a wardrobe full of flashy clothes. Stan Goethals, a big Lakers fan, offered jobs one summer to several players doing P.R. for his bank. We usually ended up at the race track. I found a tailor who also was a big fan and he got me my clothes wholesale. I looked like a million dollars in a tuxedo. In fact, I would have made a great millionaire, but I couldn't get the Lakers to go along. When the salaries started spiraling into the multimillion dollar range I'd see my mother and say, "Why didn't you wait to have me?" I could have been a millionaire. Instead, I had to play four seasons just to get a raise, and even that was just to $11,000 my fifth season. I made $11,500 my last year, meaning that I earned a grand total of $62,500 playing six seasons in the NBA. Players today get that for playing one game.

And it was a lot less if you include all the fines—including what was at that time the biggest fine ever in pro sports. The Lakers were still in Minneapolis then and we played a game in New York. Slick Leonard and I went out afterward and ended up staying out all night. By time we got back to our hotel, it was 8:00 the next morning and the team was already getting on the bus for the airport to head back to Minneapolis. There was no way we could get up to our rooms, get packed and get back down to the bus in time, so we hid out until they left, then packed up. We knew we were in trouble but had no idea how bad. We called the Lakers office and told them we missed our flight. They told us to go to the airport and there would be tickets waiting for us— which we had to pay for ourselves. When we got back to Minneapolis we heard a page at the airport: "Rod Hundley and Bob Leonard report to the Lakers office immediately." So Slick and I reported to Bob Short's office as ordered and sat outside, squirming and wondering what we were in for. The best excuse we could come up with was this cockeyed story that we went to a party in Philadelphia and had car trouble on the way back.

Short called me in first and asked me what happened. I told him we were out having fun and overdid it and blew the plane because of car trouble. I was sorry. I really was and I told him. He didn't believe it for a second, and it wasn't much of an excuse even if he did believe it. He pointed out it wasn't the first time I missed a plane, or the second or even the third. He decided it was time for strong action and fined me $1,000. I was stunned. That was 10 percent of my salary for the entire season. Could you imaging Karl Malone getting fined 10 percent of his salary for missing a plane? That was the biggest fine ever in sports. I told him it was too much, that he was making a mistake. He said it was no mistake, that it was for my own good. I couldn't believe it. I left his office and Slick asked me what the fine was.

"The big bill," I told him.

"A hundred bucks?" he asked.

"A hundred, hell," I said, "it's a thousand. And he wants to see you next."

Slick went in and got clobbered with the same fine. If we were bigger stars we knew we would have gotten away with it. I missed a plane once with Elgin and there was no fine or anything. I missed another flight once when I was with West and no one said a word. But this time it was Slick and me who missed the flight, and we paid dearly. At least for a while. Short put us on probation for the rest of the season, then gave us our money back at the end of the year.

Another year they put a weight clause in my contract. They would weigh me once a month during the season and I would get a $100 bonus if I weighed 190 or less and I would be fined $100 if I weighed over 205.

It was hard to hold onto money in L.A., and real easy to spend it. This was a town of flashy people and I was fitting in. I'm No. 33 in your program, I used to tell people, and No. 1 in your heart. Doris Day used to come to our games and sit on the front row. I met her at a party once and did the twist with her, and I sat on her lap once during a game. Another time I kissed the ball and threw it to her, right during the game. She threw it back to me, and I said, "This one's for you, Doris" and fired up a hook shot from almost half court. I missed badly but the refs were already blowing their whistles like crazy. I knelt down in front of her and apologized. "I tried, Doris, I tried."

I lived in Sherman Oaks with my wife, Flo, and our kids, right across the street from Mike Conners, who was staring in "Mannix" at the time. Every time his show came on, my daughter Kimberly would run and get me. "Daddy," she would say, "Mr. Connors is on TV." She didn't know he played "Mannix," she just knew him as our neighbor across the street, and we'd go watch him.

The best part of being in L.A. was the winning. Elgin Baylor was at the top of his game and now that we had West, we finished second in the division his first season, then won two straight division titles. Early in our first season in L.A., after a victory over the Knicks at Madison Square Garden, Elgin and I took a cab back to the hotel. He threw his arm around me and said, "Wow, 78 points. I want to tell you there's a lot of points between us sitting in this cab." Of course we both broke out laughing because he scored 71 of them. He also had 25 rebounds that game. And I had seven points. We were quite a duo. One year I wore out one side of my Converse shoe handing the ball to Elgin and running to the other side to get out of his way. He was 6-foot-5 and a great post-up player, but he was a great leaper, too. He had amazing hang time back before anyone thought to call it that. He would be up there forever. Elgin would jump and the defender would jump with him, but Elgin could wait until the guy went down, then shoot over him. At his peak he was one of the best ever, averaging 35 points and 17 rebounds a game over a three-year stretch from 1960-63. A great shooter, a great scorer and a great rebounder.

Elgin had a nervous tick and it worked to his advantage sometimes. He'd be holding the basketball squared up to the defender and look back over his shoulder, then he'd twitch. When the defender looked to see what Elgin was looking at, Elgin drove right by him. He loved to play cards too. He was always getting a game going. But when he got a full house he'd twitch and everybody folded.

Elgin loved to talk, too. Baylor played with a guy at Seattle who went on to become a captain in the military. Elgin called him one time at the base and they asked who was calling. He said, "Capt. Baylor" because he was a captain of the Lakers. They put the call right through. He was an expert on everything and was always starting arguments. He made up nicknames for everyone too, but because I already had a nickname, "Hot Rod," he always called me Rodney.

Then there was Ray Felix, a 6-11 center who called himself "Baby Ray." He was the Rookie of the Year for Baltimore in 1954 but was at the end of his career the two years I played with him in L.A. Everybody on the team had their own play except for Ray, so the coach decided once a quarter we would give him the ball and let him do whatever he wanted with it. "Let's get one for Ray," we'd say. So one game against Boston he took a hook shot in the first quarter and Bill Russell swatted it away. In the second quarter Ray went in for a layup and Russell blocked that one. In the third quarter he tried a jumper and Russell got that one too. So when Ray's play came around in the fourth quarter, he stood there with his back to the basket about 18 feet out and just whipped the ball over his head in the general vicinity of the basket. The ball grazed the side of the backboard and bounced out of bounds. Ray turned to Russell and said with a big grin, "You didn't get that one!"

One time Walter Dukes, a 7-footer for Detroit, threw an elbow and tripped Ray, and the refs threw Dukes out of the game. Ray got mad at the refs. "Don't throw him out," Ray said, "I want a piece of him." Dukes was tossed anyway, so the minute the game ended, Ray sprinted off the court and headed straight to the Detroit locker room. Dukes was sitting there getting dressed and Ray walked up behind him, tapped him on the shoulder and punched him in the mouth. By time the rest of the players got there Ray was walking out of the Pistons' locker room rubbing his hand. "Nobody does that to Baby Ray," he said.

I know the hotels we stayed in had thin walls because one time some of us were talking about the team and I said I thought we should start Ray at center. A minute later the phone rang and it was Ray, who had the room next door, thanking me for starting him. Ray was an interesting guy. He loved catfish and warm root beer.

Most players in the league smoked cigarettes in those days. The only guys on our team who didn't smoke were Jerry West and Rudy LaRusso. Elgin Baylor smoked all through his career and so did I. We'd go in at halftime and instead of giving us a pep talk, Fred Schaus, would bum a cigarette off one of us. We all fired up. The locker rooms were very small then and we had eight players and a coach puffing away. There was one big cloud of smoke in there. Then Fred would give us our halftime speech and call us into a huddle. We'd all put one hand in and be holding cigarettes in the other. We'd take that last drag, then throw the cigarette on the floor and put it out with our basketball shoes, then go out and play. One time Bobby Leonard sprained his ankle in a game and had to go to the locker room. While they were taping up his ankle he had a cigarette and when he came back out on the floor during a timeout, the cigarette was still dangling from his lips. He forgot it was there and we had to yell at him to put it out.

Most people don't realize it but I have the best coaching percentage in NBA history. I'm a perfect 3-0. I won twice finishing off games when the coach got kicked out, and I did some pretty good coaching in both of those, and I filled in once when the coach couldn't make it to the game. We didn't have assistant coaches then so if the coach got tossed, a player had to take over. Fred Schaus always thought I had a good feel for the game, a real understanding of it, so when I offered to take over for him he felt he could trust me.

One time Schaus was ejected for arguing a call late in the game at Cincinnati in the 1962-63 season. I probably helped him get kicked out, although it wasn't intentional. He already had one technical when referee Sid Borgia made a bad call on Elgin Baylor. Schaus had his back to the play, talking to a guy he was sending into the game, and didn't even see what happened. I said, "Hey, Fred, did you see that? Terrible!" Schaus jumped up and got after Borgia, so Borgia tossed him. We were down by two points with 10 seconds to play and Fred left me in charge.

I called for a full-court press and we stole the ball with about five seconds left. When the players called a timeout to set up the last play, I sat on the bench wondering who would get to take the last shot. Then someone slapped me on the back and asked me what we were going to do. That's when I remembered I was the coach and started to think hard. I came up with a play where Dick Barnett would take the ball out and throw it in to Baylor, then cut to the free throw line. Rudy LaRusso would screen for Barnett, who would get the ball back from Baylor near the free throw line and shoot. It worked perfectly to tie the score, then we beat them easily in overtime.

Another time Schaus got kicked out at St. Louis. We were down by five with less than a minute to play. I put myself in along with Jerry West and Frank Selvy, and kept our two forwards in the game, Elgin Baylor and Tom Hawkins, so we had a small, quick lineup. We went to a full-court press and stole the ball and drove in for a layup to cut their lead to three. Then we came up with another steal and scored again to make it a one-point game. After that I intercepted a pass and threw to West, who gave us a one-point lead. By then the Hawks were rattled pretty good and they threw the ball to West, then fouled him. Jerry made the free throws and we won by three, outscoring them 8-0 in the last 55 seconds.

The other time I got to coach was also in St. Louis. Schaus had some sort of personal business to attend to so Lou Mohs, our general manager, told me I would coach. It was a tough game but I was into it, and when Schaus showed up in the third quarter, we had a 77-76 lead. Schaus called a timeout and I said, "Fred, my man, I got you the lead. It's up to you to hold it." I don't think he appreciated my remark, but we won the game. I count it as a victory for me because I coached more than half the game and we had the lead when I turned it over to Schaus.

That made me 3-0 as a coach, but all those games were on the road. I always wanted Schaus to get kicked out at home once so I could have the L.A. crowd cheering me on.

I did come close once to coaching for real. When Seattle got an expansion team in 1967, Gene Klein, who owned the San Diego Chargers football team, talked to me about coaching the SuperSonics. He offered me a one-year contract for $17,000 but I wanted a guaranteed three-year deal if I was going to coach an expansion team. They wouldn't do it so I turned it down and took a job for $15,000 as Chick Hearn's analyst on the Lakers broadcasts. I said, "I think I can keep this job longer than I can keep that job up there." As it turned out, I lasted two years working with Chick and Al Bianchi, the guy they ended up hiring in Seattle, lasted two years there. But I made the right move.

I've always been interested in coaching and it might have been a good career for me. But there's no way you can walk into an expansion job with no coaching experience and expect to survive if they only give you a one-year contract. If I had an established team with some talent on it, then I would have considered a one-year contract to prove myself. For an expansion team, though, you have to have at least three years. I had no experience other than those three games filling in with the Lakers, and in those games all I had to do was make sure I kept West and Baylor on the court. But on an expansion team there is no West and there is no Baylor. You don't have anyone close to them so you know going in that you're going to get fired. I wanted the people in Seattle to show me some sort of vision of the future, an understanding that it takes time and they would work with me on building a team. But they never saw it that way. They expected me to show more enthusiasm about winning right away, about building a playoff team quickly. They wanted me to sweet talk them and paint a rosy picture. And they acted like they were doing me a favor by offering me the job. So when I turned them down they gave it to Al Bianchi instead. And they fired him in two years because they didn't make the playoffs.

It wasn't Bianchi's fault. Out of 82 games your first year you're going to win 15 to 25 no matter what, and you're going to lose badly in a lot of games. Even if they accept that the first year and bring you back for a second, you're still going to lose, and they're going to fire you. Then you're out on the street without a job. Who's going to hire you now? It's your first coaching job and you got fired in two years? That's it. You're through as a coach. It's like the guys with the Vancouver Grizzlies and Toronto Raptors. Brendan Malone lasted one year in Toronto before he was fired and Brian Winters lasted a year-and-a-half in Vancouver. It's inevitable. At least they both had experience as assistant coaches and were able to find work after that, but I didn't have that going for me. I'm sure happy I went the way I did because broadcasting has been great.

I almost had as many highlights as a coach as I did as a player. I played in two All-Star games and I was selected by the coaches both times. I'm proud of that, being picked by guys who know the game. It was a lot of fun too, running out there with Wilt Chamberlain, Bill Russell, Bob Cousy, Bob Pettit and Oscar Robertson, all those guys. The first year I played, Wilt was a rookie and he won MVP of the All-Star game. The second time I played, Oscar was a rookie and he won MVP of the game. I had 10 points in the 1960 game, outscoring Russell, and I had 14 in the 1961 game, outscoring West and Chamberlain. Those games were a little more competitive than they are today. Now it has really turned into a circus, which is fine. People like to be entertained. It's show business now. People don't guard one another. Guys today dunk everything. Back then guys hardly ever dunked. I couldn't jump that high. But it was more competitive. We played harder.

For six seasons I was one of the top 80 players in the nation. There were 80 NBA jobs and I had one of them. But I never became a star in the pros like I was in college. I didn't work at it enough. I never was in great shape. I have workout equipment in my house today and exercise three times a week when I'm home. That's three times a week more than I ever worked out as a player.

Chapter Four

CRASH LANDING IN EMMA STEFFES' CORNFIELD

oday's NBA players take so much better care of themselves than I ever did. And why not? With the money out there now players do everything they can to keep their bodies strong and healthy so they can play as long as possible. It's not easy getting through an 82- game schedule. All those games and practices are a grind and even getting to the games wears you down because of the constant travel. In the 1997-98 Jazz season, 12 of their 17 games in March were on the road, including a pair of five-game road trips. Those five-, six- and seven-game trips are draining both physically and mentally, and to have two of them in three weeks was especially rough.

The second long trip ended with an emotional double-over-time victory over the New York Knicks at Madison Square Garden. It was March 22 and the team had been on the road for all but six days that month. Everyone was eager to get home, but the five-hour flight out of the Newark Airport to Salt Lake City was delayed four hours—all because they didn't have flight attendants for their chartered plane. The FAA says there have to be attendants on every flight and because of connection problems, our crew was still in Chicago when we were ready to leave New York.

It was a miserable way to end a long trip, sitting around with four hours to kill when you're anxious to get home. But more than anyone on the plane I appreciated how much worse things could have been. I've been traveling with NBA teams nearly every year since 1957, first as a player for the Minneapolis and Los Angeles

Lakers, then as a broadcaster with the Lakers, Phoenix Suns and the Jazz. I know the worst travel nightmares today are nothing compared to the problems we routinely encountered in the past. Getting home late is tough, but that's nothing compared to ending up in an Iowa cornfield in the middle of the night.

That happened to the Lakers on a blustery January night in 1960 when our flight from St. Louis to Minneapolis never made it home. The Lakers had their own plane then, a propeller-driven DC-3, and the team was flying back to Minneapolis after a game against the Hawks in St. Louis. We left in light snow at 8:30 p.m. and shortly after takeoff our plane developed generator trouble. We usually played poker on those flights but the lights were cut when the generator went out so we couldn't play. There wasn't any heat either, so we grabbed all the blankets we could find and tried to get some sleep. That was hard to do because it was so cold, but we did our best to make the time pass.

The flight was supposed to last about three hours but we were still in the air four hours later, in the middle of a blizzard with no idea where we were. Vern Ullman, a retired Air Force colonel, was at the controls along with a co-pilot. Their instrument panel in the cockpit had stopped working and they had lost contact with the ground.

The pilots announced to us over the loudspeaker we were off course and in trouble, warning us to strap ourselves in because they didn't know what to expect. Col. Ullman had tried to climb over the storm and that didn't work so now he was dropping low to look for a place to land, not even sure where we were. We had circled a town for about 45 minutes hoping to find an airport but had no luck. Col. Ullman couldn't even find a landing strip on a farm. We were no longer just uncomfortable, we were getting scared. Elgin Baylor went to the back of the plane looking to lie down and stretch out. He said if this was his time to go, he was going to be comfortable when it happened. The flight attendants, however, sent him back to his seat. We tried joking about it, hoping that would ease the tension some, maybe even trying to convince ourselves we weren't scared, but that didn't work. I told the guys I was ready to pay off all my debts, that's how scared I was.

We started running low on fuel and with no landing strip in sight, the pilots had to find another alternative. We were getting more frightened by the minute. Col. Ullman picked out a road where he thought he could put us down and decided that was our best chance. As we felt the plane descending, the door to the cockpit popped open. We could see the pilots shining flashlights out the window trying to get some sort of vision. I looked out the windows on the side and couldn't see much of anything, just a bunch of snow whipping by. It was eerily silent in the plane, just the sound of wind whipping past as the engines slowed down. We eased down lower and lower toward the ground and couldn't have been more than 50 or 100 feet above the road we were trying to land on when suddenly the engines roared to life and the plane jerked nose-first up in the air, knocking us around in our seats. Some of the guys got sick from the abrupt maneuver. At the last moment, Col. Ullman had spotted a car on the road where he planned to land and had to abort. The pilot leveled off the plane, then continued searching for a landing site. Finally, about 1:30 a.m.—five hours after we took off—Col. Ullman picked out a cornfield under a foot of snow. That would be our landing site. He announced we were going down again and we heard the co-pilot calling out the altitude. Five hundred feet. Four hundred feet. Three hundred. ...We dropped below 100 feet and braced for another try. ... Fifty feet. Forty. Thirty. Twenty. I couldn't look but I had to look. We heard the wings slicing through the corn stalks and hit the ground hard. The plane bounced up and hit the ground again. This time we skidded wildly, hurtling through the corn stalks. It seemed like forever, but we finally slid to a stop.

It was a perfect crash landing.

The plane was silent for a moment, then once it sunk in that we were actually safe and on the ground we let out a huge cheer. There were 23 people on that plane and we all congratulated the pilots like they had just hit a game-winning shot. We climbed out of the plane into the snowy cornfield, never so happy to have our feet on the ground. The cornfield we were in belonged to Emma Steffes, who lived just on the outskirts of Carroll, Iowa, a town about 150 miles off course for a flight from St. Louis to Minneapolis. Within minutes people from Carroll were pouring out. The first car we saw pull up was a hearse. We were directed to a road about 100 yards away, tromping through the cornfield in the dark, laughing and joking and carrying on like a bunch of kids.

We spent the night at a hotel in town but we were too wound up, too excited to go to sleep. All the guys spent the night in the lobby talking. By morning all of Carroll was out there looking at the downed plane in the cornfield. There were more people there than we had showing up for our games in Minneapolis. They eventually cleared out a path in the cornfield a couple days later and flew the plane out— another big day in Carroll—but we got on a bus and headed back to Minneapolis. It was a long ride but I don't think anybody was too anxious to get back on an airplane and nobody complained about the bus. We rode right by the plane on the way out of town, sitting there in the snow and sunshine in Emma Steffes' cornfield, not a scratch on it.

I was out with Col. Ullman one night and he had been telling me about what a great plane the DC-3 was. He said, "The DC-3 is so sturdy you could land it in a cornfield." And two weeks later he landed it in a cornfield. All 10 of us players chipped in $20 apiece when we got back to Minneapolis and at a game we presented the $200 and a trophy to Col. Ullman. Twenty dollars isn't a bad price to pay for your life.

It's hard to imagine a story of that magnitude going under-reported today. If a plane carrying an entire professional basketball team went down you could be anywhere in the world and hear about it in a matter of minutes. But in 1960, long before there was cable television— and cable television networks—news was different. Sports was different. There was no CNN to dispatch crews to the scene, no ESPN to break into its regular programing with updates. A professional basketball team crash-landing was the story of the decade in Carroll, Iowa, but the reaction in the rest of the world was nothing like it would be if that happened today.

Thirty-eight years later, sitting on that runway in Newark, New Jersey, four hours late for a flight home, I was as restless as anyone on that plane and just as anxious to get home. But I also realized how much worse things could be.

Today's players think travel is a grind, and it is, but it's nothing compared to when I played in the late '50s and early '60s. Sometimes we traveled by bus or train and when we did fly, it was by DC-3, a propeller-driven plane made obsolete by the jet airliner. I played three years in Minneapolis, which was the farthest West any NBA team went then. Jet travel allowed sports teams to move to the West Coast. We were among the first people to ride in jets and it was unbelievable to us how fast they were. It would be like people today who are used to flying commercial jets taking their first ride in an F-14. I feel ancient now thinking that I was one of the first people ever to get in a commercial jet plane. Before the team moved to Los Angeles, we flew there in our DC-3 for exhibition games and had to make two pit stops for fuel. You can imagine flying over the

Rocky Mountains for the first time, looking out the window of that DC-3, putt-putting along. It took more than 20 hours with the stops.

And you never knew when you might end up in an Iowa cornfield in the middle of the night. Some players today don't realize how good they've got it. Guys who have been in the league five or 10 years remember the commercial travel: The 5 a.m. wake-up calls, the long waits at baggage claim, running through airports to make connection. Younger players haven't even experienced that. Players today skip the airport terminals and go straight to the tarmac, where they step directly onto a jet that whisks them away to the next city. When they arrive there's a bus waiting right next to the plane to take them to the hotel. And a bus is waiting for them the next morning to go to the arena for practices and games. Players are never on their own for anything.

We were. We rode buses from city to city but there were never any buses for us to get around town when we got there. That meant riding in cabs and even that was an ordeal. We were supposed to get reimbursed by the coach for our cab fare but it wasn't a sure thing, so we always worried about getting stuck with the tab. No one wanted to pay seven or eight bucks, which was most of our per diem, if we weren't going to get it back.

The last guy out of the cab had to pay for it so we flew out of the taxi, knocking each other down to get out. Vern Mikkelsen, a teammate in Minnesota my first two years in the league, was one guy everybody liked to ride with because he always paid. You didn't have to fight to get out with him around because you knew he'd take care of it. If you weren't in a cab with him, though, it was a scramble. And we came up with lots of tricks to avoid getting stuck for the cab. We all wore hats in those days so if you were the last one out you'd try to grab someone's hat and throw it back in so they'd have to get it. Elgin Baylor was great at that. He'd get in and say, "I got the cab, don't worry about it." Then when we'd get back to the hotel he'd grab someone's hat and throw it in while he took off. Or if we had lots of bags everyone would hang around the back of the cab to put theirs in last so they would be the first one to retrieve it when we got out.

One time in Philadelphia, four or five of us took a cab to the Convention Hall, which is the arena where the Philadelphia Warriors played. When we got to the arena all of us were standing in back waiting for the cab driver to open the trunk so we could grab our bags and make a break for it. We almost knocked him down trying to get our bags, and we all took off running. Usually when we ran one guy lagged behind so he'd stop and pay but this time we were all in a dead heat. No one was willing to concede so no one stopped. And the driver came running after us. We were all running with bags in our hands, giggling like little children, with the cabbie matching us step for step. Everyone thought he could outrun everyone else so no one stopped. The cabbie chased us up the street, into the arena, down the hall and into the dressing room. The coach sees this, a bunch of professional basketball players getting chased by a cab driver, and just shakes his head. He says, "You guys are a bunch of kids," and he was right. But he paid the driver.

The hotels weren't too bad when I played, but they weren't great. The worst thing about it was that everyone had to share a room. The rooms were small with two twin beds and if your roommate kept different hours than you or snored real bad, it could be hard to sleep. One time Rudy LaRusso was rooming with Bobby Leonard, and Bobby was snoring so loud he kept waking up Rudy. Each time, Rudy would go over and wake up Bobby and he'd stop for a minute, but as soon as he fell back to sleep he would start snoring again. So Rudy finally picked up Bobby's bed and dragged it out into the hallway and left him there sound asleep. The maid came by in the morning and Bobby was still out there in the hallway snoring away.

When I came into the league there were only eight teams: the New York Knickerbockers, Boston Celtics, Philadelphia Warriors and Syracuse Nationals in the East and the Minneapolis Lakers, St. Louis Hawks, Detroit Pistons and Cincinnati Royals in the West. That made travel a lot easier. We went by train to most of the games in the West, and we always took a train between New York and Boston. We'd never get a sleeper car, just seats, so we spent all our time in the club car playing poker.

In the preseason everything was by bus. We might play as many 20 exhibition games a year. Teams today are limited to eight preseason games but it was much different then. One year we might go to California and travel all over the state for the exhibition season, and another year we might to go New England and play in places like Bangor, Maine, and all these cities that didn't have NBA teams. We played in small college gyms and even high schools. We paired up with another team on these trips, maybe playing the Celtics 15 times in the preseason. Then in the regular season, because there were only eight teams, we'd play them nine more times.

In one of those preseason games up in New England, they introduced me as "Red" Hundley and Bill Sharman was introduced as
"Bob." To this day, that's what we call each other. We played teams
in our own division 13 times in the regular season. That's a lot of
games against the same team. Today you see the same team no more
than four times in a season, even if they're in your own division. If
you play them in the preseason it's never more than once or twice.

The more popular teams today can pick up $100,000 just for
playing a preseason game, but back then the games were just for
practice. I don't think there was any money to be made but we had
to play them to get ready for the season. Hardly anyone played or
even worked out in the offseason. We needed the exhibitions to
get back in shape. If you wanted to play in the offseason, you went
to a playground and found a pickup game. I never thought of touch-
ing a basketball in the summer. The guys on our team who wanted
to work out went to the beach and played volleyball or went jog-
ging. Most players today keep in shape over the summer. And for
guys who really want to work on their game, there are summer
leagues and summer training camps. They even have predraft camps
for college kids, so there are all sorts of opportunities to improve
your game that we never had.

The game itself has changed over the years. When I played
most teams had a playmaker, but with few exceptions the two guards
were interchangeable. Bob Cousy always had the ball in Boston but
that wasn't the norm in those days. The playmaker has evolved into
the point guard of today, which is a distinct position from the shooting guard. They couldn't shoot the ball as well in those days so
there was a lot more team play. Field goal percentages were below
40 percent but they shot free throws as well then as they do today.
Cousy never shot 40 percent in a season his whole career, but he
was a career 80-percent free throw shooter. It doesn't make any
sense. In 1958, the league shot .383 from the field and .746 from
the line. Field goal percentages have steadily improved but free
throw shooting has stayed about the same.

Because the shooting was poor in the early years of the NBA,
they ran a lot more plays to get guys shots. There's a lot of individual play in the game today with guys like Michael Jordan going
one-on-one. The Jazz are the exception. They run a lot of plays and
do a lot of screening with very little one-on-one play—and that's
why they led the NBA in field goal percentage for four straight
years. They've never had great open-court players. Karl Malone and

Adrian Dantley could take guys one-on-one in the low post once they got the insert pass, but neither one could break people down off the dribble.

These guys are much better shooters today and across the board they're bigger and stronger with a better shooting range. They are better players, there's no question about it. And there are plenty of reasons for it. The equipment is better. The floor is better. The lighting is better. The coaching is better. The scouting is better. The travel is better. The food is better. The hotels are better. The buses are better. The airplanes are better. The money is better.

Everything is better. Even the ball is better. The ball today has a nice feel to it. You can really get a good grip. The feel was different when I played. The ball was slick to begin with, then it would get covered with dirt and sweat to make it even slipperier. There was no such thing as Stick-Um then to help you get a grip. Once they developed the stuff it became popular in a hurry, but it got to the point where the basketball was so sticky you could palm it with one finger. So they banned the stuff and make you use rosin now. You're not supposed to use Stick-Um but I'm sure some players do. If they catch you they slap your wrist and fine you $25. Big deal. It's like the spitball in baseball. It has been illegal for 50 years, but guys still throw it. Most basketball players settle for rosin these days. It might not be as good as Stick-Um, but it's a lot better than when I played.

Eating habits are a lot better today, too. We never gave any thought to what we ate. We'd go to a game and grab a couple hot dogs when we got to the arena. You'd be filled up and ready for the game. It never occurred to us to let the food digest before we played. Nobody thought about nutrition, we just ate junk. We'd eat better on an off-day than we did before a game. On a day off we'd go to a nice restaurant and eat a hearty meal. On game days the coach wanted you to eat three or four hours before a game but we'd wait until we got to the arena and save the cost of a meal.

Even with all the differences, the best players of the '50s and '60s and '70s would be stars today. Guys like Oscar Robertson and Jerry West would eat up the players today. Look at the way everyone grabs the ball while they're dribbling. They pick up the ball, hold it, look over the defense, then bounce it and pick it up again. When West and Robertson played, that was palming and the refs called it. If they could have gotten away with that, no one would have ever stopped them. No one stopped them as it was, so could you imagine West and Robertson getting away with stuff like that? There's no telling what their numbers would have been.

Changes in the NBA have been gradual but there was something new nearly every year. The Lakers moved to Los Angeles for the 1960-61 season and Chicago Packers joined the league a year later. A year after that, the Philadelphia Warriors moved to San Francisco to join the Lakers on the West Coast, and the Chicago Packers changed their name to the Chicago Zephyrs. For the 1963-64 season, the Zephyrs moved to Baltimore and became the Bullets—still playing in the Western Division—and the Syracuse Nationals moved to Philadelphia and became the 76ers. The more teams they added, the longer the season got. We played 72 games my first season and we were up to 80 my last year. They've been playing 82 since the 1967-68 season.

Not only has the number of teams expanded but so has the size of the teams. The league has gone from eight teams with one coach, 10 players and a part-time trainer, to 29 teams with 12 players, four or five coaches, two trainers, a scouting staff, a strength and conditioning coach, a video coordinator, a team psychologist, a handful of basketball consultants, an equipment manager and in some cases, a team masseuse. On the road we always had the home team's trainer tape our ankles or we brought in someone from a local college to save expenses. Today, teams have a small army with them on the road.

When I played in Minneapolis we were responsible for washing our own uniforms. If you went on a 10-game road trip, you wore that thing 10 games in a row. It would be all wet and musty when you threw it in your bag after a game, along with your socks and jock strap. You took them back to your hotel room and rinsed them out, maybe, and hung them up. Some of these guys had a little bit healthier habits than the others. Near the end of a road trip you got on the court and the odor from some of these guys would knock you out. You had to live with that. You came out of a game and a ballboy threw you a warmup jacket. You could smell it while it's flying in the air toward you and you'd knock it down. "Whew, that ain't mine! Make sure you give me my jacket. I don't want someone else's stinking sweater." By the end of a long trip the smell could get a little strong. Everybody could tolerate their own dirty clothes but when you had to smell your roommate's, it got to be too much. Then when guys got home they gave their uniforms a good washing. Nobody was going to dry clean it, that cost money.

So they'd wash them in bleach and the colors would fade. Some guys used more bleach than others so when our team took the court we had four different colors of blue in our uniforms.

Uniforms today are washed for the players right after the game and might be back in the lockers before a player leaves for the night. Home teams will wash the visiting team's uniforms after the game, too, so players never have to worry about anything. Their uniforms are waiting for them in the next city. And there's quite a bit more material in these uniforms today because everyone wears the baggy shorts—everyone but John Stockton, anyway. He would have loved the uniforms we played in because the shorts were definitely short. The uniform from my first season in Los Angeles is hanging at Iggy's Bar in Salt Lake City, short pants and all. Those were stylish when I played but today Stockton stands out. That's the only similarity Stockton and I had as players—we both wore the same size shorts.

And shoes—these guys will wear a new pair of shoes every game or two. We wore one pair of canvas Converse for a whole season. High tops and low tops, white and black, those were the choices then. The Celtics were the only team wearing black shoes then, and they were the only team winning. Everyone else wore white. The rubber on the bottom would be smooth by the end of the year, and the canvas uppers would get smelly and stiff. Sweat dripped down and saturated the canvas. They could smell pretty bad, and when the shoes dried they would stiffen up. The only way you could get them loose the next day was to start sweating again. And by the end of the season everyone was slipping on the court because their shoes were worn down.

The tenth man in those days didn't have to worry about it because he never got in the games. The tenth man always had a nice, clean uniform. That's something that hasn't changed whether it's a 10-man roster, a 12-man roster or even the 15-man roster some teams go with today by hiding players on the injured list. Professional basketball is basically an eight-man game regardless of the roster size. You have your five starters and a sub at each position. You rotate three guards, you rotate three forwards and you have a backup at center. There are variations but usually those are the eight guys who play most of the minutes. Everyone else sits.

Another thing that hasn't changed is competition for roster spots. Do you know how many guys are trying to get your job every year? That's one thing about sports, there is no seniority. You're the best player or you're gone. I don't care how nice a guy you are, how hard you work, how loyal you've been, there are 12 roster spots and if you're the 13th best player, it's see ya, Charlie. It's a cold business. When I played there were only eight teams and 10 players on a team, so that meant there were only 80 jobs in the whole country. It was an honor to be one of just 80 in the world, but someone was always gunning for your job. Every year all the guys on the team wondered who we drafted, a guard, a forward or a center. Everybody sweated out their position.

Guys didn't take care of themselves in my day. Most of the players smoked cigarettes, probably 70 percent of the guys in the league. We drank, too. Hard liquor. Martinis, bourbon, shots. There was a place in New York called Frankie's Footlight. It was a little neighborhood bar, but it was popular among the players. Everybody in the league hung out there. We'd play doubleheaders at Madison Square Garden sometimes. Two teams would play an early game, then a third team would play the Knicks right after, and all four teams would go to Frankie's Footlight after the games. There were only eight teams then so we'd get half the players in the NBA gathered in one bar at the same time. I remember seeing Slater Martin, who played for the St. Louis Hawks, drinking a shot with a beer. I was a rookie then and I had never seen such a thing. Man, that's living, I thought. We never want to the fancy nightclubs in New York. We couldn't afford them. That was for the rich. None of us was making any money. Today's players wouldn't even walk in the places we hung out in. They wouldn't go near them.

Almost nobody smokes these days and there aren't many drinkers. Some of the Jazz players might have a beer once in awhile, maybe after a game or on an off-night. The biggest difference is that these guys might go out for a beer whereas we went out for a 12-pack. And I never see them out the night before a game.

The money has changed the game in a lot of ways. I don't think guys are as close knit as they used to be. When I played, guys did a lot of things together. Of course, everyone had a roommate on the road. When I first came in the league, meal money was $7 a day. My last year we got $10. Today it's $84. Can you imagine that? Since I travel with the team that's what I get, which almost matches the salary I got for playing, which is the biggest difference in the game today. When I was making $10,000 a year that came to about $125 a game, and today I get $84 a day just in expense money. I played six years for the Lakers and made $10,000 in each of my first four seasons. In today's dollars, that's about $50,000 a year. Today's players average close to $3 million a year and some of them get million-dollar raises for having mediocre years.

The annual NBA All-Star game is great example of how far the league has come. Long before anyone ever dreamed of a slam dunk contest or a legends game, All-Star Weekend was the All-Star game, period. I played in the 1960 All-Star game at Philadelphia and my reward was a black and white television set with rabbit ears. I played again in 1961 at Syracuse and we got leather golf bags with our names on them and a set of Sam Snead signature clubs, which were bottom of the line.

I got a nicer gift for participating in the Legends Game at the 1989 All-Star Weekend in Houston—the same All-Star ring the players got—than I ever got when I was an actual All-Star. And it keeps getting better. The NBA flew me to New York for the 1998 All-Star game at Madison Square Garden to serve as an honorary coach for one event on All-Star Saturday. Like everything the league does these days, it was first class the whole way. They spent $1,900 apiece for a pair of first class plane tickets from Salt Lake City, a limo picked me up at the airport and they put me up in a nice hotel, all for coaching Karl Malone and Tammi Reiss in the 2 ball Competition. I wasn't an All-Star or even a contestant, yet they gave me the full treatment. Thirty-seven years earlier when I was the All-Star, I couldn't have even dreamed of being treated so well.

One thing that hasn't changed is the pursuit of women, and the lies that go with it. Guys used to pay a lot of attention to the women in stands. They did that everywhere, but especially in L.A. If guys saw a woman they knew, they wanted to impress her, which was difficult to do sitting on the bench. So if they didn't start or if they played poorly, they would limp after the game and say they were injured. And if they didn't even get off the bench, a popular excuse was to say they were suspended for staying out too late the night before. They'd say something like, "Oh, there was a party at Dean Martin's last night and I just had to go." When Wilt Chamberlain's book came out and he said he had been with 20,000 women, *USA Today* asked me if I thought it was true.

I had played against Wilt in the first part of his career and was a broadcaster in L.A. and Phoenix the whole time he was with the Lakers, so I knew Wilt and had been around him quite a bit. I told the paper I didn't believe it. In fact, I told them I turned down more women than he had ever been with, and they printed that line in the paper. I saw Wilt a little later and he wouldn't speak to me. I said, "Big Fella, how are you?" He just looked at me with that turned-up nose.

Chapter Five

YOU THINK I MADE THIS UP?

I get a chill every time I'm broadcasting a game from the Forum and look up to see my No. 33 hanging from the rafters, right up there with Elgin Baylor's 22, Jerry West's 44 and Wilt Chamberlain's 13. It's a great honor to get your number retired. Of course, it would have meant a lot more if the jersey hanging up there with my No. 33 on it didn't have "Abdul-Jabbar" written across the top. Jerry West tells me, "Don't worry. Your name's on the back, against the wall." How could I mind sharing the number with Kareem Abdul-Jabbar? I'd say we gave No. 33 justice, scoring more than 42,000 career points between us. And I contributed more than 3,600 of them by myself!

OK, so maybe I don't deserve to have my number retired by the Lakers but with the right opportunity, I think I could have done more as a player. It seemed like my career got sidetracked just when it was finally taking off. The 1960-61 season was shaping up as my best ever when I was named to the All-Star team for the second time. I was averaging 18 points a game over the first half of the season and leading the team in assists. Playing against the NBA's best players at the All-Star game, I scored 14 points in just 14 minutes. I felt like a star again. It was my fourth year in the NBA and I was finally hitting my stride as a pro player. I felt like my career was finally starting to take off, that I was on the verge of something great.

But just like that it was over. When I got back from Syracuse, where the All-Star game was held, coach Fred Schaus stopped play-

ing me. He never said a word and I never asked why. I was buried
on the bench, though, just like that. I couldn't understand it. One
day I was an All-Star, playing the best basketball of my career, and
the next day I couldn't even start for my own team. It made no
sense. I wasn't going to make an issue of it, though. I didn't want to
play if I had to beg like some players do, and it wasn't my style to
go around badmouthing someone to try to make me look better. A
lot of guys do that in basketball, probably in all sports, but I wasn't
going to stab someone in the back to get more playing time. So I
sulked instead.

Jerry West was a rookie that season and Schaus had him coming off the bench for the first half of the year. By the All-Star break
Schaus was under a lot of pressure to play West more, and under-
standably so. West was a three-time All-American player in college,
the second player taken in the draft, and the best player on the
team after Baylor. He and Oscar Robertson were co-captains of the
United States' Gold Medal Olympic basketball team that summer in
Rome. Oscar was starting in Cincinnati and averaging 30 points a
game, but Jerry was stuck on our bench and he resented it. Schaus
wanted to bring him along slowly because Jerry had to make the
transition from forward to guard. Schaus thought it was best to let
West sit through the first quarter or so in the games and watch
things unfold. Schaus started Frank Selvy and me at guard with Jerry
backing us up. Even as a reserve that season Jerry made the All-Star
team. We both made it, and West deserved to start. That really bothered Jerry sitting on the bench. It still bothers him today.

So after the All-Star break Schaus finally moved West into the
starting lineup, but I didn't understand why I was the one who had
to sit. I was the best ballhandler on the team. I thought I was better
than Selvy and should have been starting with West in the backcourt,
especially with the kind of year I was having. But for the second
half of the season Schaus started West and Selvy at guard and now
I was coming off the bench.

The only thing I could come up with was that Schaus wasn't
ever going to start West and me together because the three of us
were all from West Virginia University. I think he was afraid the
other guys on the team would accuse him of favoritism if he played
us both. He started me while he was making West go through his
apprenticeship, but once Schaus decided to play West, one West
Virginia guy had to sit to make room for the other. I honestly think
the worst thing that happened to me was Schaus coaching the

team. That led to my demise as a player because I think if anyone else coached the team he would have started West and me. But Schaus was the coach and he wouldn't play me. I think that started me on the downward spiral.

I was frustrated sitting on the bench knowing I should be playing, but I didn't want a trade, either. I didn't want to be moving around. Before long I was only playing at the end of blowouts, so I started clowning around like I did in college, putting on a show for fans. It was something I did a lot of at West Virginia and I was known for it. So I started doing it again with the Lakers. Sometimes we had a 20-point lead and fans were leaving before I got in the game. When I started putting on my show, however, they stayed in their seats. I'd do some fancy dribbling and make fancy passes to liven things up, maybe toss up a hook shot from half court and play to the crowd. The fans loved it. Instead of leaving early, I kept them there till the end and made sure they got their money's worth.

The next year was more of the same. I was playing less then 20 minutes a night and not scoring much more than five points a game. We went all the way to the NBA Finals that year before losing to Boston in Game 7, but aside from that final play in regulation when I passed up a shot that might have won it, I wasn't a big part of it. The 1962-63 season was even worse. We traded for Dick Barnett to back up West and Selvy, so now I wasn't even getting those minutes. Barnett was a great shooter who went on to win two championships with the Knicks, and he bumped me to fourth guard on the team. I just didn't care any more. I accepted it and mentally, I was out of there. I don't know why, immaturity I guess. I didn't fight back. I was too busy enjoying life to care about working at basketball, something I thought I had already proven I could do. I resigned myself to the fact that no matter what I did, I wasn't going to play. I tried to make myself as popular as possible with the fans and was clowning more than ever. I was hoping I'd be enough of a gate attraction to hold onto my job that way.

I averaged 12 minutes a night and four points a game in the 1962-63 season. We made it back to the NBA Finals and lost in six games to Boston, but I wasn't much a part of it. The following summer, Schaus called me into his office and told me they didn't have room on the roster to bring me back for another year. He said he worked out a trade with the San Francisco Warriors so I could keep playing. I didn't think about it more than a few seconds before I told him to go ahead and announce my retirement. I didn't want to start moving all over the place to play basketball, so just like that I was through as a player. I was stubborn and refused to accept the trade.

There were reasons to stay in Los Angeles—my first daughter was born the previous November and I had just bought a house in Malibu— but I should have gone, if for no other reason than to get a full-blown pension. Two more years in the league and I would have had it. I do get a pension now, which actually pays me more than I got when I played. I'd like to see these guys playing today do that. There's no way these multimillionaires are going to get multi-million-dollar pensions.

I wanted to stay in Los Angeles, though, and I thought I had a job lined up to keep me there. That made it easier to walk away from the Lakers. I had been talking to Grady Lewis, who was the general manager for Converse Rubber Co., about working for them. Converse had 10 regional representatives spread around the country, former basketball stars who not only went to sporting goods stores to fill orders, but also promoted the shoes with clinics and speaking engagements, things like that. I was expecting to take the West Coast territory but Grady had other ideas. He wanted me to work West Virginia so I got that region instead. That meant moving my family across the country. We settled in Greensboro, North Carolina, and I worked that state, along with Virginia and West Virginia. The job started at $7,500 a year but included expenses and a car. It wasn't what I was making with the Lakers and it wasn't L.A., but it was a job.

The clinics and talks were fun and the sales were easy, but I was driving all over the South and I missed the Sunset Strip. I knew I didn't want to be a shoe salesman the rest of my life. I spent three years there and picked up a couple of broadcasting jobs along the way, including a West Virginia game, but it wasn't anything I thought seriously about getting into. I was still looking for a way to get back to L.A. and every time I talked to Grady Lewis I reminded him I wanted the West Coast region if it ever opened up. So when Bob Boyd, the Converse representative in the West, quit to take the coaching job at Southern Cal, I asked for his territory and got to move back. Bill Chambers, who had retired as a coach at William and Mary, was living in Virginia and wanted a job with Converse so I talked them into giving him my territory so I could take the L.A. job.

Bill was a real down-to-earth guy, a good image for Converse, certainly better than I was. So I went back and worked the region that covered Southern California, Southern Nevada and the whole state of Arizona. Today I'll bet you they have 25 people working Los Angeles alone. I didn't realize it at the time but that was my big break to get into broadcasting, because if I hadn't moved back to L.A. the Lakers never would have called. And a few months later, they called.

It was about the time I had been speaking with the Seattle people about the Sonics coaching job that Fred Schaus approached me about a broadcasting job with the Lakers. Jack Kent Cooke owned the team then and I would be working for him. Bob Short sold him the Lakers for $5.2 million about five years after the team moved from Minneapolis to L.A., and about two years after I quit playing. It was Mr. Cooke— everyone called him Mr. Cooke—who hired me to work with Chick Hearn on the Lakers broadcasts. I met Mr. Cooke a month or two earlier at a Lakers game when I went up and introduced myself. I told him I used to play for the Lakers and was working for Converse and just wanted to say hello. I think he knew who I was. He was very cordial and invited me to a little rendezvous he and his guests had at the arena after games. I dropped by and we chatted some more. It wasn't very long after that that he called. And I jumped at the chance.

It was a few games into the 1967-68 season and the Lakers had just fired Al Michaels as Chick Hearn's analyst. I flew to Boston with the Lakers and stepped in as Chick's sidekick. It was a great break for me but I'd say Al has done pretty well since then. It's remarkable when you look back on it, considering where Al has gone with his career. From there he got a job broadcasting for the Hawaii AAA baseball team, then he got the Cincinnati Reds job. After three years in Cincinnati he went to San Francisco and spent three years broadcasting for the Giants, and then to the big time when the networks picked him up.

Al is one of the all-time great baseball announcers, the lead broadcaster for Monday Night Football and he had one of the most famous calls of all time—"Do you believe in miracles? Yes!"—when the United States beat the Soviet Union in hockey in 1980. Now he's a star and one of the most respected broadcasters in the business. I've always liked Al. I even worked a few regional college games with him years ago. He never let success go to his head. He is one of the nicest, most level-headed guys in the business.

Then there was Jack Kent Cooke. What an experience it was working for that guy. I never met another man who intimidated me as much as he did. He brought me in for an interview and used the opportunity to pick my brain. He asked me how they could attract more fans and I told him to win some games. I wasn't just a broadcaster when he hired me, I was the traveling secretary, I did P.R. and had a few other duties. You wore a lot of hats in those days. It was a job, 9 to 5, but it was my break, a chance to get into telecommunications in Los Angeles.

Cooke was the toughest, tightest man in the world, both egocentric and arrogant. I can't think of anyone who liked him. Everybody was a number to him, nobody had a name. *Sports Illustrated* did a   story on Cooke in 1991 and they called people like me getting quotes about him. I told them about the time in 1968 when he gave me a very nice silver coffee warmer as a Christmas present. It probably cost over a hundred bucks so it was a generous gift, but he had *his* name engraved on it—Jack Kent Cooke—and he gave it to me. You talk about ego, he put his name on my gift. It didn't say "from" or anything like that, just "Jack Kent Cooke, 1968." There were about 100 people in the organization and everybody got one.

When *Sports Illustrated* did the fact-checking for the article they told him what I said and he claimed it never happened. "That's bushwah," he told them. He was a very intelligent man and he talked like that. "That's bushwah." I was looking right at the thing when I was talking to *Sports Illustrated* yet right there in the article, he denied it ever happened. In the restaurant I used to have in Salt Lake City, "Hot Rod Hundley's," I had a lot of my memorabilia on the walls so I made a shrine there to Jack Kent Cooke. I took the coffee warmer with his name engraved on it and had it enclosed in a glass case. Then I cut out the *Sports Illustrated* article and put it in the case right next to the coffee warmer, and underlined "that's bushwah" in yellow. It's absolutely as true as can be, yet he denied it. The funny thing is, there are 99 other people walking around with one of those "Jack Kent Cooke" coffee warmers. I should have mailed the damn thing back to him with a copy of the magazine article.

Obviously I'm not a fan of his. I never was and I wasn't alone. There was a group of ex-employees of his—people he had fired— who formed a club in Los Angeles called the Forum Alumni. You couldn't fit them all in a room, there were that many of them. They gathered for cocktail parties to celebrate not working for him anymore. He had five wives, too, and lost $49 million to his first one in a divorce settlement. The presiding judge in that case was Joseph Wapner, the guy from "People's Court." The settlement made the *Guinness Book of World Records* for what was at the time the largest divorce settlement in the world.

Cooke was the kind of boss that if you saw him coming down the hall you quickly ducked into an office. He'd walk by me and say, "Rahhhhhhhhhd, we can't get anything done standing in the hallways, can we," and he'd keep walking. He never stopped. He introduced me one day to Rod Laver, the tennis player who was playing at the Forum. Cooke walked by and said, "Rod Hundley, Rod Laver," and just kept walking. That was it. He came down the hall once with a stack of paperback books called "How to Work 24 Hours a Day" or something like that, and he put one on everybody's desk.

Cooke had a Rolls-Royce and a Bentley and he had them both parked out in front of the Forum. When people in the offices saw him pull up they would send out an alert so everyone could look busy in case he popped in on them. He had a driver, Eddie, and I guarantee you he fired Eddie a minimum of 50 times. He'd fire him but as soon as Eddie turned to leave Cooke would yell, "Eddie, where are you going?"

"You fired me."

"Go get my car and fill it up with gas."

He never paid anybody anything, the cheapest SOB I ever met. Everyone worked for peanuts. When he built the Forum, Chick Hearn suggested he call it "The Fabulous Forum." Cooke liked the name and as a reward he told Chick he could expect a little something extra in his next pay envelope. So on the next payday, inside the envelope was Chick's regular check—and a photograph of Jack Kent Cooke. It wasn't like Cooke didn't have money. He sold the team for $67.5 million in 1979, nearly 13 times as much as he paid for it 14 years earlier.

Mr. Cooke made sure everyone in his organization watched every dollar. When we were in Boston for the world championships one year we took cabs in from the airport, then went to Fred Schaus, who was the general manager then, and got reimbursed for cab fare. The first couple of guys went to Schaus to get their money and it came to $5.50. Then the team's P.R. director goes up to Schaus and tells him his fare was $5.75. Schaus tells him, "You get five-fifty, just like everyone else." Fred cheated him out of a quarter. That's how it was under Jack Kent Cooke.

Cooke liked owning sports teams but he didn't know much about basketball. Billy Hewitt out of USC was our first-round draft choice in 1968. He was a local player and he was OK, but he wasn't great and never would be. I said as much in my broadcasts. Cooke says to me, "Rahhhhhd, Chick is singing the praises of Billy Hewitt. He's going to be the next Elgin Baylor!" Chick is saying this stuff on the air and Cooke wonders why I'm not. Cooke is telling Chick to do it so he does it. Chick was scared to death of Jack Kent Cooke. And I said, "Mr. Cooke, I can't say that because Billy Hewitt couldn't carry Elgin's jock." The best thing I could say about Hewitt was that he was a nice guy, but he couldn't play. He was traded early the next season for Happy Hairston, who gave the Lakers 15 points a night for five years. Billy Hewitt bounced around the league for six years, playing for four different teams and averaging 5.7 points a game for his career. But Jack Kent Cooke thought he was the next Elgin Baylor.

One good deal Cooke did make was sending Jerry Chambers, Darrall Imhoff and Archie Clark to Philadelphia for Wilt Chamberlain. The Lakers still had Elgin Baylor and Jerry West, and the three of them combined for nearly 80,000 points in their careers. It was a lopsided trade because the Lakers were able to keep both of their stars. Wilt was making big money then and the Lakers could afford to pay him. Philadelphia couldn't. It's the same old story—they bought Chamberlain, they bought Kareem Abdul-Jabbar and they bought Shaquille O'Neal. Who else but the Lakers could afford to do that? They buy the world championship. You think if the Jazz had the money to buy Shaq they might win a championship? Or if they put Kareem with Stockton and Malone?

But teams couldn't afford to do what the Lakers have done, so now Cooke has Chamberlain to go with West and Baylor and he's giddy with excitement. He's asking people if a team has ever gone 82-0 in a season. He actually thought we could go undefeated. So what happens? We got beat the very first game of the year. We were 0-1, so that took care of an 82-0 season. Those three guys averaged 70 points a game that year but they still lost 27 times.

Cooke would say to me, "Isn't Wilt wonderful?" and I'd say, "No, Mr. Cooke, he isn't wonderful. He's a pain in the ass." He was a great player, but he was a pain. I had to serve as traveling secretary in addition to doing the broadcasting, and Wilt was my biggest headache. I handed out the plane tickets and Wilt always sat in the first row on the aisle in first class. On one flight that seat was already taken, so Wilt was in the second row, and of course he complained. He said, "Hey, baby, how come I'm not in the front row?" I told him because someone else was sitting there.

Nowadays you're on your own but back then I had to make the wakeup calls. I called everybody on the team and always called Wilt last. He'd say, "Hey, baby, what time we got to be in the lobby?" and I'd say 30 minutes. He'd say, "call me back in 15," and I would. Then Wilt would stroll through the hotel lobby, jump in a cab and take off by himself. We took cabs from the hotel to the airport and they always said be sure and get four guys in a cab, but Wilt would jump in by himself and take off. I had to reimburse the guys for the cabs, then I would turn in the receipts, and they wouldn't want to give me the money for Wilt's cab. "We said four guys in a cab," they'd tell me. And I'd say you tell Wilt that.

He was a real pain to everyone. If we'd be going to New York in the morning, he would ask me for his ticket the night before. "I'm going tonight," he said. I'd tell him I couldn't give it to him, that he would have to ask the coach, Butch van Breda Kolff. We called Wilt "The Load" and Butch would tell me to give him his ticket. "We'll get rid of the Load and make it a happy flight." I actually liked Wilt and enjoyed being around him, but he was impossible to deal with. He wasn't a very good poker player so he always tried to buy the pot. He'd try to raise us $50 and we'd say Wilt, it's a $5 game. So he'd raise us $5 and we'd call. He usually only had a pair of deuces.

Jerry West loved him though. Wilt got hounded by autograph-seekers the minute he got off a plane. The guy's 7 feet tall and very recognizable. So Jerry always waited until Wilt got off the plane, then slipped out behind him unnoticed. He always followed Wilt out of the locker room, too, letting Wilt draw the crowd while Jerry walked away unnoticed. John Stockton does the same thing today with Karl Malone.

I got serious about broadcasting right from the start. Even though I was sitting next to Chick Hearn when he was broadcasting, I would tape his games and listen to them. I was trying to get a feel for what made him so good, how he would inject lines, his timing and tempo, his voice inflections, things like that. Bill King was another great broadcaster whom I taped. He worked out of the San Francisco Bay area, broadcasting for the Warriors, the San Francisco Giants and the Oakland Raiders, and I studied him too. I would tape him and Chick and study their styles. I knew I had to develop my own, but I wanted to learn the technical side of it and those two were the best for that. Because I never took school too seriously, I had to teach myself. I read a lot of books and when people corrected my mistakes I learned from them. I wanted to get better and I was serious about learning.

Chick gave me the best piece of broadcasting advice I ever received. He said, always pretend you are broadcasting for the blind. Describe where the ball is and what people are doing with it. I never forget that. I also learned to use phrases and sentence fragments like Chick did. You can't keep up with the action if you talk in complete sentences. You have to use short cuts so you don't get behind. That allows you to get in more description: "Baseline right ... parallel to the free throw line ... on the left top to the right side ... fake right, go left ... into the paint leaning to his left ... fast break coming in from the left side with the right hand." That was a great tip. The blind depend on me to show them what's happening, and if they feel like they are there, then everyone else will too.

John Pierson is an artist in Phoenix who has done some work for me. His mother, who lives in Ogden, Utah, is mostly blind and John tells me she is a big fan of the Jazz—and me. She listens to every game and says she can tell right where the ball is. That's a nice compliment, and it showed that Chick was right.

I worked a few small college basketball games when I first got back to L.A. with Converse, broadcasting for Glendale and Fresno State, schools like that, and I kept it up after taking the Lakers jobs. I worked a lot with Ross Porter, who does the play-by-play for the Dodgers now. About the same time, Eddie Einhorn, who now is a part-owner of the Chicago White Sox, hired me to work for his company, TVS, which owned the rights to college basketball at the time. Since they weren't a network, they sold packages to independent stations in each market. On Saturday afternoons they would show a regional game, sometimes as many as 13 games going on at once all across the nation. Then Einhorn tied them all into a national game that followed. It would be a double-header and I would do the big one, usually with Dick Enberg. Of all the guys Einhorn had working for him, Enberg and I were the No. 1 team. I worked these games while also doing the Lakers broadcasts, sometimes doing two games in one day. This was back when UCLA had its great run of 88 consecutive victories and I got to broadcast the bookend games of that streak. The streak started after a loss to Notre Dame and ended three years later with another loss to the Fighting Irish.

It was a hectic pace but fun. I remember broadcasting a Lakers game on a Friday night, catching a red-eye flight to South Bend, Indiana, changing clothes in Ara Parsegian's office and getting on the air in time for a Saturday afternoon tip-off. There were a lot of times when I would walk into the arena just as the game was starting. Because I was doing color commentary and not play-by-play I could pull it off.

Einhorn operated out of a shoe box at the time but eventually sold the rights to college basketball, made a killing, and used his windfall to buy a piece of the White Sox and Bulls with Jerry Reinsdorf. Eddie offered me a job in Chicago back in the 1980s when they put together a premium cable service called Sports Channel. They showed a lot of the White Sox, Bulls and Blackhawks games each month that weren't shown on free TV, and cable viewers would pay a monthly fee for the service, just like they would for HBO or Showtime. In addition to doing broadcasting for the Bulls, Eddie wanted me to host the studio show for the baseball games. I was working for the Jazz at the time and I considered it, but the money wasn't enough to get me to leave Utah and give up my job with the Jazz.

The best schooling I ever had was spending two years with Chick Hearn. Not only did I learn so much about the technical side of broadcasting, I stole all my best lines from him. I didn't have time to make this stuff up. If I heard something I liked, I used it. Dribble drive ... Leapin' leaner ... Frozen rope ... This game's in the ol' refrigerator ... I stole all those from Chick. I read a great line about me in a newspaper article when I was in high school that I use now as my signature line: "With a gentle push and a mild arc, the old cowhide globe hit home." I stole everything.

Chick Hearn has broadcast more than 3,000 Lakers game, by far the most in NBA history. His 2,000th game came in Utah against the Jazz so we held a ceremony to honor him and gave him a bottle of champagne. His wife, Marge, told me that night she thought the Lakers should give me the play-by-play job when Chick retires. I told her I was going to retire before he does, and maybe I was right. That was more than 1,000 games ago.

I don't know that Chick ever wanted me there, though. It wasn't anything against me, he just preferred to work alone. And I think he was grooming his son to take the job. His son was keeping statistics for Chick before I showed up and would go on the air at halftime and read off the stats from the first half. Then they gave me the job and Chick never let me talk. He'd cut me off in the middle of a sentence and go on with the play-by-play. He had a signal where he would hold up a fist when he wanted me to wrap up my thought and get out of it quickly. And if he shook the fist, that meant get out immediately. So he would be asking me a question and shaking his fist at the same time. The first season I think all I ever said was, "That's right, Chickie Baby." He used to always tell people he didn't like me calling him Chickie Baby, but he'd call himself the same thing. He was funny, though. He had a lot of one-liners.

He really was a remarkable broadcaster to work with, and I learned so much from him. Because I didn't get to talk I spent the time listening to him, really listening to everything he'd say. I watched the games and listened to him, his expressions and his enthusiasm, how he'd never miss a beat on the ball.

Chick was the first in a long line of great broadcasters I worked with. Don Criqui. Al McCoy of the Phoenix Suns. Dick Enberg. Gary Bender. Brent Musburger. Al Michaels. Pat Summerall. Dick Stockton—I learned from all of those guys, when to raise my voice, the inflections. They were all very professional.

Summerall and I got to be great friends. He is an ex-football player who worked his way up and now is at the head of the class. He had never done basketball play-by-play before when he started doing the NBA games on CBS, with Elgin Baylor as his analyst. Then when the playoffs started, they fired Elgin and hired Rick Barry when he was through playing for the season. They could have waited until the season was over to make the move, but it's a cutthroat business. Pat did a nice job with whomever he was with. He really knows how to play off an analyst and does it better than anyone in sports. He has no ego about the microphone. That's why he and John Madden make such a great team on football broadcasts. He considers the analyst the expert and is willing to take a back seat to him.

There were a lot of memorable coaches along the way, too. Digger Phelps was at Notre Dame when I started doing national college basketball games in addition to the Lakers. I got along with him and we'd always kid each other. I'd say something like, "Nice suit, Digger. Too bad they didn't have one in your size." The worst insult I ever had for a coach was unintentional—and broadcast live on national television. Chuck Daly was coaching Penn at the time and I knew him from his days as an assistant coach at Duke. As soon as I started the interview my mind went blank. There I was, live on national television, and my mind was absolutely blank. "You won't believe this," I said to Chuck, "but I can't remember your name." So every time I run into him these days I ask him his name.

Al McGuire was a pain in the butt then. He wouldn't do an interview unless he could plug his company or say hello to people he knew in New York. That's what I thought about after he got into broadcasting and it was his turn to ask coaches for interviews. I'd see him on TV when he had to put up with coaches who were like he had been, trying to get them to give interviews. I got a kick out of that.

Chapter Six

I LIKED THIS JOB SO MUCH, I GAVE UP SMOKING

I had something of a falling out with Jack Kent Cooke after my second season working with Chick Hearn as the Lakers' analyst. I was getting restless for something else and when Mr. Cooke found out, he acted like he didn't want me around anymore. I wanted to get into play-by-play anyway, and I knew that wouldn't happen any time soon in L.A. If I stayed with the Lakers I was going to be behind Chick forever so it was time to move on already.

The Phoenix Suns, who joined the NBA as an expansion team the year before, were looking for a color man to work with Bob Vache, so I interviewed with them. Jerry Colangelo, the CEO of the Suns, was general manager then and he offered me the job. Colangelo was just a young kid at the time, 29 years old, but he has done a great job building that franchise. What a businessman he is. He started in marketing with the Bulls and now he runs two teams. He brought baseball to Arizona with the Diamondbacks and has been instrumental in everything, even building the arenas. He's a self-made millionaire, and it all came from sports. He was a college basketball player at Illinois, not good enough to make it as a pro, but he's been in basketball all his life.

I had to think about his offer back in 1969 because that meant leaving L.A. and moving to the desert. I never thought basketball would survive there, but I took the job. Colangelo treated me really well. He gave me a company car, which he didn't have to do. Certainly Jack Kent Cooke never would have. Soon after I accepted the Suns offer, the Los Angeles Stars of the ABA also offered me a job.

That would have allowed me to stay in L.A. but I had already committed to the Suns. Besides, whatever doubts I had about basketball lasting in Phoenix, I knew that was a lot more stable than the Stars' situation. And I was right. Nearly 30 years later, the Suns are one of the strongest franchises in pro sports, and the ABA is a distant memory. A year after I took the Suns job, the Stars moved to Utah, and there's no telling if they would have taken me with them. The Stars had success on the court, winning the ABA championship their first year in Utah, but they only lasted four more years before folding 16 games into the 1975-76 season.

The Suns did well for such a young team but with one lucky flip of the coin they would have done a lot better. The Suns and the Milwaukee Bucks tossed a coin in 1969, just before I joined the team, for the No. 1 draft pick. Milwaukee won and got Lew Alcindor—who later changed his name to Kareem Abdul-Jabbar. The Suns got Neal Walk, who wasn't a bad player, but he wasn't Jabbar. Johnny Kerr was coaching the team then and after they lost the coin toss he said, "There goes my career. I could have been the greatest coach in the NBA if we had just won that coin flip."

The Suns did catch a lucky break that summer, however, signing Connie Hawkins as a free agent when he was eligible to come into the NBA. The former Harlem Globetrotter and ABA star really put some life into this team the first year I was there. He was called "the Hawk" and he played like one. He would catch the ball in one hand on the fast break, move it around in the air and lay it in one-handed. I'd say, "the Hawk swoops" in my calls. His hands were so big he could hold a basketball with two fingers and his thumb. He pulled rebounds out of the air like he was plucking a grapefruit off a tree, just plucking the ball with one hand. He would hold the ball up in the air until the crowd reacted, then throw it down court. When he posted up, he held the ball out with one hand and had his back to the defender. He'd look over his shoulder and stare the guy right in the eye. As soon as you looked back at him, though, he'd flip the ball right over you.

He had a real love for the game and made All-NBA First Team his first year in Phoenix. We got to be good friends that year, always joking around. He had all sorts of lines that would just break me up. He asked me for a cigarette once so I lit up and handed the cigarette to him. He said, "Thank you, Hot Rod, that's very white of you." He was a fun prankster. We were standing at the baggage claim area of the Atlanta airport one time when he came up from behind and kind of slapped me upside the face, not hard but enough to get me to look. I turned around and said, "What are you doing?" He said, "I just wanted to do something that has never been done in Atlanta, Georgia, before," a black man slapping a white in the South. I got a laugh out of that.

I was still working as a color analyst when my opportunity to do play-by-play came unexpectedly, as most tragedies do. Bob Vache was big in Phoenix, doing Arizona State broadcasts, and when the Suns moved there he got that job too. Halfway through my first season as his analyst, though, he got killed in an automobile accident. We were both at a sponsors' party that night, we said good night and I never saw him again. I was in bed asleep when Jerry Colangelo called and woke me up. I couldn't believe it when he told me Bob was dead. I was just with him two hours earlier.

And Colangelo said, "There's another reason I'm calling you. Can you do play-by-play?"

The next night's game was at 8 p.m. and I said, "I'll tell you tomorrow night at 10 o'clock." I had never done it in my life and with no time to think about it, really, I was on the job.

I had really studied Chick Hearn when I worked next to him so I had some idea of what I should do going in, so I gave it my best shot. The first play of the game, the Suns get the tip and Dick Van Arsdale goes in for a layup. You would have thought we just won the world championship the way I called that play. And I never let up. By halftime I couldn't even talk, I was so hoarse. I just didn't know how to control my voice. That happened to me for the rest of the season. It took me that long to learn how to adjust to it. I even quit smoking cold turkey to save my voice. I smoked a lot then, two or three packs a day, so it was hard. But I loved this job and wanted to keep it so I gave up cigarettes. And I haven't smoked since.

When the Suns formed their expansion team they raided the Chicago Bulls. Johnny Kerr had coached the Bulls the previous two seasons and they brought him in to coach the Suns. Jerry Colangelo was in marketing for the Bulls, and Joe Proski was their equipment manager and trainer, and they both came to Phoenix with Kerr. Colangelo and Proski were still in Phoenix for the Suns' 30th anniversary in 1998, but Johnny Kerr got fired in the middle of his second season. He was Coach of the Year in his first season as coach of the Chicago Bulls. He had Jerry Sloan playing for him and won 33 games and made the playoffs as an expansion team. He was too easy-going to be a good coach, though, and the Suns fired him. This was shortly after Bob Vache died so I had just started doing play-by-play, and they put Johnny on the air with me.

In those days when you fired a coach he was still under contract so if he wanted to continue getting paid he had to do whatever you wanted him to do. Today when coaches get fired they move on, but the paychecks keep coming. In those days, though, Red had to work for his money, so they made him a broadcaster. We were already good friends so we had fun working together. We called our postgame show the Red Hot show —Johnny Red Kerr and Hot Rod Hundley. He has gone on to have great success as a broadcaster for the Chicago Bulls; he has a great wit, a lot of one-liners. He was a lot like Frank Layden and Rick Majerus that way—he knew the game and had a lot of funny stories.

When Kerr still coached for the Bulls back in 1967, he had a big center named Reggie Harding. They were in L.A. playing the Lakers and had the game won. During a timeout before the final play, Red told Reggie, no matter what, don't foul and give them free throws. So naturally he fouls and they make two free throws with one second left and win the game. After the game somebody asked Red where he was going and he said, "I'm going back to the hotel to watch 'Mission: Impossible.'" He cut Harding two weeks later.

The Suns had a lot of talent my first year in Phoenix with Paul Silas and Connie Hawkins at forward, Dick Van Arsdale and Gail Goodrich at guard and Jim Fox, who was a pretty good center, in the starting lineup. They made the playoffs and got the Lakers down 3-1 when Fox got hurt. After that they didn't have anyone who could stop Wilt Chamberlain. The Lakers had Jerry West, too, and came back and beat the Suns four games to three.

By then there was a big-time love affair with the Suns in Phoenix. The fans at the airport were unbelievable, thousands of them coming out to greet the team after the series. They were kicking the Lakers' butts when Fox got hurt, and when I saw the reception from the fans, I knew right then that basketball was going to make it in the desert.

When Johnny Kerr was fired as coach, Jerry Colangelo filled in for the rest of the season. The next year, Cotton Fitzsimmons took over as coach and held the job for two years before coming back to Phoenix in the late '80s. He's a cocky little guy, but a great cocky, a harmless cocky. He wasn't arrogant at all, just a great guy to be around. I loved him and the way he coached his team. Every time he called a timeout, whoever the last guy out of the huddle was, Cotton would pull him aside so none of the other guys could hear. It didn't matter who it was, Cotton would pull one guy back while the other four walked out on the court and deliver a personal pep talk. One time it would be Dick Van Arsdale and Cotton would say, "Van, give me five minutes. I can't win it without you." Next time it would be Connie Hawkins. "Hawk," he'd say, whispering in his ear, "I've got to have you. I need five minutes, Hawk, I can't win it without you." Or Gail Goodrich. "Goody, I can't win it without you." That worked because it was a different player every time and the other four guys never were within earshot. It was his way of pumping the team up.

That year the Suns brought in Joe McConnell to do play-by-play and moved me back to the color analyst job. Jerry Colangelo told me years later that he never dreamed I would be able to do play-by-play. He never thought my voice would be strong enough. I have such a low-pitched voice and it always went hoarse. I didn't know how to do it then, so he wasn't going to hire me back for play-by-play. I could have had the job if he had the confidence I could handle it. I didn't know if I could do it either, so he brought me back as an analyst.

I continued doing college games after I moved to Phoenix so a lot of times I worked two games in one day. I'd get back from a Notre Dame game or something like that in the afternoon and arrive at the arena in Phoenix just as they were tipping it up. I ran through a lot of airports in those days.

Between my apprenticeship with Chick and my brief play-by-play experience in Phoenix, my confidence as a broadcaster was growing. Before long I has hired by CBS to work their national NBA broadcasts. I worked two separate stints with CBS, from 1972 to 1974, and from 1978 to 1981.

At the 1974 All-Star game in Seattle, Dionne Warwick sang the national anthem and I had her on as a halftime guest on CBS. I met her the night before at the All-Star banquet. They were supposed to bring in a comedian from Las Vegas as a warmup act, then have Dionne Warwick sing. I was sitting at the CBS table eating dinner with Pat Summerall, Chuck Milton, Elgin Baylor and the other guys from CBS when one of the P.R. guys came out and told me the comedian couldn't get in from Vegas because the airport was fogged in. He asked me if I could fill in. I did a lot of speaking engagements in those days, so I had 45 minutes of material at the tip of my tongue. They only wanted 15 minutes so the only problem was deciding what to leave out. This was a basketball crowd so it was a piece of cake. I did my 15 minutes, the crowd loved it, then I walked off the stage and Dionne Warwick came on right behind me. What's funny is the comedian from Vegas was probably going to get $5,000. They sent me a thank you note with a check for $100.

At that same dinner I met Shelly Beychok, who had just been named a minority owner of the expansion franchise in New Orleans. I wished him luck; I had no idea I would be working for him in a few months.

Sam Battistone, the majority owner of the new Jazz team, offered me the play-by-play job with the expansion team in 1974, and I jumped at it. I worked five seasons with the Suns and never got another chance to do play-by-play. This was my break. Jerry Colangelo was very good about it, giving me the freedom to go with the Jazz. He said, if I can better myself, go on and do it. The only problem was that Barry Mendelson, an executive with the Jazz, didn't want me breaking away for network games so I had to give up working for CBS. I thrived with the Jazz, though. Today I'm the only ex-player in the entire NBA doing radio play-by-play. Every guy who ever played the game has been an analyst at one time or another, but they don't do play-by-play. Tom Heinsohn does play-by-play for Boston television, at least in title, but all he does is sit there and talk with Bob Cousy.

Along the way, I've worked with a lot of great and interesting color analysts, starting with Johnny Kerr. Jim Nantz is a star at CBS today and I worked with him doing Jazz games for three years. One day when Frank Layden was coaching, Mark Eaton got his fourth foul in the first half and Nantz made a statement critical of Frank for leaving Eaton on the court once he got his third foul. When Frank watched films of the game, he heard Nantz's comments and jumped all over him the next day at practice. Frank had tried to get Mark out of the game after his third foul, but Mark was called for his fourth before the sub could get in. Frank didn't appreciate some young analyst criticizing him and let him have it. Frank could be as mean as he was funny. He could get on you quick, but he also quickly forgot.

The year before the Jazz moved to Utah, Sam Battistone let me work for CBS again, which I did from 1978 to 1981. Sam knew it was good publicity for the team to have their announcer working for the network. Chuck Milton was the executive producer of basketball for CBS and the guy who hired me. He really liked me but when he switched over to football, the new guys making basketball decisions didn't invite me back. Jim Nantz always said he couldn't believe CBS didn't have me doing NBA games. CBS finally did call me one day, but they called me about Jim. I got a message to call Chuck Milton one day and he told me they were interested in hiring Nantz. They were going to do a new Saturday college football program and wanted him to co-host it. Chuck wanted to know what I thought of him and I said he couldn't do better. I think Jim is strongest in the studio and he's good at golf. Chuck asked me how I thought he would be if the numbers came in upside down— if they cued him, say, to go to Brent Musburger in Chicago and they went to someone in New York instead. How would he handle that kind of pressure? I said just like Brent, and I thought Brent was great in the studio. I gave Jimmy a 100 percent recommendation and now he's the No. 1 guy there.

Before Frank Layden took over as coach of the Jazz in addition to his general manager responsibilities, he also served as my color man on the broadcasts. That's a strange combination, general manager and analyst. Team officials weren't allowed to sit on press row but Frank did the broadcasts so he sat courtside next to me. Frank would get so caught up in the games sometimes he would throw down his headset and scream at the referees like he was the coach. The refs would tell him he couldn't sit there and he'd say, "Hey, I'm the media."

Our games were broadcast on the satellite then and while people watching the local feed saw commercials, those watching directly off the satellite would still see the arena feed. So anything you said during commercial breaks would be heard by people with satellite dishes. You had to be careful what you said, but sometimes you forgot.

We were in Boston playing the Celtics and Red Auerbach was the general manager then. Frank had the ultimate respect for Red but Red could irritate you as a coach the way Rick Barry could irritate you as a player. The Jazz were getting clobbered by the Celtics and that was frustrating too, so when Frank saw Red at halftime lighting up a cigar he says to me, "I'd like to take that cigar and shove it up his ass." Bill Fitch was coaching the Celtics then and after the game we ran into him as we were walking out of the building. He said, "Hey, Frank, you've got to be careful what you say on the satellite. We have a monitor in the locker room and heard what you said about Red at halftime. All the guys were breaking up, but you're lucky Red didn't hear it."

I did play-by-play on TBS for an oldtimers game in Indianapolis and Red Auerbach was my color man. He had mellowed as he had gotten older. So later, when the Jazz were in Boston to play the Celtics and I needed a guest for halftime, I said I'd get Red. The local TV crew we hired for the game told me I needed to find someone else, because Red doesn't come out to do a halftime show for anybody. I said I'd get him, and sure enough he came out. The crew couldn't get over that. He did that for me a few times, mainly because I played against his teams, that I went back a long way with him. We talked about the old teams and compared eras, from Bird and Parish to Russell and Cousy. He enjoyed talking about that, and so did I. It's part of what makes broadcasting fun.

Chapter Seven

THE MASK

From my earliest memories as a basketball player, whether it was in the big games or in the pressure moments of the close ones, I thrived when the heat was on. I never got scared on the basketball court. I might spin the ball on my finger before shooting a crucial free throw or crack a joke in the heat of the game, anything to keep things light. Even if I missed a deciding shot and we lost the game, I got over it. Basketball was just a game and I always had fun. I wanted to win and tried hard but it wasn't the end of the world if we lost. Compared to everything else in life, this was easy. This was my security in life.

But that was basketball. When I wasn't playing the game I don't remember ever not being scared as a kid. I never had a family and I never had a home. I never even had a childhood, really. I bounced from place to place since I could remember; I never had anyone or anything. When I was around people I always had a smile for them. I always put on a happy front, but it was a mask I put on to hide how scared and lonely I was. When I was alone, I was in a much different world. I tried never to show it, but I was scared and insecure. After a big basketball game I felt the cheers and the adulation run all the way through my body and I thrived on the attention. I wore a big grin, a lovable, addictive smile, even if I didn't know where I was going to sleep that night.

I had parents in the biological sense, but I never had *parents*. My father, Louis Hundley, was a butcher by trade, so everyone called him Butch. Even I called him Butch, maybe because he just seemed like this person I knew, an acquaintance; but he never was my father. Butch didn't have much of a taste for work. He spent most of his time in the pool halls of Charleston, West Virginia, hustling and drinking. He wasn't the sort of person who would take to fatherhood, or any other responsibility for that matter. I was a month old before he ever even saw me, my mother told me, and during my whole life he was just some acquaintance I knew.

My mother, Cora, tried to be a parent. I guess she loved me and wanted me to be taken care of, but the way my father was, she was in it alone. And that wasn't enough. She grew up on a dairy farm and moved to Wheeling, West Virginia, when she was 16. She met my father at a hotel coffee shop where they both worked. He was 22 and started courting her. He wanted to get married and she thought that would give her a home. She knew how he was, but he was so handsome, so charming and fun to be around, she thought she could change him; she thought marriage would settle him down. They got married and it was hard for her right from the start. It never got any better.

They moved to Charleston to get a fresh start, but he continued to drink and miss work. They had been married four years when I was born on October 26, 1934, and she thought having a baby would finally make him more responsible. But it never happened. It was the Depression and there was no money, and as it turned out, there wasn't much of a marriage either. She couldn't have been more alone when I was born, so she looked for help. She went looking for someone willing to take me, and then someone else when that didn't work out . . . and someone else after that. I spent my whole life growing up with strangers. I don't ever remember living with her. I can't remember that far back.

My parents divorced when I was about six months old and I was still real young, probably four or five, when my mother left Charleston. She moved to Washington, D.C., where she thought she could get a better job. The Depression was still going on and my mother was uneducated. I don't think she even finished high school. She stayed with her sister and took waitressing jobs in Washington. She tried to see me sometimes the first couple of years and she sent me money once in a while, presents at Christmas, but then the visits faded. I saw her less and less.

From the time my mother moved to Washington until I was about 16, I lived with Mamie Sharp and her husband, George. My mother just knocked on their door one night and asked these people to take care of me. They were the greatest people and they took me into their home. They were in their 50s and had grown kids of their own, but they treated me like one of theirs. They didn't have much, but they took care of me the best they could. I didn't have a room of my own; all they could afford was food and a cot for me. I slept under the stairs, where they had put up a curtain. What I remember more than anything was how cold it was sleeping on that cot under the stairs. Trying to sleep at night, I was always scared and alone. And cold. Real cold. I cried a lot, but at least I never went to bed hungry.

Money was extremely scarce then. My mother would send me some when she could, and she might have sent the Sharps money too, but it couldn't have been much. The Sharps were very poor themselves. George Sharp washed bottles for a living at a dairy. That was his job. I wish my mother would have knocked on a rich door, but she was in the wrong neighborhood for that. The Sharps were nice people, though, strict but caring. They're in heaven now, I know that.

It was hard to fit in as a kid. All my friends had mothers and fathers and brothers and sisters. And homes. I didn't have any of that. I felt strange in other people's homes, so I never developed any real close friendships. While other kids went home to their families after school, I went down to a local café where they had a sports ticker. Men would hang out there, following scores of ballgames and gambling on them, and they let me hang out with them.

By time I was 16 and in high school, I got to be more than the Sharps could handle, so I moved out. Tommy Crutchfield, a friend from school, invited me to move in with his family. His mother ran a boarding house, and I stayed in Tommy's room. He was ahead of me in school and when he moved onto college, his mother let me have Tommy's room to myself. She served meals in her boarding house, so I always could get breakfast and dinner there.

Mrs. Crutchfield tried to get me to do right and sometimes she would buy me clothes or give me money for a Coke, but she wasn't my mother. I was free pretty much to go as I pleased, and I took advantage of that. All the guys at school were jealous of me because I could stay out till all hours carousing, drinking beer and smoking cigarettes. No one got on me about studying. I strutted my freedom, but deep down I was jealous of the other guys. They had homes. They had someone who cared about them. Even in high school, with all the attention I was getting then from basketball and the freedom I had from living on my own, I went home every night and cried myself to sleep. I didn't have anyone to take my report card home to, no one to take an interest in me. So I drifted.

I didn't have a car and had to walk everywhere, but I got by. I could make some money hustling pool, and once I got known for my basketball, especially after we won the state championship in junior high school, some of the alums would give me money.

I saw my father around Charleston once in a while but even though he was in town, we never had much to do with each other. I would drop by the pool hall sometimes, after I was pretty well known around town from playing basketball, and let him show me off to his friends. He enjoyed that, so I humored him. Sometimes, though, when I was in high school, I'd see him on the streets all boozed up. He'd come up to me and embarrass me in front of my friends. I hated him for that. But other times I ran into him when he was sober and we would be all right.

I remember once in his life he tried to play father. I was living with the Crutchfields and I guess he had heard I was running around, drinking and smoking and keeping late hours. He was waiting for me at the hotel one night when I got in about 1 in the morning. He was all boozed up and started yelling at me about running around and ruining my life. He tried to throw me against the wall but I grabbed him and screamed at him. He had his chance to be my father but he ran out on me. I told him to stay the hell away from me, then went up to my room and cried myself to sleep. I don't think I ever really hated the man. He was who he was; he couldn't help who he was. How do you hate someone for that?

I left Charleston for school at West Virginia University in Morgantown, then went to play for the Lakers in Minneapolis and eventually Los Angeles. Along the way, I can't say I had ever given my father much thought. In 1965, a few years after my playing career had ended, I was working for Converse and living in Greensboro, North Carolina, when someone told me that my father died. If I had still been in Los Angeles or even Minneapolis, I never would have given any thought to attending the funeral. I probably wouldn't have even known about it. But I was only a four-hour drive away, so what the hell I went. There wasn't much emotion involved, no pent-up anger or anything like that, but no overwhelming feelings of grief or sorrow either. I remember standing over him laid out in the casket with a diamond ring on his finger. I looked down at him, not feeling much at all.

Years later, though, I realized I was wrong. I hadn't seen him since high school except for a few times in college, and I resented him for not making any attempts to see me or do anything for me. He did the best he could, though. He could hardly take care of himself, so how could I blame him for not taking care of me?

It was different with my mother. She followed the stories of me becoming a basketball star and after I had grown up and made it to the NBA, we started building a real relationship. We talked regularly on the phone once I started earning money to make long-distance calls, and I'd visit her when I came to Washington with the Lakers. I got to understand her, what she went through.

After I had retired from basketball and moved on to my broadcasting career, Bill Libby, the late, great writer from *Sport* magazine, interviewed me for a book he was writing on Jerry West. I asked him, "Why do you want to write about him? All he does is drink milkshakes and go to bed. I'm the interesting story!" I must have been convincing because after he finished the book on Jerry, he came back and wrote one about me. It was called "Clown: Number 33 in your program, number one in your heart—Hot Rod Hundley." He interviewed my mother for the book and she opened up to him about how much of a struggle her life had been.

Here's what my mother told him in 1970 about what her life was like when I was born:

> "I moved in with my sister and her husband, even though they didn't have much and were in trouble, too. They had a little girl, Patsy, who was three years old and was dying of diphtheria. They couldn't afford me, but I had to eat. I worked as long as I could, but I couldn't make much. The girl was three years old on July 8 and died on October 1. Rodney was born on October 26. I was very sick. And scared. And alone. And it was a hard birth. I was two days and two nights in labor. He was born on a Friday morning at eleven o'clock and his father wasn't there and, oh, God, I cried and I cried and I cried.
>
> "He was a healthy baby, beautiful, with white blond hair, but I didn't know how I was going to take care of him or what I was going to do with him. I was paralyzed for three weeks. I don't know what was wrong. The doctors didn't know what was wrong. But I lay on my back for three weeks and I couldn't move my legs and I could hardly hold my baby and I didn't want to live. I just

wanted to die, but then I saw I had to live. I said to myself, I got to live for my baby.

"I thought maybe when Rod was born it would change his father and he would take more interest in marriage, but before I even got out of the hospital I could see it wouldn't and I made up my mind to that. And I made up my mind and I got so I could walk and I got out of the hospital, but it was still a while before I could go back to work. I had nothing, no more than a couple dollars to my name. ...

"Rod stayed five or six different places over the years. I wanted to keep him, but, oh, God, I just couldn't make a living. I always wanted to be with him, but sometimes the people who were keepin' him didn't think he should see me so much because it made him miss me too much. One lady didn't want me to see him. I found out she whipped the blood out of him. He was seventeen months old and she used to stick his feet out in the rain to punish him. I took him away from her and gave him to somebody else. ...

"One lady beat him so bad, I found blue marks all over his little body and I started to cry and I just picked him up and I took his pitiful few belongins and I said I was leavin' with my son and that was that and we went out into the night. I was walkin' the streets with him, crying and not knowing where to go or what to do, when I remembered someone had told me about a Mrs. Sharp might be able to keep him. I went to Mrs. Sharp and it was eight thirty at night, I remembered, and I asked her if she could keep him, and she said she would. I told her I couldn't pay for it, and she said it was all right. She was a wonderful woman. And him, too, her husband. She saw I was hungry and she offered me to eat, but I said, 'I been hungry many times, and I can stand it, but if you got some food, you give it to my boy,' which she did."

As I said before, after I moved in with the Sharps, my mother moved to Washington, D.C., to look for work. She found jobs as a waitress, but every time she wanted time off so she could visit me in Charleston, they told her no, she couldn't leave. She always went anyway, so every time she got back to Washington she had to find a new job. That went on for a couple years until she finally stopped going back. She eventually met a nice man, a good man, Sam DiCicco, and married him. He was a bartender, and later they bought an Italian restaurant in a poor neighborhood in Washington. They both worked at the restaurant until he died in 1967. It was hard work, but she was working for herself instead of someone else. After her second husband died, my mother ran the restaurant herself for another year before it was burned down in the 1968 race riots. She had insurance, though, and lived off that the rest of her life.

Before then, the distance between us had grown. She would come back to Charleston sometimes, but only watch me from a distance. Once she heard people talking at a drugstore about "a great young basketball player named Rodney Hundley" who would be playing that night, so she went to see me play. She sat in a dark corner of the gymnasium watching. Once she was settled in Washington, D.C., and was married and running the restaurant, she thought about sending for me, but she never did. She thought it was too late, so she never did anything about it.

When I was in high school I would go to Washington in the summer and stay for a week or so. I wasn't happy about it. I would rather be with my friends back in West Virginia. I would go to the playgrounds by Eastern High School on East Capitol Street in Washington and play basketball with the guys. I was the best player there. I don't know who any of them were, the guys that were hanging out there, but they weren't very good.

> "Later on," my mother told Bill Libby, "when he became a big star, nationally known and a celebrity and everything, with his picture in the newspapers and magazines, he came to see me and my husband, Mr. DiCicco, at our restaurant a couple of times, and he saw how we had put his picture on the wall and how proud we were of him and it made him proud. ...
>
> "He doesn't hate me, I don't think. He's told me he don't. He knows I never stopped sending money for him. He knows I always loved him and couldn't help myself. If I was to die tonight, I'd say I did my best with my life and for my son. I swear I did. People who know me know I did. I think Rodney knows I did. I couldn't help the way things were for me and what happened. I think Rodney knows I did the best I could."

I never talked to her much when I was growing up or in school, but once I got into the pros and could afford to call, I'd call her about once a week, right up until the end when she died a few years ago. When I was playing pro ball we would go to Washington to play the Bullets and I would get her tickets to the game. She wasn't a basketball fan and didn't know much about it. She never talked about basketball, didn't have any interest in it at all, but she liked to watch me play. She didn't have any idea who anyone was except me and Jerry West, and I introduced her to Elgin Baylor.

After I retired from the Lakers and moved to North Carolina to work for Converse, I invited my mother and Mr. DiCicco for a visit. She seemed to really enjoy it, getting to know my wife and daughters. Later when I moved back to Los Angeles, I brought them out for another visit. When her second husband died, I was all she had left, and I was glad I got to know her.

By 1994, my mother was 82 and I had hired a nurse to take care of her and the house in Washington. I wanted her to sell the house and move to Phoenix where she could be with my family. The Jazz season was just about over and my middle daughter, Jacquie, had just gotten back from extensive travels in the Far East. She was in New York and didn't have a job lined up yet when she said she was going down to Washington to see grandma. I suggested she go live with her grandmother until we could get her moved. The plan was for Jacquie to fix up the house so we could get it rented, then my mother would move to Phoenix and enjoy life.

So Jacquie went back there to do just that, and she wasn't there six hours before my mother died. It was almost like she was waiting for someone to get there. Jacquie knew there was something wrong when she arrived. She asked my mother if she was all right, and she said she was fine, but Jacquie called 911 anyway. An ambulance was there in three minutes, but my mother died before she ever reached the hospital.

I was in Portland, Oregon, for a Jazz game that night and I don't know what I would have done if Jacquie wasn't there. My mother lived alone and didn't have anyone there. She took care of everything, though, the funeral, the burial, everything. My mother had it all written out and everything was paid for. My daughter was able to handle it all. The Jazz had a game against Minnesota in Salt Lake City two nights later. I was going to catch a red-eye flight to Washington after the Minnesota game, but the Jazz were very nice about it. They sent me straight to Washington from Portland and Steve Klauke filled in for me at the Minnesota game. I remember picking up the paper in Washington the next day and seeing that we got beat.

I've only missed about five games my whole career, and never because of illness. I missed two or three Jazz games when there were conflicts with my CBS work. The Jazz let me go to the 1982 Final Four where I was honored by the National Association of Basketball Coaches and I missed a game for that. Then I missed a game to attend my mother's funeral. That's it.

My mother left me her house on East Capitol Street, 13 blocks from the U.S. Capitol in Washington, so it's good property. She had it paid off from working all her life as a waitress, working in cafés, bus terminals, you name it. It's good property that I'm renting out now. That was quite an accomplishment for her. Neither she nor my father had much education, so growing up in the Depression they never had a chance to make it in the world. Late in her life when I was paying some of her bills for her on the house, my mother would pull me aside and whisper, "You know, one day this is going to be your house." I told her I didn't care about that, I was just happy to be able to help her. It's the same feeling I got being able to help my three daughters. I never had anything growing up and I wanted things to be better for them than they were for me.

In a lot of ways I succeeded, but in other ways I didn't. I did a better job of providing for my family than my father ever did for me, but in some ways I was the same kind of father. I wasn't always there for my kids, just like no one was ever there for me growing up. I don't know if that was part of the mask I was hiding behind, or if it was just that I didn't know better But it's interesting to me how everything in life seems to come full circle.

Chapter Eight

THE PROVIDER

The best way to play basketball is like a kid, playing for fun. It shouldn't make any difference whether you're a kid in your backyard pretending to take the game-winning shot in the NBA Finals, or if you're actually on the parquet floor of Boston Garden taking that shot. You do it because it's something you love to do. You do it because it's fun. Don't let the money or the pressure interfere with the fact it's a game that should be played for the pure joy of it. I've lived that way my whole life, always looking to have fun. I'm still a child in my heart. I'm 63 years old and still like to party and have a good time. I never grew up.

In a lot of ways I've been a kid my whole life. It's been a fun ride, but I haven't always been on the right road. There's a difference between being a kid at heart and being immature. I was both; I was immature for much of my life and I've also paid a price for it. And worse, I've made other people pay too, the people I've been closest to. Immaturity shortened my basketball career, and it ruined two marriages. I have three beautiful daughters that I have developed great relationships with, but it took a long time to get there. I've always been their father, but I wasn't much of a dad for them growing up. And I never made much of a husband, either.

I've been married twice, the first time in college. We were two young kids who were too young to know what we were doing when we got married. She was my high school sweetheart, a majorette, and I was the basketball star, so we were supposed to go together. Then we went to the same university and got married my junior year, which was dumb. Why do that? Why get married right when you're in the middle of college? It was doomed from the start. We drifted apart and it was all my fault, I'm sure. She went with me to Texas those few months I was in the Army, then moved with me to Minneapolis when I played for the Lakers. Neither one of us was happy, and one day out of the blue she told me she wanted a divorce. I had never thought about divorce, so it surprised me when she said that. It hit me hard, but I wanted out too. I wanted my freedom and we got it done as quick as we could.

I was naive about the procedure, though. How do you get a divorce? She already had a lawyer and I didn't have a lawyer so I went through him, which is why she ended up with everything, which wasn't much. We were renting an apartment so there wasn't a house to worry about. We didn't have any kids. All of our furniture was given to us by her father, who owned a furniture store, so she kept that. I had about $10,000 in the bank and she kept that, too. It never occurred to me to fight for the money or try to split it with her. The only thing I did fight for was my car. I had just bought a brand new Oldsmobile convertible, which I had paid cash for, and there was no way I was going to let her have it. When her lawyer asked about the car I told him I'd cancel the insurance on it and drive it into the Mississippi River before I'd let her have it. So I got to keep the car and she got everything else. Which was fine.

We divorced in Minneapolis in 1959 and I haven't seen her since. The basketball season was just ending, I had my car and just enough money for gas, so I drove. I spent the summer in Fort Lauderdale, Florida, staying with Mike Holt, a teammate of mine at West Virginia. He had an apartment on the beach and I hustled pool for money.

At the end of the summer I drove back to Minneapolis for the start of basketball season, and that's where I met my second wife, Flo. We started dating, and I was still going with her when the team moved to Los Angeles after the 1959-60 season. Maybe that's why we ended up getting married. If I had stayed in Minneapolis, maybe I never would have. L.A. was a lonely old town, so big and spread out and I didn't know anybody. Flo and I weren't engaged when I moved out there with the team, but we kept in touch. She'd write me and I went back once or twice to visit. Rudy LaRusso and I went out to L.A. together and he was my roommate at first, but he got married not much later and moved out. Then I was really lonely. I had been running around with him, but once he got married I was hanging out all alone. The next time I flew back to see Flo I asked her to come out to California and get married, and she agreed. Flo and I were guests on an L.A. television show and received a $300 tab at a Las Vegas hotel for it. So that's where we went to get married and have our honeymoon.

Once we got there we hopped in a cab and told the driver we wanted to get married, so he took us to the Silver Bell Wedding Chapel right on the strip. All three of us went in and the cabbie served as the best man. The meter, of course, was running the whole time. Then we got back in the cab after the ceremony and he took us back to the Stardust Hotel. The fare came to about 10 bucks. I gave him a $5 tip plus an extra five bucks for being my best man. They made a 45 rpm record of the ceremony and wanted $5 for that too.

I had just ended one marriage, though, when I jumped into another, and I just wasn't ready for it. Then I started having children and I thought that would change things, but it really didn't because of my immaturity.

The first of my three lovely daughters was born in 1962, early in what turned out to be my final season as a basketball player. The Lakers were leaving on a road trip and I dropped Flo off at Santa Monica Hospital on my way to the airport. We had a game in Baltimore the next day and at the airport Fred Schaus happened to ask me how Flo was doing. I told him I had just dropped her off at the hospital and she was going to have the baby. He says, "What are you doing here? You can fly out tomorrow." So I grabbed my bag and went back to the hospital. Sure enough, Kimberly was born that night and I flew out the next morning to catch up with the team in time for that night's game.

I bought a house in Malibu on a hill overlooking the ocean. I paid $45,000 for it, but less than a year later I was out of the NBA and on my way to North Carolina to work for Converse. When we packed up and moved to Greensboro I had trouble selling my house, barely getting what I paid for it. It's worth about $1 million today and I had trouble selling it new for $45,000.

I settled down in North Carolina, and that's when Jacqueline, my second daughter, was born. I was a better family man there, because there wasn't as much to do. We lived in a family-oriented neighborhood and did things with other families. I golfed a lot and stayed home at night. In Los Angeles I was always out till midnight running the streets, afraid I might miss something if I went home. I was terrible, and while I was doing this, my kids were growing up on me. I liked North Carolina and it was good for our family, but it was too small for me. I wanted to get back to L.A. so bad. When Converse had an opening there I almost begged them to send me back, which they did.

So then Flo and I were back in L.A. and we had two daughters. I wasn't back three months when the Lakers called and I got my break in broadcasting. I was back in the city that was up all night, plus I was traveling with the team, so I was gone a lot. If I want to use a very weak excuse for not being a great family man, the one thing I had was my job. I was never at home. I don't know how these guys who play basketball stay married. Professional athletes are very vulnerable; everywhere they go people treat them special because they are athletes. The women want your company and the men want to buy you drinks. The temptations are there.

After two years back in Los Angeles, the Phoenix job opened up, and we moved to the desert. That's where my third daughter, Jennifer, was born, in September of 1970, just before my second season with the Suns started. Now we had three kids and I was still never home. Kimberly and Jacquie were almost ready to go to school and Flo was raising the kids by herself. As I look back, what I did was never include her in anything, and that was totally wrong. I was doing my single thing and I knew I could get out because she was going to be there with the kids. I didn't have to worry about the girls because Flo was a great mother and I knew she was taking care of them. I used that as my excuse. We started growing apart because I never included her in anything I did.

When I got the job with the Jazz in New Orleans, I bought a house there. Flo and the kids moved out later, but they hated New Orleans. Flo looked at the French Quarter as a dump, and I thought it was the greatest place I'd ever been. She said, "This place is terrible. I don't want my kids growing up here." They all wanted to go back to Phoenix. I didn't have our house in Phoenix sold yet, so they had a place to go back to. They went back to Phoenix, I stayed in New Orleans, and we haven't been together as a family since. I went to Phoenix every chance I could when the girls were growing up and stayed with them. We'd have a family Christmas party every year, but every year we grew a little more apart.

Flo and I remain married after all this time, even though we haven't been together in nearly 25 years. Flo is a devout Catholic and doesn't want a divorce, and our daughters don't want us to get divorced, either. So she lives her life in Phoenix, and I live my life in Utah, and our daughters continue to love us both. Flo is a great lady and a great mother and I'd do anything for her. To this day, I take care of her. I feel obligated to, just like I felt obligated to take care of my kids. She's the mother of my children and a part of my life.

Maybe I took after my own father. Who knows? I didn't have a close relationship with my parents when I was growing up, and my kids didn't have a close relationship with me when they were growing up. Later in life my mother and I started over and became close, and my daughters and I have started over and we've become close, too.

I've gotten to know my children so much better in the last few years, and we've come to an understanding. They know I wasn't a good father growing up. The one thing I've always done for them was to be a great provider. I've paid for everything; I paid for all of their educations, which I'm proud of. Flo hasn't had to work a day since our first daughter was born in 1962. I bought her a house and provided her with everything she needs, and I always will. It doesn't make up for not being there for them growing up, but it's something. There are so many women in this country who had kids, got divorced and neither the mother nor the kids ever got one dime from their father, no help at all. That's the only thing that makes me feel like I've done something. I did one thing right at least, providing for my family.

My oldest daughter, Kimberly, graduated from the University of Utah and is a newspaper reporter in Wichita Falls, Texas. Jacquie, my second daughter, graduated from Arizona State and is a school teacher by trade, but she is in Los Angeles now going to cartoon animation school. And Jennifer owns a hair salon in Scottsdale, Arizona. So all three have got degrees, are working and doing well. We're all spread out, but they're all close to NBA cities so I get to see them regularly. Kimberly comes to games in Dallas when the Jazz are in town, Jennifer comes to games in Phoenix and Jacquie comes to the games in L.A.

All three of my daughters have seen me play basketball once in a legends game. Kimberly saw me play in a West Virginia University legends game at Morgantown in 1980, Jacquie saw me play in an NBA Legends game in Houston in 1989, and Jennifer saw me play with the NBA Legends in Salt Lake City in 1993.

In the game Kimberly saw at West Virginia, Jerry West captained one team and I captained the other. We played in the new coliseum neither Jerry nor I had played in. We drew about 12,000 people. They kept talking about having that game and West and I were the keys. I said if you're going to have this game you better get on with it. I was 46 and Jerry was 42. I said, how do you expect us to get up and down the floor? We had a great time, and that was the only time Kimberly ever saw me play.

I was 54 when I played in the NBA Legends game in '89 and Morganna the Kissing Bandit came out and kissed me. After she kisses you she takes off running and I said hey, come back here and went running after her. It was a complete surprise. Afterward Jacquie asked me why that woman came out and kissed me. I said, who else is she going to kiss? Morganna sent me a picture of her kissing me. She signed it, "Still my bosom buddy." That was kind of a feather in your cap, getting kissed by her. She kissed Cal Ripken once when he was at bat in Baltimore. She jumped over the railing and ran over to him and planted a kiss on him right there in the batter's box. As soon as they got her off the field, he hit a home run on the very next pitch. She also got Frank Layden when he was coaching the Jazz at the Salt Palace.

The last NBA Legends game ever held was in Salt Lake City in 1993. My daughter Jennifer was there and I was 58, the oldest player in the game. My daughter, watching me play for the first time, said, "I read a lot about your playing, but you don't seem to be as good as the others."

I'm closer today than ever before to balancing fun with family, responsibility with independence. I'm so proud of the fact all three of my daughters went to college and struck out on their own, pursuing careers that they love. I admit I was a terrible father. There's nothing I can do about it now. It seems there are two roads you can go down, the good one and the bad one. I started down that bad one early on and could never get turned back. I just never can get turned all the way back. I'm still out there thinking, "What am I doing?" I get along a lot better with my wife now than I ever did living with her. She has never lived in Utah, but she has become a huge Jazz fan. We get along fine. We've accepted that I'm here and she's there.

And that's where we are. I talk to my kids about us. They're mature young women now. We can have intelligent conversations about me and about their mother and about the two of us together and about them as children. We can have serious talks about the way things were and the way they can be now. We have a much better relationship, and they know me for who I am.

A provider.

A kid at heart, still trying to grow up.

Chapter Nine

I WASN'T ALWAYS HOT ROD

Basketball was king in West Virginia, and from junior high on, I was king of the basketball courts, at least around Charleston. I wasn't very fast, but I had quick reflexes and I could shoot and dribble with both hands, even in junior high school. I was tall for my age, too. By eighth grade I was 6 feet tall and I grew to 6-feet-2 by ninth grade. I didn't have any money, but it didn't take money to play basketball or baseball on the playgrounds, so that's where I spent all my time. I had some natural ability and I played all the time to develop the skills I had. I played all the sports on the playgrounds with kids from the neighborhood, but basketball became my favorite.

I lived a couple blocks away from a playground on Clendenin Street and went down there every day at 3 o'clock and played with the kids until it got dark. I even shot hoops in the winter. I went down there with a Mackinaw coat and gloves on and shoveled the court off so I could play. That place has been wiped out now, replaced by the Charleston Civic Center. Ironically, that's also the site of the West Virginia Basketball Hall of Fame, and I was elected to the hall in 1967, putting a plaque in my honor on the same site of my childhood playground.

I spent a lot of time playing at the Charleston YMCA, too. I never could afford a membership, but a guy named Red Hartman let me sneak in all the time. He could have jeopardized his job for that, but he knew I was going to be a player and he helped me. He was very instrumental to my success. There was a buzzer at the front desk he pushed to let the members in, so he would have me stand over by the door and when he buzzed someone in, I followed them through the door. Then I was in for the day. I was in junior high and I played with the high school and college kids in town. I really worked on my game, too. I started out by taking a basketball into the handball courts and throwing it off the wall. I marked an X on the wall and threw the ball behind my back with either hand and hit that X nine times out of 10. Then I would pass it again, catch it, dribble it, and throw another pass. I used to do that for an hour, left-handed and right-handed, then I went to play. There were two gyms there at the Y, one where kids mostly my age played, and another where the high school kids played. I was 14 at the time and told the kids my age I wasn't going to learn anything beating them and went to play with the high school kids.

I played on my first organized team in seventh grade, but it wasn't a school team. I played for an independent team coached by Frank Polk called the Charleston Reds. I played both baseball and basketball for the Reds. Teams like that were sanctioned by the state of West Virginia to play school teams. Kids who couldn't make their school's team played for them, then they would schedule games against the schools and it would count as one of their games. Today there's a million independent leagues, but they don't play school teams.

I wasn't real good at first because it was my first team, but I enjoyed it and really worked at it. By time I was in eighth grade at Thomas Jefferson Junior High in Charleston I was a pretty good player. Our junior high coach, Bob Jameson, taught physical education classes and saw me play. He told me I should be playing for him. He said there was nothing wrong with the Charleston Reds but I was the best player in the school so I should be playing on the school's team. He said, "You're going on to play in high school and you're going to college and you're going to go get scholarships."

He explained the whole thing and it made sense. He said, "No one knows who you are playing for the Charleston Reds," and he was right. So I went to Mr. Polk and was scared to death. It was like being on an NBA team and telling them I wanted to quit, like telling your boss you're going to quit your job and go somewhere else because you got a better offer. I was a young kid and he was an imposing man who had been nice to me. I was going to be his star and he didn't like it. But he understood.

So I went to play junior high ball, and as an eighth grader I was one of the best players on the team even though most of the guys were in the ninth grade. I made All-City in Charleston, which was the biggest city in the state. I started and averaged 14 points a game. That got my picture in the Charleston paper quite a bit and people started talking about the kind of high school career they thought I would have. We had a state tournament in West Virginia for junior highs just like for the high schools. It was big, with sectionals, regionals and finals.

We played full-court man-to-man defense, and I developed a lot of sound fundamental skills because of it. It forces you to use good footwork. You're learning how to use your feet without even knowing it. If you've got to guard that guy man-to-man and you're chasing him all over the place, you don't run, you slide your feet.

By ninth grade I was getting fairly well known for basketball. I set state records that year for averaging 20 points a game and scoring 441 points for the season. My high game of 37 points also set a state record. Of course, I also took more shots than anyone the state had ever seen. We never lost a game that year, going 22-0 and winning the West Virginia state championship. We whipped Chapmansville, 57-24, in the finals of the state tournament, and I had 26 points in that game. It was the seventh time that season that I single-handedly outscored the team we were playing. Mr. Jameson, my coach, later said we were a better team that year than a high school championship team he had coached in Ohio.

People started telling me I was going to be a star. I didn't know where I was going to sleep at night, but I was supposed to be on my way to fame and fortune. I loved the attention, though. It was about all I had going for me. I knew it was the way to go and I took it seriously. Things just kept rolling for me when I reached Charleston High School. I was lucky to play for a coach named Clay Martin who drilled fundamental skills that lasted a lifetime. He was a great small-college player in his day and really knew the game. He really knew how to teach it, too. We'd go to practice and work for an hour without anyone ever taking a shot. We worked on all the fundamentals—passing, dribbling, defensive footwork. We were a sound fundamental team. I was fortunate to have two great teaching coaches growing up, one in junior high and one in high school, who really stressed the fundamentals.

I scored 23 points a game my sophomore year and we had a 15-5 record, ending a streak of losing seasons. We did even better in the state tournament. I made some last-second shots in the regionals to send us to the statewide finals at Morgantown. In the first of many games to come for me at the West Virginia University field house, we beat Huntington Central by 10 to advance to the championship game against Beckley.

The place was packed with 6,000 screaming fans. I knew this was the life for me. Guys were throwing up in the locker room before the game because they were so nervous, but not me. I scored 30 points that day but Beckley beat us by eight to win the championship. We led 17-3 early in the game, but we choked. Four guys fouled out and we blew it in the end. Guys were crying after the game. I was sad, but there was no reason to cry because I knew I did all I could.

It turned out that would be the closest we ever came to a state championship. I had two more chances but never got any closer. I averaged 24 points a game my junior year, but seven of our top players from the year before had graduated, and we lost early in the tournament. By my senior year I had grown to 6-foot-4 and filled out to 200 pounds. I had been a scrawny kid up until then. I averaged 33 points a game and totaled 672 for the season to set the West Virginia state record. We were a better team that year, but there were a lot of distractions. Everywhere I went, college recruiters were tripping over themselves to talk to me and watch me play. They were at practice and at games and everywhere else. Clay Martin, our coach, hated the disruptions. We went 19-1 that year and after our only loss, to South Charleston, I headed to the airport for a tryout at North Carolina State. When Coach Martin heard about it, he went crazy.

In the first game of the state tournament, we won by 58 and I only took one shot. I scored one basket early, then spent the rest of the game passing. That game came so easy to us there wasn't any reason to shoot. We won the second game by 25, but then the competition got much tougher. Against East Bank—Jerry West's school—we were way behind early but we rallied to win by two. In the semifinals it was another two-point victory. Then came a rematch with Beckley in the finals. I made eight of my first 10 shots and scored 34 points in the game, and I had 15 rebounds and 10 assists. But we lost by six.

After the game, Beckley's coach, Jerome Van Meter, called me the greatest high school player he ever saw. He is in the high school Hall of Fame, so it was a great thrill to hear him say that. But who was I to disagree with him? I was the best high school player I've ever seen too, and that includes Jerry West. I haven't seen a lot of high school players, but it came so easy to me at that level. I was the best ball handler in the state of West Virginia. I could dribble behind my back, do all that stuff with either hand. Shoot it, everything as a high school player. I could play every position, handle the middle of the fast break, play point guard, play center, I could play anywhere. I had hook shots and everything.

I hated Beckley, though. They beat us in the state tournament all three years that I was in high school. In junior high we beat Beckley in state semifinals, but the same guys on that team beat us when I got in high school. There were five junior highs in Charleston that fed into Charleston High School and all five starters my senior year played together at Thomas Jefferson Junior High.

I made all-state my junior and senior years of high school and I should have made it as a sophomore, too, but there was an unwritten rule then that sophomores didn't get such honors. In my senior year, a national publication, *Dell Magazine*, named me to its All-America team, first team. I was the first player from the state of West Virginia to be a high school All-American.

I was chasing girls, sneaking cigarettes and swigging the occasional beer then, but I was still Rodney Hundley. The flamboyant "Hot Rod" was waiting to emerge, but I didn't have the nickname yet. That came in college when I started clowning around. I guess "Hot Rod" is the obvious nickname for a guy named Rod, and in college the name started to stick. But I was serious on the basketball court in high school and no one called me that then.

The recruiters started coming from all over the country. More than 100 schools were sending telegrams and mail and coaches my way. They told me they would make me a star and pave the way for the riches of pro ball. They sent me plane tickets and travel money. They threw parties for me and set me up on dates with beautiful college girls. They never talked about specifics but they made it clear I wouldn't have to worry about money once I got to their school. I even was quoted in a newspaper as saying, "I want to go to a school where they'll treat me right and take care of me, not where I can make the most money." How's that for perspective? It would be tough for any 17- or 18-year-old kid to keep his feet on the ground even with parents to help him through it, but I was on my own. And I loved it. I loved the attention. I wasn't in any position to make a mature, level-headed decision but I was on top of the world.

After my senior season they had an all-star game in Ashland, Kentucky, for the best high school players in West Virginia and Kentucky. It was my kind of game—10,000 screaming fans, player introductions with a spotlight on me in a dark arena and great competition. I fed off the crowd and the moment. It felt like I was unstoppable, pouring in 45 points, which is still a record for that game. Adolph Rupp, the legendary Kentucky coach, was there and he offered me a scholarship. That night I laid awake in bed, the crowd noise still ringing in my head, and I knew how things could be. I was 18 years old and it seemed like everyone in the world wanted a piece of me. Everyone wanted a piece of Rodney Hundley, and I loved it.

Chapter Ten

TWO BAD KNEES, TWO GOOD STORIES

My first serious basketball injury came in 1951. I tore the cartilage in my right knee during a game my sophomore year in high school and needed surgery to repair it. I went down giving my all to my team, a courageous victim in the battle on the hardwoods—at least that's how the story went later in life. The truth is, I injured my knee in the summertime goofing off at Dreamland, a pool in Huntington, West Virginia. A cute girl caught my eye at the pool and I was flirting with her. I chased her around the pool and slipped in a puddle of water. That's how I really blew out my knee, clowning around at a swimming pool. The knee has bothered me off and on the rest of my life. Even today it acts up on me sometimes. Even though I never was that fast, it slowed me as a basketball player by affecting my mobility.

By my junior year in high school, colleges from all over the country were calling. West Virginia University recruited me heavily, but so did every other big school. I got letters and telegrams from scores of schools, and 48 solid scholarship offers. Duke, Western Kentucky, LSU and the other schools from the Atlantic Coast Conference and the Southeastern Conference wanted me. I heard from schools in the Big Ten and even the Far West. WVU was the most desperate of those 48 schools because I was from the state and schools couldn't afford to lose their local heroes.

Red Brown, the coach at West Virginia, was a good coach and a great guy, but my first choice was North Carolina State. I liked coach Everett Case, and along with Kentucky they were the biggest thing in the South. I could tell Coach Case knew a lot about basketball and they had a lot of talent in their program. I went there for a couple visits and they treated me well. He had invited me down there illegally for a tryout my sophomore year in high school. That summer they put me in a basketball camp and got me a job as a lifeguard at pool on the N.C. State campus, even though I couldn't swim. I was assigned to the wading pool, but mostly I got paid for laying in the sun. It was like Grand Central Station the way they had kids coming in from everywhere in the country. I've never seen anything like it. They put me up in a dorm and I spent my days lying by the pool and spent my nights driving a fancy Olds and wearing the fancy duds they gave me. I was loving it. Like I said, they treated me well.

A little too well, maybe. The Atlantic Coast Conference declared 14 of North Carolina State's players ineligible because they were brought in for tryouts as high school students, which was against the rules, and the National Collegiate Athletic Association was starting to investigate the school's recruiting practices as well. The NCAA was looking for even harsher penalties for both the school and individuals, and my name got mentioned. N.C. State wasn't doing anything other schools weren't doing. They just got caught. But I was one of the ones they brought in for illegal tryouts and I was scared. If I went there now, would I be jeopardizing my career?

Red Brown at West Virginia still wanted me, so that's where I decided to go. He couldn't wait to get the word out, he was so excited. So I made the 155-mile move from Charleston to Morgantown. That's where everyone in Charleston wanted me to go in the first place, so it was front-page news in the *Charleston Daily Mail* the day I accepted the scholarship and became a Mountaineer. They gave me room, board, tuition, book fees and $15 a month for laundry and expenses, which was the most schools could legally offer then. I enrolled in summer school and moved in with Coach Brown. He became my legal guardian and treated me like a member of his family.

But I never made it easy on him. I dropped out of school twice during my freshman year, and I even tried out for a pro team before I ever played a single varsity game. The first time I left school, I went home to Charleston telling everyone I was going to enroll in a hometown school, Morris Harvey College, which is now the University of Charleston. Even though I didn't have a home to go to, I was homesick. I missed my friends and I missed Charleston.

I decided to return to West Virginia and talked my way back, but it wasn't long before I was gone again. This time it was a big mystery where I had gone and why. I came back to WVU after a couple days' disappearance, though, and Red took me in again. A sportswriter asked me why I left and I said, "Don't know." He asked me why I came back and I said, "Same reason." I didn't want to tell him I was off chasing a girl. I had been dating a girl, Nancye Hertnick from Weirton, West Virginia. She was attending Miami University in Ohio. I was restless, and going to see Nancye in Ohio seemed like a good excuse. It was a mistake. After a couple days, I called Red Brown and begged him to take me back, begged him for one more chance. I could tell he was disgusted, but he always gave me one more chance.

The real problem was that I never was cut out for a class-room. I was too restless. I'd rather spend my time playing basket-ball or reading basketball magazines. I knew about all the All-Ameri-cans, even the guys out in Utah like Arnie Ferrin and Vern Gardner, because I read about them. And the pros like Bob Cousy and Dick McGuire. Cousy was my idol then. He could do all the fancy stuff and that's what I liked to do. He started playing for the Celtics when I was just starting high school. They didn't have games on TV the way they do today, where every game is on satellite, but I could follow him through the magazines. I did a lot of reading in college, it just wasn't the textbooks I was supposed to be reading. A text-book couldn't hold my attention but a basketball magazine could. It wasn't that I wasn't smart enough for the classwork, it was just difficult to sit in a classroom. That's why I was always wanting to drop out of school.

I came close a few more times. Once in particular I was hav-ing a terrible time and thinking of quitting for good. I was sitting in the student union when I heard a page for me, telling me I had a long-distance phone call. I figured it was my coach or somebody from the team. Instead, it was Bob Cousy. I couldn't believe it. My basketball idol was on the phone talking to me. Fred Schaus, my coach, played five seasons in the NBA so he knew Cousy and got him to call and talk to me about staying in school. I can't remem-ber what he said (and neither can he for that matter) but it worked.

I never did play for Red Brown. He coached the varsity while I played on the freshmen team my first year. Then when Legs Hawley, the WVU athletic director, died before my sophomore year, Red replaced him as athletic director, and a new varsity coach was hired. That was Fred Schaus, and I never made it easy on him, either.

As much of a headache as I was for Red Brown and the other people at West Virginia, I still played a full season my first year. Freshmen didn't play varsity back then, so I had to play on the freshman team. I scored 50 points in my very first game and had 62 in another. It was so easy I didn't even bother to try to score sometimes. Even though I had those big games it wasn't much fun because the competition was so bad on the freshman level. There was no one who could stop me. It was boring to play that kind of basketball. There were no challenges. One night we played a road game and a writer there asked me if I was going to break the arena record. It was 40 points, set by one of that school's heroes. I told him I didn't want to remove a legend from the record book so I would only tie it. Once I got to 40, I didn't take another shot the rest of the game. The night I scored 62 against Ohio University I was four points short of Legs Hawley's record for the state of West Virginia. Legs was the athletic director at the time. I could have broken his record but I held back. I said at the time it was "out of respect for a great Mountaineer." Through the first 16 games of the season I averaged 40 points but I was bored. I looked for other things to do to make the games interesting and over the last six games I hardly took a shot. I still averaged 34 points a game for the season.

It was during my freshman year that I started showboating and clowning around. I always could handle the ball and do pretty much what I wanted to with it, so clowning came easy to me. I worked on my left hand to make it as good as my right and I was one of the first guys to put the ball behind my back. I used to do all that stuff. I would dribble with my knees, where every other dribble I would hit the ball down low below my leg and hit it off my knee, then pick it up off the floor. I would stand there and go right leg, left leg, off the knees. I could dribble the ball like a magician. Sometimes defenders tripped over themselves trying to keep up. That's how it all started.

One night as I was driving down court, the guy guarding me got tangled up in his own feet and fell to the floor. We had a big lead at the time, so I stopped. I put the ball under my arm and, with a smile on my face, reached down with my free hand to help this poor soul up. The crowd went nuts! Everyone stood and cheered. It was an electrifying moment the way the crowd reacted. I drove to the basket and whipped a behind-the-back pass to a teammate, and the roar of the crowd got even louder. It was magic. The crowd was buzzing and I thought, what have we got here? I played off that energy and had to do more.

The next time down the court I started doing the jitterbug with the basketball, dancing and dribbling. I was playing to the crowd now and the people loved it. They loved me! I felt it right down to my bones. I was on such an emotional high, something I had never felt before. The games had become almost boring because it was so easy then, but suddenly I was onto something. It was like I was born to be a clown and now I was doing it on the basketball court. I made it a part of my game. I started coming up with more stunts like that, adding more and more things as the season went on. In no time the crowds had come to expect it. The basketball had become so easy I found something else to hold my attention. Before long, fans started pouring into the field house just to see what I would do next. We started getting more fans to our freshman games than the varsity did. If you saw our varsity that year you'd know why. They only won half their games. So people turned out to see the freshmen play. And they were expecting me to put on a show.

I stopped working so much at getting better as a basketball player and started working on my clowning. I didn't care much for practice anyway. Coaches and teachers got on me, trying to get me to be more disciplined about basketball. And they worried about me as a student, too. But our freshman team was having a lot of success on the basketball court, winning a lot of games. As much fun as they were having watching me clown around, they were even more excited about the prospects for the varsity squad when I moved up the next year.

I almost didn't get that far. Just before the start of my sophomore year I flew to Hershey, Pennsylvania, to try out with the Philadelphia Warriors of the NBA. Mark Workman, a former WVU star, arranged for me to work out at the Warriors' training camp. Eddie Gottlieb, who owned the Warriors, liked me and I could have made their team. But because I had already signed a commitment to play for West Virginia, NBA rules said I couldn't sign with a team in their league until my class graduated. Gottlieb owned another team, though, the Philadelphia Sphas, who toured with the Harlem Globetrotters. He offered me a spot on the Sphas roster until I was eligible to play for the Warriors. I worked out with the Warriors and did OK, basketball-wise, but I was so much younger than everyone else I felt out of place. The offer was a tempting, though. I loved basketball but couldn't say the same about school. Here was a chance to play and not worry about the classroom. Before I could make up my mind, though, I hurt my other knee. This time I really was playing basketball when I tore the cartilage in my knee, I just wasn't where I was supposed to be.

It looked like I would need knee surgery and I wondered if my career was already over. Gottlieb was prepared to take care of me, but he called Red Brown at West Virginia first. Red was athletic director then and he and Fred Schaus agreed to take me back—and to take responsibility for the injury.

When I got back to WVU, school had already started and Red didn't have a place for me to stay. I was able to go through late registration to get enrolled in classes but housing was a problem. That's when he set me up with Ann Dinardi. She was a wonderful woman who lived close by, not 50 yards from the field house in a little white house. She was a real friend of the athletic department— and the whole town. She was the Morgantown Woman of the Year at least five times. All she does is give. Red talked her into putting me up there when I needed a place to stay so she fixed a room up for me and watched out for me. It was one of the best things that ever happened to me. I never had much direction in my life and she tried hard to get me on track. I used to sleep till noon and cut classes. I just didn't want to go to school. I only wanted to play basketball. Ann was a short, wide Italian woman who wouldn't put up with anything. She used to get on me, hitting me with a pillow saying, "You lazy son of a bitch! Get up and go to school!"

She loved basketball but wouldn't go to see me play. She'd say, "Honey, I can't go. I get too nervous. They beat up on you." She'd say the same thing to Jerry West when he lived there later on. "Oh, they always double-team you, they always foul you guys." So she stayed home and listened to the games on the radio. She'd buy milkshakes and burgers for me at the drugstore and say, "Don't tell the other guys I'm doing this for you." I used to smoke cigarettes then and she'd buy them for me too. "Don't tell anyone I do this," she'd say.

She never charged me a dime's rent, which was good because I didn't have any money. She enjoyed having us around and started letting other athletes stay there, including West. Jerry grew up poor just like I did and he couldn't afford rent either. He had a tough childhood, growing up in a poor coal mining town. He wasn't as poor as I was because he had a family, but they didn't have much. He got out of there, though, and Ann helped. I don't know if you'd call Jerry a great student but he certainly was a good one. He got his degree and was on line from the start, working as hard in the classroom as he did at basketball. He never had any problems with school, he studied on his own and did everything you're supposed to do when you're in school. His parents were a strong influence.

I watched how well Jerry did in school after I left and wished somebody had told me what to do when I was a student. But I'm afraid the truth is, people did tell me. I just didn't listen to them. Ann Dinardi was one of them. She was like a mother to me, and Red Brown was like a father. Those two people saved me. They did everything they could to keep me in school, keep me pointed in the right direction, even if I wasn't as cooperative as I should have been. Regardless of what I did wrong, they stayed after me. They never gave up on me.

One time Jerry West and I were flying back East somewhere together and had to change planes in Pittsburgh. We were only 75 miles from Morgantown and thought about Ann, so we decided to give her a call. Jerry talked to her first, then handed the phone to me and I talked with her for a while. When I hung up I asked Jerry what she told him. He laughed and said, "She said I was the best basketball player ever to play at West Virginia, but don't tell you she said that." I said, "She told me the same thing, but don't tell Jerry." She should have been a politician. On her 90th birthday, they threw a big party for her in Morgantown and all the ex-players who stayed with her came back. She is a great woman.

I had an operation on my left knee, the one I hurt during my tryout with the Warriors, in November of 1954. Before long I was back on the court for West Virginia University. Doctors told me to lift weights for an hour a day to build my knee back up, but I did more than that. I couldn't wait to get back on the court. I wore a weight boot for an hour every morning and every night to speed up the process. And I was in uniform for our first varsity game of the season. By the third game I was in the starting lineup.

But then I was playing on two bad knees. I still have identical four-inch half-moon scars on my knees. Today they make a tiny cut and you're out of hospital the same day of the surgery. They don't even put you to sleep. In a week you're walking and in two weeks you're playing again. It's unbelievable what they do today, but I wasn't that lucky. I had butchers operating on me and it affected my career. I lost all of my jumping ability. I was like Larry Bird, I couldn't run or jump. I never had any speed but at least I was quick. I could get a first step on you and that's all basketball is. If I get the first step on you in a half-court game, I've got you beat. But after two knee operations I had lost some of my mobility.

I still wasn't excited about sitting in classrooms but I was re-signed to it. If I wanted to play pro ball I had to go to college, so I stayed at WVU for good. There were some alums who were happy to help me out financially. It wasn't a lot, $10 or $20 here and there. Somebody gave me a car to drive, and I could get free clothes at a local store. Word got back to the NCAA and the Southern Confer-ence, though, and they were about ready to crack down when Red Brown heard about it. He asked me if it was true. I never lied. When I told him about it I got scared, wondering once again if my basket-ball career was over. Red thought we should beat the conference to the punch, to tell them about the infractions before they could call us on it, and say we were sorry and it wouldn't happen again. We asked for a hearing before they had a chance to strike first. I told them the truth and Red asked for mercy. It worked and I was allowed to keep playing.

We went 19-11 my sophomore year, 21-9 my junior year and 25-5 my senior year. We won the Southern Conference champion-ship all three years, and my senior year we finished sixth in the country in the polls. We weren't a national power, though, and all three seasons we got beat in the first round of the NCAA tourna-ment at Madison Square Garden.

My senior year was our best team. Our only losses were to Duke, Utah and Iowa in the Dixie Classic in Raleigh, North Caro-lina, to Penn State in the regular season, and to Canisius in the first round of the NCAA tournament. But we also beat two of the teams that beat us, Duke and Penn State, and we beat some other good schools as well, such as Pitt twice, Villanova, Florida State, North Carolina State, St. John's and NYU.

In my three varsity seasons at West Virginia I scored 2,180 points, becoming just the fourth player in college history to top 2,000 points. I averaged 24.5 points a game and I had a career high of 54 points in a game. I also scored 711 points my first season to set a national record for sophomores.

Even though the knee operations cost me some of my quick-ness, I was still a better ballhandler than anyone else so I was able to maneuver through the defense. I liked taking a one-handed jumper from the free throw line but I also could drive to the basket or pull up and hook with either hand. I played forward but usually was the middle man on fast breaks. Fred Schaus said I ran the break perfectly, as good as anyone in college basketball.

In a lot of ways it was still too easy for me, even on the varsity,

and because of that I never really worked at getting better. I had
been working on fancy ballhandling since I was in junior high school
and got by with that because the competition in our league wasn't
the best in the country. Some games I hardly shot at all. I would
rather make a spectacular pass than an easy basket, and I led our
league in assists all three years. But I also made some wild passes
and took even crazier shots. You wouldn't believe some of the
stuff I did. I'd spin the ball on my finger at the free throw line, then
hit it with my fist to shoot the ball. I was a good shooter but my
field goal percentage was terrible because I took so many terrible
shots, shots that had no chance of going in. I took "Chris Morris"
fliers, running across the lane from 16 feet out and letting go with
a left hook even though I'm right-handed. I shot behind my back,
from half court, behind the backboard—I took all kinds of crazy
shots.

When we played New York University at Madison Square Garden my sophomore year, I scored 38 points and grabbed 22 rebounds. But I also had nine turnovers and took about eight bad
shots, and we lost by one point, 79-78. I got some mention on various All-America squads that year but people were skeptical. They
didn't know if I was a serious basketball threat or just a clown
playing in an easy conference.

Because of the reputation I built for clowning as a freshman,
people weren't just interested in my basketball, they wanted me to
entertain them. I had a whole bag of tricks by then and loved pulling them out. I would dribble between my legs, or even the
defender's legs, on my knees or with my knees. I'd pass the ball
from one hand to the other, rolling it across my shoulders, or spin
the ball on my fingers. And I would shoot lying down or sitting
down and sometimes bounce the ball off the floor and in the hoop.
I was a Globetrotter playing college basketball. The fans ate it up
and I thrived off the attention. The more they enjoyed it, the more
I wanted to do it.

Once against Pitt, I scored 38 points and we had a big lead so
Schaus took me out early. With about three or four minutes to go,
the fans started calling for Schaus to put me back in. They were
stomping their feet and chanting, "We want Hund-ley! We want
Hund-ley!" Coaches don't like to give in to that so Schaus tried to
ignore them. He just sat there stone-faced, staring straight ahead,
not even acknowledging the chants. Of course, I encouraged the
fans. I turned to the crowd and cupped my hand around my ear

like they weren't loud enough. They got even crazier but Schaus still didn't budge. So I walked down the bench and sat next to him. I stared straight ahead like he was doing and the crowd loved it. The chants got even louder. Then I turned to Schaus and said, "What do you think they want to see, the game or the show?" He broke out laughing and sent me in, so I went back out and did my stuff.

I had all sorts of crazy shots, like one that got dubbed the praying mantis. In a game my sophomore year, while the rest of the team was back playing defense, I was down by our basket kneeling on the floor. I didn't want the other team to see me so I was crouching down. Pete White, the captain of our team, stole the ball and started breaking down court. He figured he was going to get a wide open layup but he looked up and there I was under the basket, still on my knees and hollering for the ball. So he threw it to me and I never got up. I just shot it from one knee, a one-handed push shot from about 10 feet away and it went in.

If I missed five or six shots in a row I would climb up the basket support as if to inspect the net and see if that was why my shots weren't falling. Sometimes I hung from the rim and yelled for my teammates to pass me the ball.

Our first big game my sophomore year was against Richmond and by then my knee had healed enough from the surgery that I could play the whole way. We led 72-66 with a minute and a half to go and I had the ball. I decided to dribble out the clock so I went into my fancy dribbling, going all over the court with the Richmond guys chasing me. I did this all the way down until there were just three seconds left on the clock, then I heaved the basketball toward the rafters and ran off the court laughing. Schaus went crazy because there was still time left on the clock, and the other guys wondered what I was doing. But I just strolled away with a happy grin on my face. And just as the final horn sounded, the ball dropped to the floor.

I guess that's the stuff legends are made of because fans now were coming to games expecting to see a show. I was happy to oblige them. Maybe a little too happy early on, and it might have hurt us in a couple of games. Because Schaus took over as coach my sophomore season, he had never recruited me. Now he had to put up with me. He knew what he was getting into, though, when he agreed to coach the team and he had shown a lot of tolerance for my clowning. He knew he needed me to win and didn't want to stifle me, but one game I had the ball stolen from me twice while I was clowning around and it hurt us. We played Duke in the Dixie Classic and had a big lead in the first half. I rolled the ball from one hand to the other across my back like I often did, and they stole the ball and got a layup. Just to show them it was a fluke, I did it again. And they stole it again. Suddenly the game was tied and we ended up losing by 13 points. Two turnovers weren't the difference in a loss that bad, but Schaus was furious.

It wasn't fair to the other guys on the team to work so hard to have one guy give it away by goofing off. He was ready to take his right foot and kick me right out the door. He looked like he thought about kicking me off the team, yelling at me in the huddle. I didn't help things by mouthing off, but he was right and I knew it.

We talked later and cleared the air. He said he realized the fans enjoyed the way I played, and so did he, but he wasn't going to put up with it if it jeopardized a game. He said he didn't care if I drop-kicked the ball in the basket if we had a 20-point lead, and I promised him I wouldn't ever clown again when the game was on the line. The next time we had a 20-point lead, though, I drop-kicked the ball toward the basket.

I'm not sure he was entirely convinced I was serious about winning, but I was. The next year against Villanova at the Palestra in Philadelphia, we were down by a point in the closing seconds. I was at the free throw line for two shots. I needed to make one of them to tie the score and both of them to win the game. I looked over at Fred, smiled and flashed the OK sign. Then I shot the first free throw and missed. I shrugged, knowing I could still get the tie. I looked over at Fred again and smiled again. I gave him a wink as if to say, don't worry, coach, I'll get this one. I missed that shot too and we lost by a point. In the dressing room after the game, Fred was kicking lockers. I told him I tried but I don't know if he believed me. He saw the wink and the OK sign and wondered if I was serious, but that had nothing to do with trying. I really did try.

The seniors on the team resented me at first because I was just a sophomore and hadn't proven myself. They especially resented it when they felt my clowning led to turnovers. I won them over though, especially when I made it clear to them I wouldn't ever clown again until the outcome was decided. I took the games more seriously. I still played to have fun, but I also made sure I did everything I could to help us win. I had my eccentricities. I always shot free throws from the far left side of the lane, even when I didn't fire up hook shots or shoot from behind my back.

Once my teammates got to know me they accepted the way I played. Soon when we built big leads they would say, "Hey, Rodney, why don't you go into your act?" Before long, they were even joining me in it. We did some Harlem Globetrotter stuff where the five of us would line up in a T formation and run a football play. I'd take the snap, drop back and fire a long pass to the wide receiver who rolled in for a layup. The refs would be blowing their whistles like crazy but the crowd went nuts.

I wasn't a great defensive player because I didn't work at it. For me, when we were on defense it was time to rest so I could have energy for offense. But when I put my mind to it, I could be a pretty good defender. My sophomore year, George Washington had a senior All-American named Corky Devlin and he was going off early in the game. It was the finals of the Southern Conference tournament and he was just blistering us. George Washington only lost three games that year, twice to us and once to San Francisco, who had Bill Russell. I told Schaus to put me on Devlin and as soon as I switched to him, Devlin started egging me on. He was calling for the ball even more, yelling to his teammates, "Hey, I've got Hundley on me. Give me the ball." But I guarded him for 18 minutes and he only scored one basket the whole time I was on him— and that was taken in frustration from about 30 feet out. We won the game in overtime, 58-48, and I scored 30 points.

I got booed a lot on the road because of my showboating, but the crowds loved it, too. I might have been showing off but I never did anything to show up an opponent, and fans appreciated that. They would have turned on me if I did, but it was all in fun and they like that. In a game against St. John's at Madison Square Garden in New York, I missed my first five or six shots and the fans really let me have it. But just like that I got hot and hit five or six shots in a row. So I cupped my hand behind my ear as if to ask what happened to all the booing. They loved it! They still booed me the rest of the night but it was all in good fun. By then I had really won them over. They were having a ball and I was, too. We won the game but afterward they asked me for autographs and thanked me. Can you imagine? I'm an opposing player who just beat their team and they thanked me! How often does that happen?

My junior year there was a big game against Furman in Charlotte, North Carolina, and the place was packed. We ended up winning 76-73, but the game was tight the whole way. I was guarding

Fred Fraley on one play and he was trapped. I whispered to him, "Hey, Fred, throw me the ball and I'll throw it right back to you. The crowd will love it." I was serious, too. If he would have given me the ball I would have given it right back. But he wouldn't do it. "I can't," he said. "My coach will kill me."

I said, "What do you think my coach will do with me?"

In another game that year I was triple-teamed and hemmed in pretty good, so I just sat down on the floor while keeping my dribble. They guys defending me were so surprised they just stood there. Then I spotted a teammate wide open under the basket so I stood up, fired the ball to him and he got an easy layup out of it.

I played my best when I was loose and those antics helped keep me loose. West Virginia basketball was getting noticed around the country like never before, and we were packing the place like never before. Mountaineer Field House only seated about 6,000 people, but they rarely drew crowds that big before I came along. My freshman year, the crowds for our games were bigger than the varsity's. My sophomore year we averaged more than 5,500 fans a game and my junior year it was more than 5,900. By my senior year we averaged more than 6,400 fans a game at home. On the road in the bigger arena, the crowds were huge. We were getting crowds of 12,000 and 15,000. And everybody was coming to see the show. Once when I was into my act the ref blew his whistle and called me for traveling. I said to him, "You really think all these people came here to watch you make that call?"

School remained a struggle, though, not so much because the classes were difficult but because I had a hard time going. One local fan offered me $2 for every class I went to, but I was making that much not going. I shouldn't have remained eligible but professors cooperated. One prof gave me an oral history test and the only question he asked was how many points I scored in the last game. I told him 32. He looked up the box score in the newspaper and said, "That is correct." So I passed.

I had great fun in college even when I wasn't playing basketball. If it wasn't for classes, it would have been perfect. I was a disc jockey with my own local radio show, I played a lot of pool and table tennis and won some tournaments.

Sam Huff, the great linebacker, played at West Virginia then and we became friends. Football players usually didn't care much for basketball players but we got along great. I joked with the football players that the crowds coming to see me play basketball generated enough money to support the whole football program. I got along great with Pappy Lewis, the football coach, too. Pappy once threatened to put me in pads and send me out on the football field, then to call Fred Schaus over and tell him he thought I'd make a great quarterback. Fred would have had a heart attack. Pappy also put me up to calling Red Brown and telling him I wouldn't play the next game unless he promised me half the gate. I told Red I knew they were making a ton of money off me because I was packing the place. At first Red was sure I was kidding but I played it straight. Then he started taking me seriously and getting real nervous. But I could not keep it up and broke out laughing.

The last home game of my college career was against William and Mary. We won easily, 80-57, and with the game just about over I called time out. I went over to the William and Mary bench and shook hands with coach Boyd Baird, whom I had tormented throughout my college career. I sat on his bench once in a game and when he tried to kick me off I told him there wasn't any rule that said I couldn't sit there. Then I shook hands with Fred Schaus and walked off the court for the final time. More than 6,800 people had packed the place that night and they were all yelling and stomping their feet. It was one of the greatest moments of my life, a heartfelt show of support that brought tears to my eyes.

As soon as my senior season ended, though, I was through with school as far as I was concerned. The pro season was still several months away so I was looking for work. But I sure didn't want to *work*. Abe Saperstein asked me if I was interested in touring with a group of all-stars on an 18-game tour with the Harlem Globetrotters. I asked him for $500 a game—$9,000 for the tour. Abe almost had a heart attack because the most he ever paid a player was two years earlier when Tom Gola got $3,000 for the tour. They went on without me, which might have been their mistake. I might have been better suited to be a barnstormer than an NBA player. Who knows? If I had gone on that tour I might have ended up being a "white Globetrotter" one day, making Abe Saperstein a whole lot of money.

Instead, I formed my own group of all-stars and went on a barnstorming trip of my own all across West Virginia. Hot Rod Hundley's All-Stars played 30 games in 30 nights and I netted $7,000. We played the same team every night. The only thing that changed was what we called them. That changed every night depending on where we played. One night it would be the West Virginia College

All-Stars, another night it would be the Morris Harvey College All-Stars. And the players had different names from night to night, too. We had a couple players everyone knew but most of the other guys were from YMCA leagues or something like that. Actually, we had a lot of good players and the games were competitive.

I wrote introductions for each player and really hyped them up. Every guy would be "a local favorite," "a rookie sensation" or a "perennial all-star." Jim Sottile would be introduced as, "player-coach Jumpin' Jim Sottile, the Bristol Bomber from Bristol P-A!" And I loved the way "Villanova" sounded so every night someone would be introduced as an All-America from Villanova. One night in Morgantown there was an injury and we needed an extra player, so I recruited a bar buddy of mine, Pickles Hines, to play. He hadn't played in five years and wasn't that good when he did play. But that never mattered on Hot Rod Hundley's All-Stars. When it came time to introduce him, the announcer belted out, "And now, a two-time All-American from Villanova, Pickles Hines!" I was introduced last and the crowd roared. I played the whole game, did all my tricks and the crowd was entertained.

I lost 20 pounds on that tour because all I ever ate was junk, but that $7,000 I walked away with was more money than I had ever seen in my life. I ate pretty well after that.

Chapter Eleven

THEY'LL NEVER FORGET YOU

West Virginia is a great place to be a basketball player. They treat you well when you're playing, and they never forget you once you've moved on. I make it back there as often as I can and I'm always moved by how warmly I'm greeted. I broke away from a Jazz road trip in March of 1998 long enough to spend a whirlwind day in my home state. It was more than 40 years after I finished my college basketball career and I still received a hero's welcome everywhere I went.

The Jazz played in Charlotte, North Carolina, on a Wednesday night and were off until Friday night in Philadelphia. That was long enough to squeeze in a quick trip to West Virginia. Pete White, who was the captain of West Virginia's basketball team my sophomore year, flew down to Charlotte with a couple of pilots in a private plane to pick me up right after the Jazz-Hornets game. Then they whisked me off on the 30-minute flight back to West Virginia. I guess my reputation preceded me because there was a fifth of scotch, a fifth of vodka and two six-packs of beer waiting for me on the plane. When we landed someone asked me how long the flight was. I said, "Two Budweisers."

When we got to Charleston late that night, Pete and I ducked into a bar to get a beer and right away I was recognized. This guy came up to me and said, "I'll be damned, Hot Rod Hundley," and he shakes my hand.

Later on this guy came back up to me and said, "Buy me a beer."

I said, "Wait a minute. You want me to buy you a beer? Why should I buy you a beer?"

He says, "Because tomorrow I'm going to tell everyone I run into that you bought me one."

I said, "Well, that's better than telling them that I didn't," so I went ahead and bought him one. He walks away saying, "Man, I'm going to tell *everybody* Hot Rod Hundley bought me a beer. He's my buddy."

The next day I had a full schedule, starting with a speech at a fund-raising luncheon for the Boy Scouts there in Charleston. Talk about not forgetting—the luncheon was held at the Marriott, where they have a suite named after me. Room 1522 at the Charleston Marriott is the "Hot Rod Hundley Suite," and there's even a plaque on the wall saying so. They also have suites there named after Sam Huff and Bruce Bosley, a couple of West Virginia football stars, and Sen. Jennings Randolph.

After I gave my talk at the luncheon they took me across the street where the state high school basketball tournament finals were being held. There was a kid named Brett Nelson, a junior in high school who averaged 30 points a game for St. Albans. West Virginia University wanted him real bad for their basketball program. Duke University was really after him too, but WVU was hoping to keep him in his home state.

Tex Williams, an old friend of mine, was his coach and they lost by one point that day. He took me into the locker room after the game and introduced me to all his players. They just got beat in the state tournament by a point so they were all down and I told them, hey, I've been there myself. I got beat twice in the state tournament when I was in high school. So while I was in there I met this recruit. I mentioned that I had heard a lot about him and he said, "I hope all of it's good." I told him, "everything but Duke University." He laughed and I made my pitch for West Virginia.

Then I hopped in a car and drove to the other end of town to Capitol High School to film a public service announcement about the importance of reading to your children, similar to the one Jeff Hornacek and his kids were filming in Utah about the same time. I recorded five different announcements, then it was back in the car to drive to Logan, West Virginia, about 75 miles south of Charleston, to speak at a banquet, which also was a fund-raiser for the Boy Scouts.

As fate would have it, that was the same day West Virginia was playing the University of Utah in the NCAA tournament, the Sweet

16. My oldest daughter, Kimberly, graduated from Utah and called me in West Virginia that day to tell me the Utes were going to kick West Virginia's butt. It was a fun game, but a tough one for me emotionally. I had lived in Utah a long time and knew a lot of grads and boosters there, but I had to pull for West Virginia. And of course everyone in West Virginia was going crazy because that was the best the Mountaineers had done since Rod Thorn played for them in 1963. They were playing on the other side of the country in Anaheim, California, about as far away from West Virginia as you can get. Not many people could make the trip, so naturally everyone was glued to their televisions.

I had to go to Logan, though, for the fund-raising dinner and the game was going to start right about when the dinner was over, so they got a limousine with a TV in it so we could watch the game on the way back to Charleston. The reception wasn't very good, though, so we ended up listening to it on the radio. We got back to Charleston when the second half of the game was still going on so we headed to the Embassy Suites where there was a big gathering for the game. They had a couple big screen TVs and hundreds of people were there watching. The local television stations were covering the party because this was a huge event for the whole state. The TV stations grabbed me for interviews and during a time out they introduced me to the crowd and the place went crazy. It's amazing how they remember you back there after all these years.

There was a lot of disappointment that night when Utah won the game, but they were happy the Mountaineers made it as far as they did. I was pulling for them, but once Utah got by West Virginia I was hoping they would go all the way, which they nearly did.

And of course when I got back to my hotel room that night, there was a message from my daughter waiting for me.

That was my day in West Virginia. The next morning the same plane flew me up to Philadelphia to meet up with the Jazz, who were playing the 76ers that night. This time, though, there was only one pilot and me on the plane. I saw him sitting there alone in the cockpit and the thought of just me and him on this plane was a little unsettling. I said, "You OK, big guy? Drink some coffee and stay awake."

Chapter Twelve

ZEKE FROM CABIN CREEK

B y my junior year at West Virginia, I was well on my way to setting just about every record the school ever had for basketball. But I did something that season that ensured I wouldn't hold them for long.

I helped recruit Jerry West.

Jerry grew up in Cabin Creek, West Virginia, about 30 miles outside of Charleston where I grew up. He went to East Bank High School and played in the same county conference I did, the Kanawha Valley Conference. East Bank was one of the best teams in the state his senior year. Actually, they were a pretty bad team, but Jerry was that good. Without him they wouldn't have won five games, but Jerry was so dominating—he could get 30 points, 20 rebounds and five blocked shots in a game—they made it to Morgantown in the state tournament and were the odds-on favorite to win the championship.

In West Virginia, the final eight teams in the Class A tournament would advance to Morgantown. Our coach would then pick eight guys off the team to serve as hosts for these schools. Each guy was assigned to a team and we would show them around. The teams stayed in the athletic dormitory and we would eat meals with them and sit on their bench during the games.

That made it seem like a big deal for the kids but it also gave us a chance to do some subtle (and not so subtle) recruiting. It was a chance for our players to tell the top high school players what a great basketball program we had at WVU and get them thinking about coming there. Jerry West was the best high school player in the state and I was the All-America, so it was no coincidence I hosted his team.

I was with him for three or four days, sitting on their bench in the games, going into the locker room with them before games and at halftime, and eating meals with them. At halftime of the state championship game I told them, if you guys want to win this thing you better get the ball to Jerry. They did, and they won.

The first time I met him I walked into his dorm room and he was making his bed. He was quiet and shy, but he knew who I was. We talked about his team, and we talked about college. I told him I knew he had scholarship offers from every school in the country but if he liked his home state, this was the only school in the state for him. I told him I wasn't the easiest guy in the world to handle but they did everything in the world for me. And I told him Fred Schaus and Red Brown were always straight with me. We played as good of a schedule as any team in the country, including two games a year at Madison Square Garden in New York. We played Pittsburgh, Alabama, Duke, North Carolina State, Villanova and LaSalle. We played in Florida, and every year we had two trips to New York City to play St. John's and NYU. If you're an All-American, that's where you're going to get noticed. So he ended up going to West Virginia—and breaking all my records

By the time I finished my college career I had set about 25 school records, everything from scoring average to career points to points in a game. I even set an assist record or two. Attendance soared while I was playing, bringing in a lot of revenue to the program. I'd tell Jerry, "I want you to understand I'm the one who's making the payments on this field house." My records didn't last long. I was a better high school player than he was, but by time he got to college he had passed me. Three years after I finished school, Jerry was finishing off most of my records. He broke my record for points in a season and points in a career. He passed me in career scoring and career 20-point games. He broke my records for field goals in a season and a career, and my free throw records too. I still hold the school record for points in a game, 54, and there were two records he could never come close to—shots in a game (48) and shots in a season (814). I should hold those forever. No one has ever shot without conscience the way I did.

To this day, Jerry holds about 15 school records that once belonged to me. He averaged 24.8 points a game for his career in

My mother bought me this soldier's suit when I was eight years old.

My Thomas Jefferson Junior High school team won the West Virginia state championship in 1950. That's me in the middle holding the ball.

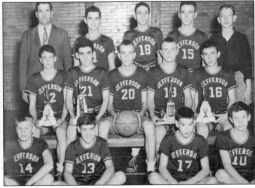

Here I am in my senior year at Charleston High School.

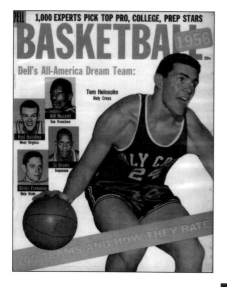

Forget the 1992 U.S. Olympic basketball team, I was on the "original" Dream Team in 1956. *Dell Magazine* said so.

This was my first full game following knee surgery my sophomore year. With three seconds left I threw the ball in the air and trotted off the court. The ball hit the floor just as the final buzzer sounded. (Photo courtesy of West Virginia University)

West Virginia Athletic Director Red Brown, who was a father figure to me in college, presents me with the Southern Conference Player of the Year award in 1957.

Jerry West and I were just two of the many athletes Ann Dinardi took in at West Virginia University. She was one of the greatest influences in my life.

I'm up to my usual tricks at West Virginia.

What a great looking bunch! Hot Rod Hundley's All-Stars Fred Schaus, Mike Holt, Leland Byrd, John Holt, me, Jim Sottile and Clayce Kishbaugh.

Jack Fleming, the longtime voice of the Mountaineers, introduces me at Mountaineer Field House.

Here I'm taking some time to sign autographs after a game in Philadelphia my rookie year. (Bill Naylor)

I'm teaching Ryne Duren of the Angels the proper grip for a curveball in our league. (Los Angeles Lakers photo).

I spent six years with the Lakers, three in Minneapolis and three in Los Angeles.

Chuck Connors, "The Rifleman," played two seasons with the Boston Celtics before going to Hollywood.

For participating in the 1961 All-Star game, we all received a set of Sam Snead signature golf clubs.

Fred Schaus was my coach at West Virginia and later with the Los Angeles Lakers.

I couldn't jump high enough to block Zelmo Beaty's shot, so I had to settle for grabbing his arm. Bob Pettit, No. 9 for the Hawks, was one of the all-time greats. (Peter Banks)

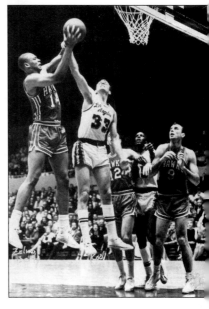

Red Robbins, who played eight years in the ABA, including stops in New Orleans and Utah, was my color analyst in 1978. Here we are working a Jazz game at the Louisiana Superdome.

Here I'm posing with three bartenders at Pat O'Brien's in the French Quarter.

Bill Russell offers a few pointers on the game. We worked together at CBS for several years.

The golf tournament I sponsored for five years raised funds for the Shriners Hospital for Children. I participated in the ground breaking for the Salt Lake City Hospital.

Bobby "Slick" Leonard and I toast the good old days. The longtime player and coach has been a broadcaster for the Indiana Pacers the past 13 years.

I used to think Pat Riley was overrated as a coach when he started out with the Lakers, but over the years he has proved me wrong.

Magic Johnson has the greatest smile in sports and before going on the air I'd tell him to, "Light 'em up, Magic, light 'em up."

Jerry West (front), Magic Johnson (middle), Rudy LaRusso and Byron Scott (back) pose with me at a Lakers fantasy camp in Palm Springs, California.

Chick Hearn (center) and former teammate Rudy LaRusso (right) at a Lakers fantasy camp. Chick would do play-by-play of the games we played and give tapes to camp participants.

Chubby Checker taught me a few things about doing "The Twist." I ran into him at several celebrity golf tournaments, including my own.

Mickey Mantle was my idol growing up so it was a thrill to get to know him. Here we are at his golf tournament, posing with Indianapolis 500 winner Tom Sneva.

Here are two of Utah's favorite athletes. San Francisco 49ers quarterback Steve Young (left), who played football at Brigham Young University, and 7-foot-6 Shawn Bradley with me at a charity auction in Salt Lake City.

Jerry Sloan (center) and Phil Johnson make a great coaching tandem. Jerry was *The Sporting News* Coach of the Year in 1998 and Phil was the NBA Coach of the Year in 1975.

Utah Sen. Orrin Hatch (left) is introducing me to Muhammad Ali at the Senator's golf tournament in Park City.

This guy's pretty good, isn't he? Michael Jordan has always been gracious to me with his time.

Having a laugh with former Green Bay Packers great Jim Taylor and relief ace Rollie Fingers at my golf tournament.

One of Utah's favorite actors, William Brimley, is a longtime Jazz season ticket holder.

I'm standing with the only owners the Jazz have ever had: Sam Battistone (left) and Larry H. Miller (right).

Frank Layden and I rode with Karl Malone in the Pioneer Days parade shortly after we drafted the Mailman. The Utah holiday falls on Karl's birthday, July 24.

Ron Boone, who holds the professional basketball record for consecutive games played, has been my color analyst longer than anyone. (Utah Jazz/Don Grayston)

Jazz owner Larry H. Miller and Frank Layden in Frank's coaching days. Frank eventually handed the coaching reins over to Jerry Sloan and was promoted to team president.

Charles Barkley, one of the league's colorful characters, had his best years in Phoenix and was always an interesting interview.

Karl Malone ices down his knees after every game to help recover from the pounding of an NBA game. (Utah Jazz/Don Grayston).

Karl Malone is one of the greatest interviews in the NBA. He always has something interesting to say. (Utah Jazz/Don Grayston)

John Stockton usually brings one of his kids with him to post-game interviews. (Utah Jazz/Don Grayston)

My middle daughter,
Jacqueline, is a school
teacher by profession.
She currently is in
cartoon animation
school.

Two of my daughters:
Jennifer (left) and Kimberly,
my oldest. Kimberly is a
newspaper reporter in
Wichita Falls, Texas.

My youngest daughter,
Jennifer, owns a hair salon in
Scottsdale, Arizona, called
Chameleon.

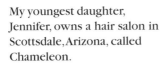

"You gotta love it, baby!"

(Utah Jazz/Don Grayston)

93 games. Because his teams did well in the NCAA tournaments and we always got knocked out in the first round, I played in 89 career games.

I only played against him once in college, my senior year when we had our annual preseason scrimmage with the freshman team. They were a good team because of West and Willie Akers, who was the other top high school player from West Virginia that year. Akers' team lost to West's team in the state championship game the year before. Freshmen weren't allowed to play varsity then, but if we had those two guys on our team, we never would have lost a game. I guarded West in that scrimmage and he guarded me. I'll tell you what, he was as good as anyone I played against my entire college career.

I only saw him play once when he was on the varsity at West Virginia because I was with the Lakers then. The Mountaineers had a game at Madison Square Garden while the Lakers were in New York so I went to see him. He was only a sophomore but he already was a great college player. I didn't see him much after that until his rookie year with the Lakers. I did run into him once, though. He said, "Hey, Rod, you know that field house you were paying for? Well it's paid in full."

Rod Thorn arrived at West Virginia as a freshman when Jerry was a senior and replaced him as the varsity star the year after West graduated. So for nine straight years, the Mountaineers' program was in great hands. We were without question the three biggest names ever to play there and we were all three years apart. I finished in 1957, West finished in 1960 and Thorn finished in '63. Those were the glory days at West Virginia University, and to this day they remember the three of us as their own.

My team never made it past the first round of the NCAA tournament, but West's team made it all the way to the championship game his junior year in 1959, losing by a single point to California. West made it back to the Sweet 16 his senior season, and Thorn's team advanced in 1963. In fact, Thorn's team was the last one to make it that far in the NCAA tournament until the 1997-98 season, when they lost to Utah in the Sweet 16.

Thorn and I always argued over who was the second-greatest player in West Virginia. There was no question Jerry West was No. 1 so Rod and I argued over who was second-best. He said he was tired of always hearing about Jerry West and Rod Hundley, that he had a better shooting percentage, was a better all-around player. He was going on and on about being the second-best player at West Virginia. Finally I said, "Rod, you've got it wrong. Jerry West is second-best player at West Virginia, not you."

When they announced the All-Time Southern Conference team, Brian McIntyre from the NBA office called to congratulate me for making first team. Well, I knew if I made it then Jerry West had to have made it, so I asked him if Rod Thorn was on it. He said Rod was on the second team. There have probably been 20 teams that played in the conference at one time or another, maybe 6,000 basketball players, so I sent Rod a telegram congratulating him for being one of the 10 best out of all those players, that being honored on the second team, was a great accomplishment. "P.S.," I added, "Jerry and I made the first team."

Jerry West made himself into a great basketball player. Everything he did on the court was all right-handed but he worked on his left hand until he was adequate with it. He was never great with his left hand but he was good enough, and that was the only weakness he ever had with his game.

He was blessed with four things that helped him excel at the game: He had extremely long arms, he was a great leaper, he was unbelievably quick, and he had a tremendous desire and work ethic that was second to none.

Because of his long arms he could go up against bigger players. He was 6-3 but played like he was 6-6. He was sneaky about it too. You didn't realize his reach was that long until you took a shot and this little guy blocked it. And on the other end of the floor when he drove on you, he'd go up for a shot you'd think you were going to block it and he'd get it over you. Then to go with that was his leaping ability. He could jump out of the building, really get up in the air.

Maybe the biggest thing he had going for him was his competitiveness. You can't be as great of a player as he was without talent, but he also maximized his ability. He had a real passion for the game, a burning desire to win and to make himself a great player. He never, ever was contented with how well he played. West was just like Karl Malone and John Stockton. In their minds their best game is still out there. They play every night like that, always looking to put together that one great game. West was the same way. He never was satisfied. He had a huge heart and he worked hard at the game. He was a no-nonsense basketball player. He was about winning.

Elgin Baylor joined the Lakers two years before Jerry West

and immediately made a difference in terms of the quality of basketball we played and establishing a winning attitude, so it was his team. By adding West we became one of the elite teams in the NBA, assuring success for years to come, doing for the Lakers what John Stockton and Karl Malone have done for the Jazz. West and Baylor played together for a solid decade and both averaged more than 27 points a game for their careers. Baylor had nicknames for everyone on the team and he started calling West "Zeke" because he talked a little like a hillbilly back then. Zeke from Cabin Creek.

Baylor was the focus of our offense, our go-to guy, and West was our second option. But with the game on the line, when we needed one basket, we went with West. His other nickname was "Mr. Clutch." That says it all. You talk about icewater in a guy's veins, this guy thrived on pressure. His whole life was about winning. He's always trying to do better in everything he does, just an incredible work ethic. He made himself great. His one weakness was his left hand, but he compensated for that with his quickness. If he got a step on the defender, it was over.

Jerry was a great defensive player, too, with unbelievable quickness, probably the best defensive player in basketball. He could be just two feet away from you and yet he had enough time to react to anything you did. If you tried to get a bounce pass by him, he would swoop down and snatch the ball before it ever hit the ground. And if you tried to whip a bullet pass over his head he would jump up and catch it, just swipe the ball out of the air. You talk about superhuman reflexes, I've seen him do that standing two feet away from the guy he was guarding, he was that quick. In basketball, quickness is more important than speed. He was quick as a cat. That's what made Bill Russell so great. He was a 6-foot-9 center who stopped people with his quickness.

The only player Jerry West ever had trouble defending was Oscar Robertson, who was probably the best offensive player in basketball. West couldn't stop him but then, who could? The two of them were co-captains of the U.S. Olympic team in 1960 and they entered the NBA together that year. Only one other time in the history of the NBA did two of the all-time greats come into the league at the same time. That was in 1979 when Magic Johnson was drafted by the Lakers and Larry Bird went to the Celtics. Oscar was the first player drafted in 1960 when the Cincinnati Royals used a territorial pick to get him from the University of Cincinnati. The Lakers drafted West with the second pick. They were two of the greatest players of all time and I had the privilege of being on the court with both of them, playing with West and against Robertson. They had great admiration for each other and both would say the other one was the best.

We played Cincinnati the first game of the season their rookie year so I got to defend Oscar Robertson in his first game as a pro. Because Fred Schaus had Jerry coming off the bench the first part of his rookie year, I started in the Lakers backcourt with Frank Selvy. Jerry came up to me before the game and warned me about Oscar, because I would have to try to guard him. I had heard about him but I had never seen him play. Jerry knew all about him from the Olympics and came up to me before the game and said, "You're going to guard the greatest basketball player in the history of the game." Here Jerry West was, a rookie in the NBA, and already he was great judge of talent because he was right. Larry Bird, Magic Johnson and Michael Jordan are all right up there, but they all came along much later.

At the time Oscar was the greatest to ever play the game, and he still might be. You couldn't stop him. He could get a shot anytime he wanted, but he was a great playmaker, too. His second year in the league he averaged a triple-double for the season, and he came close to doing it four other times. He was strong enough he could back in the defender then turn and shoot with whatever arc he needed to get the shot off. He could shoot a frozen rope, a mild arc or a rain-maker, and he shot them all with the perfect touch.

By comparison, Oscar had more talent than Jerry, a much more complete all-around game. They both had just one weakness. Jerry's weakness was his left hand and Oscar's was his mouth. He yelled at his teammates too much. He could not tolerate anything less than perfection from the guys he played with. West would never yell at you if you messed up a play. He'd just let it go, but Oscar jumped all over you.

So that first game, West told me I had one chance against Robertson. He said, "When the referee throws the ball up to start the game, reach over and pull Oscar's shirt out of his pants." I told him to get serious and he said, "No, really, pull his shirt out. Then reach down inside his pants, get him by his jock strap, pull it out and step in there with him because getting inside his jock with him is your only hope." We held him to 21 points that night. West scored 20 and I scored 13, but the Royals beat us by 17.

Now when I tell this story I say that I went out there for the opening tip and said, "Hey, Oscar, you won't believe this, but this isn't my idea ..."

In all those years playing together with Elgin Baylor—10 solid seasons of averaging 27 points apiece—they never won a championship. They came the closest in 1969 when Jerry was MVP of the Finals even though they lost to the Celtics in seven games. That's the only time in NBA history a player on the losing team won MVP of the Finals. That was Wilt Chamberlain's first year with the Lakers. West and Wilt finally did win a championship in 1972, but Baylor had retired by then.

Jerry retired during the exhibition season in 1974. He still averaged more than 20 points a game the year before, but he saw his game slip before anyone else could. In a preseason game when he chased after a loose ball and a younger player beat him to it, that was it. He had always been quicker than everyone else, but suddenly he didn't get to a ball he used to get. He had such tremendous pride in his game that if he couldn't play at the top level, he wasn't going to play at all. He went to management and announced his retirement. They were stunned because he could still play. But he went out on top, and I always admired him for that. So many guys hold on too long.

He averaged 27 points, 6.6 assists and 5.7 rebounds for his career. He led the league in scoring once and assists once, and he was an All-Star all 14 years he was in the league. He retired as the leading scorer in Lakers history with 25,192 points. He was a shoo-in for the Hall of Fame and was named one of the 50 Greatest Players in NBA history. He was the master of the frozen rope jump shot. He shot a line drive right at the back of the rim; it was like a bullet. They say the shortest distance between two points is a straight line, and he didn't waste any space on his shots. My co-captain as a senior at West Virginia was Clayce Kishbaugh. You ask him what the shortest distance between two points was and he'd say "half way." But for everyone else it was a straight line and that's how Jerry West shot.

A couple years after retiring as a player, he came back as coach of the team and had some success, but he never really enjoyed it. He was too much of a perfectionist and couldn't understand why everybody didn't look at the game the same way he did, why they didn't play it with the same dedication. In three seasons he had a 145-101 record and won a division title, and he made the playoffs every year, but he got out of it.

After that he spent three years as a consultant for the team, then came back and sat on the bench when Pat Riley took over as coach. They were called co-coaches, but West wanted to make it clear to everyone he wasn't the coach, he was just helping out Riley. He sat on the bench until Riley felt comfortable, then went back to the front office. He was promoted to general manager and in 1995 was given the title of vice president, basketball operations.

He's one of the best ever in that role because he's a tremendous judge of basketball talent. That's probably the No. 1 responsibility of the job, and he excels at it. You have to know who to draft and what to look for in trades. It's no surprise he has done so well in that job, because he's the kind of guy who can be good at anything he takes up. He's competitive at everything he does. He is just a pure athlete. He's a good volleyball player, a good softball player, tennis, you name it. He's a tremendous gin rummy player— better than I am, and I taught him the game.

West is the best golfer I've ever seen who didn't play the game professionally. Ralph Terry, the former pitcher for the New York Yankees, and John Brodie, the former quarterback for the San Francisco 49ers, both had success on the Senior PGA Tour, but West was better than both of them. In my mind, he could have been a great player on the senior tour but he didn't do it. I've always said if there's a 20-foot putt to win the Masters, I'd rather have him putt it instead of Jack Nicklaus. Jerry loves to golf, but he only wants to go to the country club in Bel Air and play with his friends. He didn't want to deal with the travel and the fanfare of playing on the senior tour even though he could have had great success at it. He had no desire to give up his privacy and return to professional sports.

He never plays in celebrity golf tournaments, either, so I had to twist his arm to get him to Utah to play in mine. I really laid it on thick about it being a benefit for a hospital, for children. The first year I held the tournament I asked him to come just this once to help me get this thing off the ground.

I told him on the first day we would give him the last tee time in the afternoon so he wouldn't have to fly in from Los Angeles until that morning. Then the next day we would give him the first tee time of the day so he could head right back to L.A. He's a fast golfer and the course would be wide open ahead of him because he would be leading the pack. He could leave at 11 a.m. one day and be home by noon the next. He asked, "Where am I staying overnight?" I knew by then I had him. I told him we'd put him up in a nice hotel with all the other celebrities. He didn't want to do that, so I offered to let him stay at my house. "All right, then, I'll do it." He came in and did his thing and left. He finished second and didn't even know it, because most of the golfers were still on the course when he was flying back to L.A.

They say opposites attract and we were the best of friends. On the basketball court I liked to clown around and he was serious as hell, but we got along. It was the same off the court. I'm a party person and I like to have fun and not get hung up on anything too serious. He's the exact opposite, very high-strung, very serious. We'll go out to dinner and I'm content to sit in the restaurant and he's always anxious to get out of there. When we're together we don't talk about basketball because there's so much else to talk about. I couldn't think of anything negative to say about him. I think he would do anything for me, he's that good of a friend. I love him like a brother, and I'm so proud of him for going as far as he did considering where he came from. I'd like to think I had a hand in it, growing up in West Virginia.

Chapter Thirteen

A LITTLE SLICE
OF HEAVEN

Steve Hamilton, the long-time pitcher for the New York Yankees, also played two seasons in the NBA. He was 6-foot-7, which was good size for basketball and great size for a pitcher. He was my teammate on the Minneapolis Lakers for two years, but when the Lakers moved to Los Angeles, Steve got into baseball full time. We got to be friends while we were teammates and whenever the Yankees came out West to play the Angels, Steve got me tickets to the baseball game. Mickey Mantle, the Yankees slugger, was my idol, so one day Steve took me into the clubhouse to meet him. I was tickled to get the opportunity, but when Steve introduced us I was shocked. Mickey says, "Hey, Hot Rod Hundley," and starts pretending he's dribbling an imaginary basketball, through his legs, behind his back, spinning it on his finger. Mickey Mantle knew who I was! I couldn't believe it. It was a little slice of heaven, one of the great days in my life.

I got to know Bill Mazeroski and Ralph Terry, too. Mazeroski hit that famous home run for Pittsburgh off Terry to clinch the 1960 World Series, and they both played in my celebrity golf tournament. Ralph was a good golfer who had a nice career on the Senior PGA Tour after finishing with baseball. He asked me once why I never played in Mickey Mantle's golf tournament. I told him I was never invited, so Ralph said he would take care of that. Sure enough, my invitation came through and I was the only basketball player there. I played four years in a row, up until the year after Mickey died. One year they had a reception at night and about

1,000 people were there. Roy Clark was the entertainment and this ballroom was packed. Before Roy took the stage, Stan Musial was up there playing the harmonica and stomping his feet. It was fun for a while, but he didn't want to leave. Mickey finally had to go up there to try to get him off because Roy Clark was waiting to go on. I sat down with Mickey later on and we started swapping stories, about who the best ballplayers were and things like that. He loved Joe DiMaggio. Next thing we knew, it was 2 a.m. and the place was empty, just the two of us sitting there.

Earlier in the night, Jerry Lumpe, a second baseman who used to be Mickey's teammate, told a story about the time he was playing against Mickey. It was a tie game in the ninth inning, the bases were loaded and Mickey was at bat. Al Lopat, the manager, ordered the infield in because if a run scored, they'd lose the game. None of the infielders would move up, though. They knew how hard Mickey hit the ball and they were afraid they'd get killed. Lopat was screaming at them to move up so finally they did. And Mickey hit a screaming shot right at Jerry Lumpe that actually went through his legs in the air and kept rising. The ball made it all the way to the outfield wall on the fly, that's how hard he hit it. So Lumpe was telling this story and Mickey was smiling. He loved hearing stuff like that.

Mickey didn't play in the tournament. Instead he hung out at one of the par-3 holes and played that hole with every group as they came through. Everyone who participated got a baseball autographed by Mickey, and if they drove closer to the pin than him on this hole, they got another one. I beat him that day so he signed a baseball, "Hot Rod, great shot, Mickey Mantle." One of my most cherished pictures is one with me, Yogi Berra and Mickey taken the year before he died.

I had met Stan Musial years earlier and that was another thrill. The legendary St. Louis Cardinal was a big basketball fan and went to a lot of Hawks games when the team was in St. Louis. The first time we met he came up to me and said hello. Again I was shocked. Stan Musial approached me! To this day I have a baseball he autographed on my desk.

I came to realize when you're in the sports business you cross paths with so many other professional athletes. We all knew one another from the sports pages. I knew every football player from reading the paper and every baseball player too. So I guess it made sense they knew who I was too. We were all in this together.

I've met so many people like that over the years, crossing paths with them and they knew who I was because I played basketball, especially in L.A. with all the movie stars. When I got into broadcasting I'd usually spot someone in the crowd I knew, or at least had met, and ask them to join me on the air at halftime of a broadcast. I've interviewed Peter Falk, Nick Nolte and Jesse Owens. Fred Couples has become a good friend I met through Jim Nantz and over the years I've gotten to know a lot of other golfers who are basketball fans, like Ray Floyd and Phil Mickelson. There always seems to be somebody at the games.

Once when I was with CBS, I interviewed Bob Hope at halftime. I couldn't even hold my microphone steady I was so nervous. You don't get any bigger than Bob Hope. I had a radio show when I was in New Orleans and interviewed Bill Bradley of the Knicks one day. I was sitting there talking to this basketball player thinking, this man is going to be president of the United States one day. And there I was talking to him about basketball. I've done more interviews with him over the years, after he made it to the United States Senate. I still think he's got a chance to be president.

During my second tour with CBS in 1979, we were in Los Angels to broadcast the fourth game of the Seattle-Lakers playoff series on a Sunday. Game 3 was in L.A. on a Friday night, so we planned to watch that game to prepare for the Sunday broadcast. Since I was in town, the Sonics asked me to be a guest analyst on Game 3 for their broadcast back to Seattle. So I did. For a halftime guest I got Walter Matthau to join me. The Sonics were down by 10 at halftime so I asked Walter what he would do if he coached the team. He said, "I'd have them all eat Limburger cheese, then when they came out, have them blow their breath right in the other guys' faces. We'd take this game over."

I knew a lot of people in broadcasting, either from being interviewed as a player or from working with them once I got in the business myself. Howard Cosell got to be a good friend, and he was an easy target, too. He always treated me well, but I could see how he rubbed people the wrong way because he was a bit on the vain side. I first met Howard when I was in college at West Virginia. He had a radio talk show nationwide and he had us college All-Americans on with him. Over the years I got to know him well, running into him often during my playing days with the Lakers, and even more during my broadcasting days with CBS.

When I was in New York for the 1968 NBA All-Star game, Johnny Kerr and I went to dinner with Howard at the Four Seasons, one of the most exclusive places in town. I didn't normally hang out in the fancy joints but Howard was buying, so why not? Howard had a show called "Speaking on Sports" at the time and he introduced it by saying, "This is Howard Cosell . . . speaking on sports!" Johnny, Howard and I sauntered into the Four Seasons and as we got past the entryway overlooking the room, I used my best Howard Cosell voice to holler out, "Ladies and gentlemen, Howard Cosell speaking on sports!" Johnny and I then ducked under a table, leaving Howard standing there by himself with the whole room watching. He was ready to duck under a table himself.

Howard never let a prank go unanswered. Once when I was staying at the Beverly Hills Hotel while I was in town to broadcast a Lakers playoff game, Cosell was staying at the same place while in town to do a "Superstars" show for ABC. I went out by the pool on a day off and all the CBS guys were there, Rick Barry and all the producers. They were all sitting by the pool with Howard when I walked out. And Howard said to me in that unique style of his for all to hear, "When did it dawn on you, Hot Rod, that you had no talent for this business?" He could knock you, then sit down with you and talk. I'd see him in a coffee shop and he would holler for me to come over and sit with him. We'd talk for hours at a time. In New York City he would drive me around in his limo. I know he irritated some people but he was always nice to me.

The best anyone ever got me was in 1974. I was in Milwaukee with CBS for the NBA Finals between the Bucks and Celtics. Our whole crew had dinner one night at Sally's, a great steak house in the hotel where we were staying. We usually ran up about a $500 tab at those things, which the producers picked up. After dinner they told me that the chef wanted to meet me and get my autograph, so the waiters took me back into the kitchen. I meet the chef and gave him my autograph and told him what a great restaurant it was and how much we enjoyed the food. He introduced me to his assistants and I signed autographs for them too. We chatted for five or 10 minutes and they all seemed to enjoy meeting me. But when I went back to my table, everyone was gone. Every single one of them had left and the check was sitting there in the middle of the table. I was the only one left to pay for it. They had set me up perfectly. It was about a $500 tab waiting for me. So I just wrote CBS Television, New York City on the bill along with the address and told them to send it there, they'd take care of it. When I met up with the group later on they were all still laughing.

The best I ever got myself was in Milwaukee for that same series. The night before one of the games there, everyone from CBS was at a bar called Major Goolsby's and we were toasting the network. "To the eye!" they were saying. They were drinking shots of peppermint schnapps with beer backs. I had never had schnapps in my life, but I joined in. The next day while we were broadcasting the game I had the worst headache of my life. I made it to halftime and I thought we were off the air when I said, "Man, I could use a Cutty and water." We were still on the air, though, and that went out to the entire country. I'd never touch a drink on the day of a game, I just said that. CBS thought a truck load of Cutty Sark was going to show up at my house because I mentioned them on the air. The next day I was running through the airport and some guy yelled out, "Hey, Hot Rod, you get that Cutty and water?"

Being famous has its advantages sometimes, but not always. In 1974, Brent Musburger and I were working an afternoon game in Chicago, and we raced out of the arena the second we got off the air to catch our flights home. The timing was tight and we were trying like hell to catch our planes because if we missed our flights we had to stay over until the next morning. We got a cab that raced us to the airport and we were running through the terminal, the two of us heading for different flights on the same airline. We were doing OK until we got to the security check. There was a huge line to go through the metal detector. Brent told me to follow him and we went to the head of the line.

This was Chicago, Brent's hometown, and he was the No. 1 announcer for CBS. Everyone knew who he was and he figured he was going to talk his way through the line. It didn't work, though. They didn't recognize either one of us and they made us go to the back of the line. "They must not have any TVs on this side of Chicago," he said to me.

One guy I never did meet but wish I had was Harry Caray. He seemed like my kind of guy. He was a homer and wasn't ashamed of it. Vin Scully was more middle of the road. He wanted the Dodgers to win but was very professional about it. I think that's the best way to approach it and that's what I try to do. But Harry Caray related to the fans and his style seemed to work for him. Jim Foley, the Houston Rockets' color analyst, told me about a time he caught up with Harry when the Cubs were in Houston to play the Astros.

The two of them were out on the town when this excited young man comes up to Harry and says, "You're Harry Caray! You're the greatest baseball announcer I've ever heard! Can I buy you a drink?"

Harry said, "Son, the last time I turned down a drink, I misunderstood the question." Foley told me that story and I use it all the time myself. I love that line.

As a former professional athlete you run into a lot of people on the celebrity golf circuit. I met Wayne Walker, the former Detroit Lions linebacker and kicker, at a celebrity tournament and now I'm playing in his tournament, which he co-hosts with Jerry Kramer, the old offensive lineman of the Green Bay Packers. They hold their tournament at Cactus Pete's in Jackpot, Nevada, and one night after golfing we went in the lounge and Chubby Checker was playing there. He was bringing people up on stage to do the twist. He started singing, "Meet me baby on 42nd Street at the Peppermint Lounge" and I was ready to go. That was my song. I can do the twist and I've been to the Peppermint Lounge in New York. That was my day, the '50s, and we'd do the peppermint twist at the Peppermint Lounge when it first opened. Here we are now years later and Chubby Checker was calling people up on the stage to dance with him so I jumped at the chance.

I went up there with him and did my two minutes, and he ran me off and brought someone else up. He played it for an hour, bringing up people from the audience to do the twist with him. We all went up there, but Jerry Kramer held back. He was the host, though, so they kept trying to get him up there. Finally he got up there and that big son of a bitch, he stalked Chubby. He got down in a three-point stance like he was lining up for the Packers and Chubby kind of took a step back and gave him a wary look. Then Jerry stood up and started doing the twist. He was good at it, too, better than any of us. He brought the house down. The next year we went back and Chubby was still there. We got it going again.

After playing in a lot of those tournaments I decided to hold my own. The first year I had a lot of basketball players like Jerry West, Elgin Baylor, Bob Cousy, Gail Goodrich, Jerry Lucas and John Havlicek participate, but football players (Gale Sayers, Jim Plunkett, Jerry Kramer) and baseball players (Enos Slaughter) as well. Even Tom Sneva, the race car driver, and Earl Anthony, the bowler, played too, so I had my bases covered. Stella Stevens, the actress, was the only woman to play. She said, "I can't play golf, but I love being around all these men."

Bobby Knight, the Indiana basketball coach, was there just to piss everybody off. He could piss off anybody, anywhere. Bobby saw Ed Marinaro walking by and they're friends, but he still said, "Aw, Ed, don't ruin my day. I'm having a good day and I sure as heck don't want to see you." Ed broke up. The two of them used to work camps together and actually liked each other, but not everyone liked Bobby Knight. He played in a foursome one year with three Mormons and by the end of the round the three of them were steamed. Bobby was arguing religion with them the whole time they were on the golf course.

Billy Kilmer, the Washington Redskins quarterback, played in my tournament. We come from the same mold; Billy never wanted to go to bed because he was afraid he might miss something, and I was the same way. He was a ballplayer's ballplayer. He was great with people and everybody liked him.

Arte Johnson, the actor from "Rowan and Martin's Laugh In," brought a camera with him to photograph the other celebrities. He was on the practice tee with Wilford Brimley and asked Wilford to pose for a picture. No problem, Wilford said. He was wearing shorts and had his hands strung through his belt loops. Just as Arte was going to snap the picture, Wilford spun around and dropped his shorts, mooning the camera. Arte took the picture of Wilford's big butt and said, "I'm going to have that picture blown up and put it on the back wall of my garage. Every time I open my garage door, that's what I'll see."

Jerry Kramer played too, and he was great. Not only did we raise money for the Shriners Hospital, we raised awareness for their cause, too. They have children's hospitals all over the country and provide free care to those who need it. We would bring in kids from the hospital and have them at the first tee where they got a chance to meet the celebrities and get autographs. Kramer was great at this. There's this big, rugged guy, voted the greatest offensive guard ever to play football, but he's a real softie with the kids. He told this one little kid he had something he wanted to show him, then pulled a pouch out of his golf bag. He opened it up and it was his Super Bowl ring. The ring was huge, and he handed it to this kid and let him hold it. He told him how he got it, playing for the Green Bay Packers. This kid's eyes got big as saucers. It's something he will never forget

Jim Taylor, Jerry's teammate with the Packers, played in my tournament one year and won the low net. He strolled in there with a 19 handicap and shot a 77 or something like that and won the tournament going away. Everybody thought he was a ringer and they were all complaining to me because it's my tournament. They asked me what I was going to say to him and I told them, hey, he's a football player. I'm not saying a word. His calves are bigger than my waist. You got a problem, you tell him. The next year he came back and played again, but this time we cut his handicap to a nine. We took 10 shots off because he won it the year before, so he went out and shot 90 twice. He was right at the handicap he had the year before when nobody would believe him.

One guy who wouldn't play in my tournament was Paul Hornung. I've know him since we were in college in 1956. I got the Dapper Dan award for the college basketball player of the year and he got the award for football. They had a banquet in Pittsburgh and that's where I first met him. I've run into him so many times over the years. We both worked for CBS when I was doing college basketball and he was doing football. I saw him at the NBA Finals in Chicago in 1997. He said, "I want to introduce you to my wife. Now don't hit on her." We both laughed. But when I called him up years earlier to play in my celebrity tournament he said he'd play for $10,000. I said, "Paul, you can't even break 100 and I'm going to pay you 10 grand to play? I love you, buddy, but I don't think so." He did send me an autographed picture to put up in my restaurant, though. Didn't even charge me. But he never came out to play.

Gale Sayers, the former Chicago Bears running back, played one year. He wasn't a very good golfer. I don't know if he could break 100, but he tried. I was the starter for the tournament, introducing everyone when they came to the first tee. Gale took his first swing off the first tee and the ball just dribbled a few feet in front of him. I told him to hit it again, and he did the same thing. We were in a tournament so every stroke was supposed to count, but when he finally hit a good one and I said go play that one. I was impressed, though, that he came out. He knew he wasn't much of a golfer but it was for charity so he didn't hesitate to help out.

On the flip side there was Rick Barry. He could hit the ball about eight miles and had a three or four handicap. I played a practice round with him and couldn't believe how good he was. The No. 5 hole at Jeremy Ranch in Park City, Utah, was a par-4 down hill that doglegs right. It's a lay-up hole. There's a creek cutting across the fairway so most people hit to a spot in front of it, about 180 yards from the pin. Then it's about a 7- or 8-iron to the greens. I pulled out my 4-iron to tee off and I see Rick pulling out his 3-wood. I said, "Rick, that's too much club. If you hit it too far you'll be in the creek." He looked at me like I was crazy. He said, "I'm not laying up, I'm going for the green." And sure enough, he clobbered that ball and reached the green with his 3-wood. I couldn't believe it. A driver would have been too much club for him.

Rick was a fierce competitor, very proud. He wasn't just a great basketball player, he was a great tennis player and a great golfer too; just a great athlete. And he knows everything—just ask him. He is a very intelligent guy. When I worked NBA games with Rick, Brent Musburger sat between us doing the play-by-play while Rick and I were the analysts. Brent liked to pick fights with Rick, and I played along. Brent would ask Rick something then tap me on the leg under the table as my cue to say the exact opposite of whatever Rick was going to say. Like if there was a blocking foul called, Brent would ask Rick what he thought of the call. If Rick said it was a bad call, that he thought it should have been charging, Brent would hit me on the leg and ask me what I thought. I'd say, "No, it was a blocking foul all the way. Good call." After he got Rick and me to disagree, Brent always sided with me, and the two of us would jump all over Rick.

We would have production meetings the night before those CBS games and Rick always thought he was the producer-director. He always had a better way of doing things, always telling everyone what to do. He was just making suggestions but everybody would be elbowing everyone else saying, "There he goes again." The guys finally told him, "Dammit, Rick, you just broadcast the game. We'll call the shots."

I like Rick personally, and I like his kids. We got to be good friends from working together at CBS. But Rick irritates people. He's a high-strung guy. He could be rude to fans. I always thought Jerry West was a great judge of basketball talent and he says Rick Barry is one of the greatest basketball players of all time. If you list the top five or 10 players of all time Rick should be on that list, but he's always left off. No one ever picks him because of who he is. Everyone respects how great a player he was, but they didn't like him personally. He was a holier-than-thou kind of guy, a walking rule book and a coach. He was an expert at everything he's never done.

Most celebrity tournaments are one-day events but mine was two days with the scores from the first day carrying over. Gene

Mauch, the baseball manager, came in one morning on the second day and said, "Are we playing by the same rules today or has Rick Barry changed them?" Rick was notorious for that. Everybody had to do things Rick's way. Even a baseball guy like Gene Mauch knew that.

Neil Lomax, the quarterback, won my tournament the first year with a two-day score of 5-under. We played at Jeremy Ranch, which was where the Senior PGA Tour stop was at the time, so that was a great score on a tough course. Jerry West was second at 3-under and Rick Barry was third at 1-over. I don't remember what I shot.

People here in Utah couldn't believe all the celebrities I was bringing in. I used to have guys come up to me and ask if they could play, like Doc Rivers. He said I had the best golf tournament in the country. Craig Bolerjack, who recently started with CBS, used to work as my color man on Jazz broadcasts. He always asked me why he wasn't invited to participate. I told him because it was for celebrities, and we'd both laugh. I stopped hosting the tournament after five years because I didn't like the way it was run. It got too big and we were spending too much money and not giving enough to charity.

When I was broadcasting for the Suns I owned a bar in Phoenix called the Court Jester. To attract players on the team we gave them half off everything, and most visiting teams would hang out there, too, along with guys from the minor league hockey team they had at the time. Dave DeBusschere would come in and we nicknamed our draft beer "DaBush."

The American Airlines Master Jet golf tournament was held in Phoenix and it attracted a lot of the biggest names in sports, baseball and football players, primarily because it was in basketball season. Joe DiMaggio, Willie Mays, Joe Namath, Johnny Unitas, everybody played in this tournament. Lance Alsworth and Wayne Walker, too. Johnny Kerr and I played because we were with the Suns. We were the only basketball guys in it because everybody else was working. It was basketball season. I was trying to get all of these athletes to come to my bar and when they showed up, I bought drinks for them. I wanted them to stay because it was great for business. I was on the phone to everyone I knew to get them to come down and meet these famous athletes.

Ray Nitschke stopped by, the great linebacker for the Green Bay Packers who passed away in early 1998. Ray had a notorious reputation for tearing bars up in Green Bay. He would just start wild brawls. So he came in and I asked him what he wanted to drink.

"I'll have a glass of orange juice," he said.

I couldn't believe what I just heard. I knew he had a reputation so I said, "Orange juice?"

"Yeah," he said, "I quit drinking." I asked him why and he said, "When I have a few drinks I start throwing bar stools right through the wall."

"Well that's not too bad," I said. I'd been in the bar business and had seen worse.

"Yeah," he said, "but when I throw bar stools there's someone still sitting on them."

I said, "Give this man an orange juice."

Chapter Fourteen

DRAFTED TWICE IN THE SAME MONTH

I was driving through the hills of West Virginia on my barnstorming tour in 1957 when I heard the news on the car radio: I was the No. 1 pick in the NBA draft. I thought the New York Knicks were going to make a deal to get me with the second pick, so I was surprised to hear someone else took me first. I was looking forward to going to New York, but I was headed to the Minneapolis Lakers instead. The NBA draft is a big production today, carried on national television with big crowds at every arena, but not then. The Lakers never even called me after the draft. There was no telegram or anything. Good thing I had the radio on or I may have never known.

Someone wanted me even more than the Lakers, though. I withdrew from school after my last basketball season at West Virginia ended to go on my barnstorming tour in April. Because I no longer was in school I was eligible for the military draft. Uncle Sam didn't waste any time calling for me, either. Within a month after the Lakers made me their No. 1 pick, Uncle Sam made me a first-round draft pick too. I was drafted into the Army and sent to Fort Jackson, South Carolina, for processing.

My basketball career was now on hold. I passed my physical even though I had two bad knees, then was shipped out to Fort Hood, Texas, for basic training. I was the same age as Elvis Presley and he was sent to Fort Hood too, while I was still there, but I never saw him. About the closest I ever got to him was staying in the same hotel room he had stayed in back in West Virginia. A buddy of mine in Charleston owned the Daniel Boone Hotel there. I always stayed in the presidential suite when I was there, and that's the same room Elvis stayed in when he did a concert in Charleston. The owner told me later he sold every thing in the room that Elvis touched to collectors: The key, the bedspread, sheets, towels, everything.

As soon as I got to Fort Hood, things started going my way. On the first day there were about 40 of us assigned to this company and the drill sergeant, Sgt. Robinson, asked if anyone had been to college. I raised my hand and looked around. Out of 40 guys I was the only one. So he put me in charge! Just like that I was the platoon leader. I got an arm band with temporary stripes and everything. They had a chin-up bar in the mess hall and they would pull guys out of the chow line and make them do chin-ups before they could eat. They grabbed me the first day and Sgt. Robinson saw them line me up. He went up to them and said, "Hey, he doesn't do that. That's my man. I don't ever want to see him at the chin-up bar again."

Sgt. Robinson was a career man, gung-ho about everything that had to do with the military, but he was mad we weren't at war. He wanted to fight. He told me to pick four squad leaders, one for each of the squads in the company. So I picked four of the buddies I met on the train ride to Texas. This was after the sergeant gave us the talk about how he's the man, he's going to whip our asses and make soldiers out of us, then he makes me his right-hand man. He called me "Hut." He'd say, "Hut, I want you to kick their asses." And I'd say, "Yes sir!" One time we were upstairs in the barracks and everyone was goofing off, but I could hear Sgt. Robinson coming up the stairs. So I jumped up and started barking out orders to these guys, really getting on them. Sgt. Robinson comes upstairs just in time to see me yelling at these guys and says, "Hut, you're kicking ass! Keep it up!"

The other break I got was getting into special services right after basic training, playing on the base's baseball and basketball teams. During an inspection the base commander, a three-star general, singled me out and said, "How do you like this Army life?"

I said, "I love it, sir."

He says, "How do you like the food?"

"It's wonderful, sir."

Then he says, "Are we going to have a good basketball team?" That's when I knew he was a basketball nut. While the rest of my unit was preparing to ship out to Worms, Germany, for two years, I was getting ready to play baseball that summer and basketball in the winter.

My knees were really bothering me because of all they exercises they had us do, so I kept going to sick call. That never helped, though. They might give me an aspirin, but nobody really looked at my knees. Joe Marconi, a good friend of mine who played football at West Virginia while I was there, knew my plight and told me I needed to get to the orthopedic clinic. Joe had a great career at WVU, then with the Chicago Bears in the NFL. He had the same problem that I had with his knees in the Army because of a football injury. He had heard about the troubles I was having and he wrote me a letter telling me what I had to do, just one Mountaineer taking care of another one.

I eventually made it over there and of course there's a huge wait. The place was a zoo, worse than any waiting room in any doctor's office. There were probably 100 guys there waiting and I was there about three hours before I got to see a doctor. When a doctor finally looked at my knees he asked me how I ever got in the Army in the first place. I told him I was just drafted and took my physical like everyone else. He looked at my knees and shoved papers around, signing stuff while he talked to me. He asked me what I would do if I got out of the Army. I told him I'd try to play professional basketball, which I probably shouldn't have said. Fortunately he had no idea who I was and never asked how I could expect to play professional basketball on a pair of knees that I was trying to convince him weren't good enough for the Army. I told him if I couldn't play basketball I would go back to school. Another doctor came to look at me, and they were talking to me casually, talking to each other casually, but in a hurry, shoving papers around the whole time. Then just like that, the first doctor handed me some forms and said, "Give this to the company commander when you get back. You'll be a civilian in two weeks. Next."

I was shocked. I went back and turned in my papers to Sgt. Robinson. He didn't follow basketball either and never questioned me about getting out of the Army so I could go play professional basketball. He just looked over the forms and said, "I guess you're out of here." I never said a word to anyone else. Not a soul. The Army still owned me for another week or two while they processed the paperwork, and I wasn't going to make any noise at all. One day I just disappeared and my buddies probably wondered where I was. The last stop was an out-processing place and that was where you really got harassed. I did everything they wanted, though. I made it that far and I wasn't going to mess up now.

That was 1957, in between Korea and Vietnam, and there wasn't anything going on. A lot of people were getting discharged. If there was a war going on, there was no way I would have gotten out, so the timing was right. Just like that I was out of the Army. I drove back to West Virginia, called the Lakers and told them I was on my way.

Chapter Fifteen

FUNDAMENTALISM

Like a connoisseur appreciates a work of art, I've always had a great appreciation for fundamental skills on the basketball court. It's something that was drilled into me since I was a kid. After my playing days ended, I've put on clinics for Converse, run basketball camps and continued to study the game, all with an emphasis on fundamentals. A young player learning the game can pick up so much by watching the fundamentally sound pros play. It also helps fans enjoy the game and appreciate the good players.

I had my own basketball camp for several years at Salem College in West Virginia and the emphasis was on how young kids should play the game. We did all sorts of drills that focused on ball-handling skills. We stressed the little things like squeezing handballs to build hand strength. That way when you drive to the basket they can't knock it away from you. Anyone who has ever seen Elgin Baylor play knows what great hands he had. You couldn't knock the ball out of his hands. Karl Malone has a powerful grip too.

There are so many basketball camps out there, some by big names and some by no-names, but they all teach the same things. Fundamentals is the name of the game. Here are some things every young player should learn, and what fans can watch for to raise their appreciation for the game.

Passing

The No. 1 skill all great basketball players have is the ability to handle a basketball. If you can do that, there's always a place for you on the court no matter what other skills you have. All ballhandlers can play. Guys like John Stockton and Jason Kidd today and Bob Cousy when I played could do so much with the ball. They handled it so well it opened the door to so many other things.

You have to be able to pass and dribble without looking at the ball. A good pass comes from the wrist, flipping the ball so it rolls off your fingertips with a good follow-through. You need the timing, knowing when to throw with both hands, when to pass off the dribble like Stockton does. He doesn't pick the ball up and throw it. It's just one smooth motion, passing the ball with one hand as he bounces it off the floor. That skill didn't just come to him, he worked at it for hours on end.

You have to know how to pass the ball on the run so you can hit your teammate in stride, to lead a guy so he can do something with the ball when he gets it. What really kills a guy on the run is having to reach down to his feet for a pass or reach behind his back. That's hard to do. Watch teams that are good at finishing the fast break. The guy leading it probably does an excellent job of timing the pass to the basket. Stockton excels there. He knows where his teammates like the ball and he makes sure that's where they get it. Some guys have great hands and can catch it anywhere, but with other guys you have to put it right out there, tell them, "Here's where it's coming, baby, be ready for it."

The two-handed chest pass is the most overrated pass because good defenders can get a hand on it. It's important to set the defender up, to fake one way and throw another, to be looking left and throwing right. If the defender is in the classic defensive position, squared up to you with his left hand up and his right hand down, you look down to freeze him, then throw it past his right ear where he'll never have time to react to it. Don't just hold the ball and throw it, you've got to move the ball around. Fake one way, pass the other. Fake, pass. The defender's going to follow the ball so watch him react and throw it where he gave you an opening. Stockton is great at faking a high pass to get the defender up, then throwing it under him. Small guys have got to learn to do that because they are always guarded by bigger people. They have to get the pass around them or over them or under them by getting them to commit one way and firing it the other.

Jeff Hornacek is good at setting up the defenders with his passes and surprisingly, Chris Morris is sound fundamentally. We always see him freewheeling out on the court but he can really handle the ball. He can dribble with both hands, pass and shoot from either side. The problem is his timing. He uses his left hand when he should be using his right and his right hand when he should be using the left. He drives you nuts but fundamentally, he's a sound player.

Most passing is one-handed these days. The only exception is the two-handed overhead pass. You want your big men to rebound, turn outside and fire the outlet pass without ever bringing the ball down where the little guys can get it. They need to keep the ball over their head and with two hands they can get a lot of zip on the pass to get it to the guard quickly to start a fast break. Wes Unseld and Bill Russell were great at that. Mark Eaton did a nice job of leading the man down court with the outlet pass. They always turned the correct way, too. Some people have a tendency to turn toward the middle of the court but that's where all the congestion is. You're either going to get your pass batted away or your point guard is going to get stuck in traffic once he does get the ball. The rebounder needs to turn the other way, toward the closest sidelines and look for his point guard there, then lead him with a nice pass. With the right outlet pass you give yourself a good chance of having an easy possession.

The toughest pass is the one-handed baseball pass that covers most of the court. If you don't throw it with a perfect overhand motion, you're going to put a funny spin on the ball. And when you throw it that hard and that far with a funny spin, the ball is going to curve in all sorts of odd directions, making it tough to handle on the other end. That's why Stockton's one-handed baseball pass downcourt to Karl Malone to help clinch Game 4 of the 1997 NBA Finals was so spectacular. John winged it with one hand off the dribble to get it away quickly, but he also threw it perfectly on target—over the heads of the defense and in a straight line so Malone could handle it. The ball didn't knuckle and curve like most one-handed passes that long do. It's hard to throw that pass with the proper rotation. It's something you have to work on.

The pivot

Pivoting is a fundamental skill that goes hand-in-hand with passing. You get so many guys who change their pivot foot and get away with it. It's a good way of keeping defenders away from you, spinning away from them. One drill that helps teach this is to throw the ball and run after it, then come to a jump-stop, pivot away and throw the ball again. Then run and catch up to it, jump-stop, pivot and throw it again. And you need to use a different foot sometimes so you're not always pivoting off the same foot. You need to drill it so it happens by instinct instead of having to think about it and getting yourself trapped. You get your feet working with your mind that way.

Dribbling

Dribbling is one of the most overused phases of the game. Players have to be able to handle the ball but too many guys dribble too much. Big guys want to put the ball on the floor too much and the little guys try to dribble through traffic when a pass would work better. That's where most of your turnovers come from. You get double-teamed, you put it on the floor and boom, they've got it.

Players have to learn how to dribble with each hand. It's something they have to work at. And they have to learn not to watch the ball. I always tell kids you don't have to watch the ball to know someone stole it from you. When you're looking ahead and dribbling on your side, if you bounce the ball down and it doesn't come back up, right then you know the ball is in someone else's possession. You don't need to watch him take it to know he took it, so don't watch the ball. If you're watching the defender instead of the ball, you've got a better chance of keeping it away from him.

All NBA point guards are good at dribbling or they never would have gotten that far. Magic Johnson was one of the best ever because at 6-9 he was able to get away with dribbling high if he wanted to. He was real effective with that, but he could do it any way he wanted—long strides, short pitter-patter dribbles—however he cared to do it. It's important for kids to stay up with today's game and incorporate techniques the pros use. The crossover dribble has always been there but these guys today can do it with machine-gun speed—between their legs, right hand-left hand. Isiah Thomas was as quick with the dribble as anyone I've ever seen, and Pete Maravich was great at it too. Both of those guys had tremendous talent, but they also put in the time. You have to work at it.

The best place to go to work on your dribbling is a handball court where you have lots of walls—and no baskets. It takes discipline to work on your ballhandling for an hour or two at a time. When you go to a basketball court, even if it's your intention to work for an hour or two, you get tempted to dribble or pass for a minute or two, then go shoot baskets. Everyone loves to shoot baskets but the ones who improve as players are the ones willing to work on the other things. The hoop is too big of a lure, so if you go to a handball court, the temptation is removed. You can really focus on your dribbling and your passing. Put an X on the wall and throw bounce passes that hit the target. Pump fake to the right then throw a bounce pass to the left, aiming for the X. Work on a one-handed pass off the dribble. And more than anything, work on your off-hand.

Ballhandling drills are important, even showy stuff like spinning the ball on your fingers, rolling the ball across your back and down your arms and dribbling through your legs in a figure-8. You're not going to use these things in a game, but they're all good because they speed up your hand-eye coordination. Pete Maravich did a speed drill where he would bounce the ball from his right hand to his left through his legs, then take the ball with his left hand and bring it around to the front and bounce the ball back through his legs to his right hand. When you have your rhythm down, you appear to be going a lot faster than you really are and that builds your confidence in addition to your coordination. Pete tried to see how fast he could do it and soon he was just slapping the ball in a speed dribble. It's real good for developing touch.

The behind-the-back dribble is a showy play but players need to learn it as a weapon. John Stockton is not a flashy player and he rarely goes behind his back, but he can do it when he needs to. When he does it, it's for a purpose. If he can't get the ball past a defender in front of him then he will flip it behind his back with his right hand, use his body to shield the defender, then pick it up with the left hand on the run. Now he's got a step on the defender and keeps going.

Shooting

Everyone has a unique shooting style that is comfortable to them that may or may not be fundamentally sound. I've always felt if you can go to a gym and make nine out of 10 shots doing it your way, go ahead and keep shooting that way even if you have horrible mechanics. But if you're missing consistently, then you need to work on your form, breaking it down and building it back up using the proper fundamentals. Tim Hardaway has a horrible shot. The rotation isn't there, it's just a knuckleball. It floats up there and rattles around, but it goes in. He shoots about 45 percent for his career, which isn't bad for a perimeter player. And he's a 35 percent 3-point shooter, which is excellent, so trying to "fix" his shot now probably would only mess him up. For guys with ugly shots who aren't successful, though, they do need to change the way they shoot.

The proper way to shoot a basketball is to keep your eye in the front of the rim and shoot with your wrist, trying to get the ball to drop in just over the front of the rim. The ball should be on your fingertips, not in the palm of your hands, and roll off your fingertips to get a nice backspin and followthrough with your wrist. Chris Morris has a good release. Dale Ellis, one of the best 3-point shooters in NBA history, has a perfect shot. Every time he shoots it you think it's going in. Same with Jeff Hornacek; the way they release it is the way it should be done. They have a quick release, too, making it impossible to block.

Eddie Johnson, another picture-perfect shooter, might have the quickest release of any of them. I called him "Fast Eddie" because he'd catch it and boom, it's gone. Larry Bird had to work at it but he developed a quick shot. He was big and slow but he mastered the quick release. He'd have someone throw him the ball and he'd work on catching and shooting, working to make it an automatic shot and getting quicker with it at the same time. You saw it best at the 3-point shooting contest every year at All-Star Weekend. Bird won the shootout the first three years it was held. He would show up in the locker room before the event and tell the other contestants they were all playing for second place. Then he went out there and backed it up. He displayed a picture-perfect form and a quick release. One shot would still be in the air and he was already releasing the next one. And that all came from hard work. He was a great shooter in college but continued to work on his shot, adding to his range and getting a quicker release.

All of those guys had one thing in common: They never changed their release. Wrist flip, back spin. And it always looks like it's going in.

Ballhandling and shooting are related. A good ballhandler can do things to get his shot off. Jerry West worked for hours on end taking a one-bounce dribble and popping up to shoot his jumper. It was no casual dribble, it was bam! and the shot was off. He was so damn fast at it you couldn't even follow it. You'd be looking down at the floor reacting to the bounce and he was already up in the air releasing the shot over your head. He'd catch a pass and bam! One lightning-fast bounce and the shot was off. Ballhandling can do that for you.

Not many players today shoot bank shots but Sam Jones and Rudy Tomjanovich had that shot mastered in their day. They always used the glass. Tim Duncan uses the bank shot quite a bit today but you don't see it as much as you used to.

Free throws

Free throw shooting is a very important part of basketball. It's all concentration. You shoot from 15 feet out and should be able to knock that shot down. You get a comfortable stance and follow through. It's a very fundamental shot, a 15-foot one-handed shot standing on your feet. It's a shot everyone takes throughout their career regardless of the position they play. Everyone should make over 70 percent of them.

Rebounding

Rebounding more than anything is a matter of wanting to do it. It helps to be tall and to jump high, but mostly it's determination to go get the damn thing. The player with the most success is good at first finding his opponent and putting his body in front of him to block him out. Then he times the shot and guesses at the angle, and goes to get it. That's what Dennis Rodman does, and he's relentless. If he doesn't get it on the first try, he tries to at least deflect it and he keeps after it until he grabs it.

A lot of big men when they get a rebound want to put the ball on the floor, and once they do that they're putting it where the little guys can take it away from them. Greg Ostertag does a good job of keeping the ball up high. Bill Russell and Wes Unseld were great rebounders, but they were great at the outlet pass, too.

A good rebound drill is a figure-8 exercise bouncing the basketball off the backboard. Catch the ball on one side of the rim, bounce it over the basket to the other side, step over and catch it and throw it back. That helps footwork and handling the ball, getting the mind, hands and feet all working together. Tip drills help too. Instead of catching the ball and throwing it, you tip it off your fingertips. The repetition helps players in the games where they react to the ball. Another variation of the drill is to catch the ball at the end and turn to the outside to make an outlet pass.

Defensive footwork

Gary Payton is a master of defensive footwork. He has quick feet and is always in great position. He stays in front of his man, always between him and the basket. Some guys try to beat the system with their quickness and gamble defensively. Bryon Russell and Shandon Anderson do that. They're quick and come up with a lot of steals that way but sometimes it's uh-oh, too late. If they miss the ball, their guy is by them and headed to the basket. The No. 1 thing defensively is to stay between your man and the basket. That's position defense, using your body to block the other guy out. Jeff Hornacek does that well. He can't jump high but he's always in position, so it's hard to beat him. Payton does both things well. He's always in position but he also is quick enough to gamble and come up with steals. He also forces you into a lot of charges because he gets to the spot ahead of you, he's that quick.

Shot-blocking

Bill Russell may have been the greatest shot-blocker of all time. It helps to be tall, but timing and quickness are just as important. It's a reaction. Most great shot-blockers are born with it. What they have to learn is using their off-hand. If you're right-handed your instinct is to go up with your right hand to try to block it. But if the guy shooting is right-handed you have to reach across your body if you use your right hand to try to block it. By then it's too late. If the guy facing you is going up with his right, you have to use your left hand to go after it because you get there quicker. Some guys try to block every shot with the same hand but all the great shot-blockers used both hands. It's just like shooting. You've got to learn to shoot the ball with both hands.

Russell didn't just block the shots taken by guys he was defending, he would come across from the weak side and help out. He came across quick and he came across hard. He was like a 6-9 cat with great hand-eye coordination. And what really was amazing was the way he could tip a shot to a teammate. I always marveled at the way he could go up and concentrate on blocking the shot and still see his teammates or know where they were. He wasn't just watching the guy who was shooting, he knew where his teammates were and he'd tip the ball to someone when he blocked a shot.

Wilt Chamberlain used to swat the ball into the balcony. So what? The crowd went nuts because it was fun to watch, but what good did it do? You're just giving the other team the ball back. Sure, if a guy's getting a layup you block it any way you can and don't worry if the ball goes out of bounds, but why fly-swat it into the stands for no reason? You could barely tap it and get the same effect, but then you've got a chance to get the ball. It's not how hard you block it, it's just a matter of getting your hand in the way. One finger changes the shot. Wilt wanted to make a show out of it, but there was a real art to the way Russell blocked shots. If he couldn't get the ball to a teammate he'd at least keep it alive on the court. That way his team had at least a 50-50 chance of picking it up. He practiced blocking shots and keeping the ball alive.

Mark Eaton was a great shot-blocker mainly because he was 7-foot-4. He would just hang out in the middle and go after anything that came his way. The one problem he had was not keeping his arms up. He would extend them and block the shot, but then he brought them down across the body and was called for the foul. Instead of trying to knock your hand through the ball, all you have to do is make the ball go through your hand.

Most blocks occur before the ball has left the shooter's hands but the ones swatted out of the air, after they've left the shooter's hands but before the ball starts down where it would be goal-tending, really excite the crowd and excite the players about playing defense. Antoine Carr is good at that. That's a beautiful defensive look when you can pick it right out of the air. Jerry West was really good at that too. He was only 6-3 but he had long arms and would swat the ball back on the floor.

There are so many players out there who have no passion for the game and that's a shame. They only play basketball because they're tall or they have the natural ability, but they don't enjoy it. And if you don't enjoy it, you're not going to work at it. You can't just show up and play, you've got to work at it. If you enjoy the game and want to get better at it, though, put in the work and make yourself a player. The most important thing is desire.

Chapter Sixteen

MARDI GRAS

The New Orleans Jazz were starting from scratch in 1974 when they hired me as their broadcaster. They wanted me in town several months before the start of their first season to help them begin marketing the team. I arrived in mid-July to work the town with promotional appearances and speaking engagements, to let the people know we were there. I had never been to New Orleans in my life so I didn't know what to expect. It was 110 degrees and beautiful in Phoenix the day I left, and 88 degrees and miserable in New Orleans. I couldn't believe how hot it felt. I remember my cab ride in from the airport because the driver refused to turn on the air conditioner. As hot as it could get in Phoenix, I would never sweat there. But now I'm sticking to the seat of this taxicab, absolutely miserable and riding through the filthiest city I had ever seen. I'm saying to myself, "What have I done taking this job?" I wondered if I hadn't made a big mistake.

The Jazz had their offices in the Braniff Place Hotel across the street from the French Quarter, so I took a room there. After checking in I met up with Pat Screen, who was a vice president with the Jazz. He had been a quarterback for LSU and a good one, and he went on to become a lawyer. He got the job with the Jazz because he knew everyone in New Orleans, but he didn't know basketball. Here's a football guy and he's an executive for a basketball team. That's the way things were when the Jazz started out. Pat Screen was a hero there, a party guy—my kind of guy. We got to know each other and became great friends. He later went on to become the mayor of Baton Rouge, Louisiana. I met him for drinks in the hotel bar on my first night in town, then he wanted to walk me over to the French Quarter and show me around. He stopped at the bar on the way out and ordered a couple of Scotch and waters. I asked him what he was doing because I thought we were leaving. He said, "I'm getting a couple drinks to take with us."

"To take with us?" I asked.

"Yeah," he said, "they'll serve it to you in a paper cup and you can walk down the street with it."

I said, "Man, I'm going to like this town after all."

New Orleans is a lot like New York, where there's always something going on. You hate to go to bed because you're always afraid you're going to miss something. After a month in town my eyes were crossed.

I never got used to the weather there, especially the hurricanes. The people who grew up there seemed to like them—or at least the parties that went with them. One afternoon that first summer I was in New Orleans, the sky turned black and it got quiet as hell. I was looking out the window at the Braniff Place Hotel and it looked like midnight even though it was 2 o'clock in the afternoon. I was wondering what was going on and it was a hurricane, the quiet before the storm. Everyone was taping up their windows to get ready for it. A friend took me to a hurricane party over on the high side of the river. The whole French Quarter was underwater once the storm hit, including my hotel. I came downstairs and was wading through the lobby. Cops were everywhere, evacuating the Quarter. I was scared to death. But then I went to this hurricane party and everyone was in a festive mood. They had the TVs on watching the hurricane. Every channel had the weather on and the weathermen were loving it. They were charting the storm and all that stuff. I thought, man, what a town. I was scared we were going to get blown away, but these people were having the time of their lives. They just partied away. I thought, if people are like this for a hurricane, what could Mardi Gras possibly be like? I've never seen another city like it. Everybody in the country owes it to themselves to go to New Orleans on vacation one time.

In a lot of ways the Jazz were run in those days like everyone was on vacation. Every day was Mardi Gras. I knew right away that the Jazz were doomed in New Orleans. I could see the beginning of the end when I first got there. Sam Battistone was an absentee owner, still living in Santa Barbara, California, and things in New Orleans were way out of control. The team had trade-outs at every major restaurant in town where they would give away tickets in exchange for meals. I'm with Pat Screen and Bill Bertka, who was a vice president with the team, and we went out to dinner at Diamond Jim Moran's, a very expensive restaurant in the Quarter. We had drinks and food and everything, and when the tab came they just signed it and that took care of it. I'm thinking, man do I like this! Where are we going to eat tomorrow night? We were in the French Quarter every night, meeting all the high rollers of New Orleans, and nobody was spending any money. They were just signing and I thought, oh boy, Sam must have millions and millions and millions of dollars. It got out of hand in a hurry. They were mismanaged totally.

Bill Bertka, who was an assistant coach with the Lakers, got Sam Battistone involved with the expansion team. Sam was a big Lakers fan, and he hired Bertka as vice president of basketball operations. I used to tell Sam his biggest problem when he owned the Jazz was that he was still a Lakers fan. Other people involved in the team's ownership included Sheldon Beychok, a lawyer out of Baton Rouge; Andrew Martin, who was in real estate and the oil business in Tibideaux, Louisiana; and Fred Miller, a car dealer in Los Angeles. Fred Rosenfeld, a lawyer in Los Angeles was made president of the team. All these guys had a piece of the action and Sam was the majority owner.

These guys did not have the financial backing that Sam had, and Sam got a lot of help from his dad, Sam Battistone Sr., who was keeping the ship afloat. Sam Sr. owned the Sambo's Restaurant chain. The restaurant had a black Sambo logo they had to get rid of. Elgin Baylor coached for the Jazz and always joked with Sam that he took a baseball bat to the logo in Washington, D.C. He said, "I knocked that damn thing down."

There were other problems from the start. While we waited for the Louisiana Superdome to get built, our home was New Orleans Auditorium, which seated about 6,000 or 7,000. We also had to play a lot of our games at Loyola University Field House in New Orleans. They had a tin roof and it sounded like machine gun fire when it rained. The court was on a stage and they had a net around the court to keep players from falling off the stage. I announced the games from an orchestra pit on the side of the court with my head barely sticking up over the floor level. The place only seated like 4,000 or 5,000 people and we still couldn't sell the games out, even with Pete Maravich.

We finally got in the Superdome and the configuration was pretty good for basketball. I think it's the best dome in the country. But the Superdome was a big part of Mardi Gras and we couldn't get in there during the month of February to play a game.

We were giving away tickets like mad. We had a shoe store that sponsored us and we gave them tickets for 50 cents apiece, which they would give away when they sold a pair of shoes. Kids would buy a $5 pair of shoes and get a free ticket. We would get 35,000 people at a game, but 25,000 would be in the balcony for 50 cents apiece.

Things were just as bad on the basketball side. They hired a guy named Barry Mendelson to be a vice president. His resume consisted of being an agent for Gail Goodrich and two years later, Mendelson traded a future first-round draft pick to get Goodrich. That draft pick went to the Lakers and it turned out to be Magic Johnson. We got Gail Goodrich, who was 33 at the time, and we only had to give up Magic Johnson to get him. This was the second-worst trade the franchise ever made.

Their worst trade ever also happened to be the first trade they ever made. The first year we traded the whole team for Pete Maravich. We gave away expansion picks and draft picks for years to come to the Atlanta Hawks, mortgaging the franchise just to get Pete Maravich. It was a debt they could never get out of.

Pete was an unbelievable player and a phenomenal gate attraction; I understand why they did it. He played for Louisiana State and was a big draw in New Orleans, but it was the worst trade the franchise ever made. Pete couldn't win on his own, and now they had no chance of putting anyone good with him. He was a 6-5 guard; you aren't going to win a championship with him on his own, and there was no hope of getting any help. They traded away their first-round draft choices for the next two years, plus two second-round picks. Those picks ended up being used for guys like David Thompson and Alex English. That was deadly for an expansion team. They were so far in the hole they were never going to get out.

As bad as those deals were for the New Orleans Jazz, though, it worked out for the state of Utah. If they hadn't traded for Maravich and got some of those other guys instead, and they got Magic Johnson, the franchise would still be in New Orleans.

The mistakes they made, though, were unbelievable. Bill Bertka was the only basketball guy in the front office, and he couldn't do it alone. They later hired Lewis Schaffel as general manager and he was a players' agent too. He represented Truck Robinson and said if they gave him the job he'd get Truck to New Orleans. So they made the deal with Schaffel, then signed Robinson as a free agent. Never in the history of the NBA has there been anything like it. They put us so far in the hole we couldn't get out of it. Schaffel then went to Atlanta, where he was on the board of directors of both the Hawks and the Braves, then on to New Jersey, before he teamed up with Billy Cunningham to start the Miami Heat expansion franchise. Schaffel teamed up with Barry Mendelson, who was in the Hollywood crowd. They didn't even know the basketball was round, neither one of them, and they were running the franchise! They hated each other, too. It was just a circus. The team was getting deeper and deeper in debt and everyone was spending the money, living like high hogs.

Scotty Robertson was the first coach and he only lasted 15 games. He has been a coach around the league for a long time now but he had never coached in the NBA before the Jazz hired him. He was coaching at Louisiana Tech at the time, long before Karl Malone ever got there. They were looking for names and even though he only had small college coaching experience, Scotty was a big name in Louisiana, so they hired him. Then they hired Elgin Baylor and Sam Jones as his assistants, two more big names. They had never coached in their lives and were hired as assistants to a guy who had never coached the pro game. All they had going for them was their names, and you're not going to win many basketball games with just your name.

The starting lineup for the first game in Jazz history was Pete Maravich and Stu Lantz at guard, E.C. Coleman and Bud Stallworth at forward, and Walt Bellamy at center. That wasn't the sort of lineup you could win a lot of games with. Bellamy had a great NBA career but he was through by time the Jazz got him. Opening night was the only game he ever played for the Jazz. He averaged more than 20 points and nearly 14 rebounds a game for 13 years, he was the league's Rookie of the Year in 1962 and later made it to the Hall of Fame. But he had nothing left for the Jazz. He played 14 minutes, scored six points and was waived the next day. Lantz didn't last much longer. He was traded to the Lakers 19 games into the season. It was a good move for Stu, though, because after his playing days he eventually returned to the Lakers as Chick Hearn's color man, a job he held longer than anyone, working more than 1,000 games with Chick. Coleman was a starter for three seasons before signing with Golden State as a free agent. Stallworth also played for three years before retiring, but he eventually lost his starting job to Aaron James.

Maravich was our leading scorer that year, averaging 21.5 points a game. We had a 23-59 record, which wasn't bad for a first-year team. The next year we improved to 38-44, which wasn't bad for a second-year team. But that was about as good as we got in New Orleans. We won 35 games the following year and 39 the year after that. In our fifth year in New Orleans, our final one there, our record was 26-56, a giant step in the wrong direction. They never made the playoffs in the five years that we were there.

We drafted Rich Kelley our second year, making him our first-ever first-round draft choice because of all the draft picks we sent to Atlanta for Pete Maravich. Rich was probably the most unlikely guy to play in the NBA, a real unique character. He was like a hippie, always in blue jeans, T-shirts and low-cut Converse tennis shoes. He loved to get in his van and drive all over the United States when the season was over. He was a beer drinker, one of the guys. He loved to tell stories and enjoyed life. He was just a happy person. You liked being around him because he picked you up. He comes from a nice family, a great mom and dad who enjoyed life, too. They used to travel to every Olympics and had a great perspective on life and the world. Rich had that, too. He was an intelligent, studious guy, a Stanford graduate, and a pretty good basketball player for a guy who couldn't jump. He played center because he was 7 feet tall, but he really didn't have the body for it. He was very thin for that position, weighing about 235, but he was very smart and a good competitor. His teammates always respected him.

Rich played four seasons with us in New Orleans and along with Pete Maravich and James Hardy, they were the only guys to play for the Jazz in both New Orleans and Utah. Rich didn't make the move with us, though. He was traded to New Jersey for Bernard King just before we moved, but in the 1982-83 season he was traded back to us and played two seasons in Utah.

The same year Kelley was selected in the first round, we drafted Jim McElroy in the second. He went to Central Michigan, a school that put out some good players in those days, like Ben Poquette, who played for the Jazz in Utah and Dan Roundfield, who played for Atlanta. They were good, solid players in the NBA. McElroy had a nice physique and the biggest thighs I have ever seen in basketball. He looked like he should have been a football player.

Bernie Fryer, who is an NBA referee now, played for the Jazz that year. He had a good career at Brigham Young and played one full season with Portland, then was cut. He played 31 games with the Jazz and nine games in the ABA, and that was it for his playing career. I think he's a pretty darn good official. The only criticism I have is that he seems like a guy quick with the trigger, like he's got a chip on his shoulder. I've played in a couple golf tournaments with him and we talked golf and he's always been nice to me. But I see the way he reacts to things sometimes. He's fast on the trigger. It may have hurt him some as a player, I don't know.

Pat O'Brien's in the French Quarter was my headquarters when I lived in New Orleans. They sold more alcohol than any bar in the world, and they didn't even sell food. They had seven bars and the place was packed day and night. There was always a waiting list to get in there. Sonny Oechsner, who played football at Tulane, owned the place and he loved the Jazz. The last thing I would say on the air was "Win or lose, I'll see you at Pat O'Brien's." They took care of my tab for that. We had a New Orleans Jazz reunion a couple summers ago and a lot of the old players and other team personnel were there. Gail Goodrich, Butch van Breda Kolff, Jimmy McElroy, Rich Kelley, Paul Griffin, Aaron James, Nate Williams, David Fredman, they were all there. We ended up the last night at Pat O's. Sonny wasn't there but one of the bartenders from back when I was there was now general manager of the place. Our tab was $500 and I wrote, "Sonny, thanks for everything," and put a $100 tip on there and gave it to the bartender. I told him don't worry, Sonny will take care of it. I never did get a bill from him so I guess it was OK.

While the Jazz were just starting out in the NBA, I was getting my feet wet as a play-by-play man. I introduced every game by saying, "They call San Francisco 'The City,' New York 'the Big Apple'; now swing with me to the land of jazz, New Orleans. Tonight, the Chicago Bulls are in town ..." I had to change my intro when the team moved to Utah, though. Now swing with me to the land of ... what? It didn't sound right. So I stole the old Brent Musburger intro and today it's: "You're looking live on a Saturday night at the Alamodome in San Antonio, Texas ..." For the teasers just before the game they wanted me to say "Jazz basketball is coming up next. You gotta love it, baby." I said no, it's the NBA we're selling, the whole league, not just the Jazz. So I say, "NBA basketball is coming up next. You gotta love it, baby." You want to make it as interesting as possible. If you focus strictly on the Jazz, what if they get beat by 50? Then everyone goes away disappointed. But if you cover the whole NBA, then you can appreciate the other team winning by 50. You've still got a shot at lovin' it. Sure, I'd love to see the Jazz win every game, but that's not realistic. You hope they win as many as they can and when they lose, you hope it's an entertaining NBA basketball game. When your team gets beat it isn't always because they were bad. The other team usually had something to do with it. And when your team wins you like to look at how well they played, but the other team is probably wondering how they let that happen.

A lot of people comment about how I can keep interested in a 30-point blowout, how I can have the same enthusiasm for a good play when the game has long been decided as I can for one that directly affects the outcome of a barn-burner. I take pride in my job and want to be the best at it. I think I'm right up there at the top and I want to stay there. It's an entertainment business and my job is to entertain. You can't be excited when the Jazz are winning but let your attention wander when they're losing. If my enthusiasm dies down, that's being a homer. I work for the Jazz and most of the listeners root for them and I would like to see them win, but I also want to tell it like it is. I want to have credibility. It's a fine line between being the home team's announcer and being a homer. If the other team steals your pass, was it a bad pass on your part or a great defensive play on their part? Was the ball thrown away or was it intercepted? Once in a while John Stockton actually does throw a bad pass. It isn't often, but sometimes he does make the wrong decision and I say so. And I'm his biggest fan. Or if an opposing player drives in for a layup, was it a sensational move on his part or bad defense by your player who got faked out? You have to be honest. You have to decide and give credit where credit is due. I said in New Orleans that I hoped I could make a John Havlicek basket sound as exciting as a Pete Maravich basket, and today I hope I can make a Kobe Bryant shot sound as exciting as a Stockton-to-Malone play. If someone on the other team makes an incredible move, it's all right to appreciate it.

Besides, if I have no enthusiasm because the Jazz are losing, who would want to listen? You don't want to go overboard with your enthusiasm. You don't want to say "we" or "us" when you're doing a broadcast. I'm paid by the Jazz, but I'm not on the team.

There's a big difference between saying "I can't believe they didn't give us the ball" and "I can't believe they didn't give the Jazz the ball." It's the difference between showing enthusiasm for your team yet maintaining credibility, and crossing the line. When I played in college at West Virginia we almost always won on our home court at Mountaineer Field House. The home-cooking of the referees might have had something to do with it. When the ball would go out of bounds and someone asked the refs whose ball it was, instead of saying white's ball or blue's ball, they'd say, "It's our ball," and point in our direction. You don't want the refs to be homers, and I try not to be a homer as a broadcaster.

Chapter Seventeen

PISTOL PETE

Pete Maravich was a junior at Needham Broughton High School in Raleigh, North Carolina, the first time I saw him play. I was working for Converse then and living in Greensboro so I went to watch him. He already was something special. He played for three high schools in two states before he landed at LSU where he led the nation in scoring all three years he was eligible to play varsity. It's amazing for someone to have one season like he had, but he got better every year. He averaged 43.8 points a game his sophomore season, 44.2 points as a junior and 44.5 as a senior. I set a West Virginia record by scoring almost 2,200 points in my three-year college career, but he scored over 3,600 points in his three years at LSU. That's how proficient he was. And they loved him at LSU. He could have run for governor of Louisiana, he was that popular. I don't know if he would have made a very good governor, though, because Pete seemed like a very honest person.

LSU games were showtime back then, much like the NBA is today. They'd turn the lights out during player introductions and the announcer would call out "Pistooooooooooool Pete!" He would run out on the court spinning the ball on his finger. It was like a Globetrotter show. He never won, though. I remember watching LSU play Kentucky on television and he scored 64 points, but Kentucky killed them.

In his prime, Maravich did some unbelievable stuff. What an incredible ballhandler he was, the best ever. He would flip the ball between his knees, whirling and spinning the whole time. In one drive to the basket he would go behind the back or over the back with the ball, wrap it around his body and spin it off the glass, make it and get fouled. He had an around-the-body pass you had to see to believe. He would be dribbling with his right hand and throw the ball to his right by first flipping it in front of his body to his left hand, then behind his back to a player on his right. He was so smooth and quick. You saw where the ball ended up, but you had no idea how it got there. He was an attraction, bringing people to the games, home and away. He would just come down and fire away shots, throw spectacular behind-the-back passes and entertain the crowd. We lost a lot of games, but Pete made them fun. He would score 30, we'd get beat by 40 and everyone went home happy.

He heads my all-time broadcast team, along with Connie Hawkins, Adrian Dantley, John Stockton and Karl Malone, because no matter the outcome of the game, you knew these guys were going to give you something to talk about on the air every time out. I got to broadcast Pete's games all five years the Jazz were in New Orleans, plus that first year in Utah. Pete blew his knee out our last year in New Orleans. He raised his leg trying to flip the ball through from behind. He hit his leg with his arm, knocking himself to the floor and tearing up his knee. The guy he was throwing to was standing there all alone under the basket. He always tried to make a fancy pass, even when a simple one worked better.

His dad, Press Maravich, was a college coach and former professional player. He had Pete playing basketball when he was four or five years old. Every day he would come home and practice the fundamentals. His father had all sorts of drills Pete would do; he got all this coaching from a coach he lived with. From where Pete lived as a kid it was a two-mile walk to town. He made that walk often, dribbling a basketball the entire way. He'd go to a movie when the theater wasn't too crowded, pick out a seat by himself on the aisle, and dribble the ball all through the movie. He developed an amazing feel for the ball by constantly dribbling it. Pete could get a ball spinning on one finger, then move it from finger to finger, roll it down his arm and wrap his hand underneath and pick it up on his finger again. He could get the ball to do anything he wanted, flicking it in front or behind him, seemingly changing directions in mid-air, he was such a magician.

Pete wasn't a great defensive player, but then his dad never taught him, he only worked on shooting and ball-handling. Jerry Sloan played against him for six seasons and he never liked the way

Pete played. He thought all that flashy play showed him up so he took it personally. Jerry made it his mission to shut Maravich down. If Pete put the ball behind his back in front of Sloan, Jerry would knock him on his ass.

Pete's teammates didn't always like him either because he shot too much. They were jealous of him in Atlanta because he took all the shots. On top of that, he'd throw showboat passes that ended up in the crowd, and they were getting beat. He had the reputation of being a ball hog and that followed him around.

It was a little different in New Orleans because we had an expansion team and he was the man. When Pete signed a new contract with the Jazz, the team held a press conference at Jim Moran's in the French Quarter. Barry Mendelson, the G.M., was running it and someone commented that it was a good thing they signed Pete because without him, they wouldn't even have a team. Barry said, "In our negotiations with Pete, he made that quite clear to us."

Who knows, it might have been different if he had played on a great team. He played with some pretty good players, like Truck Robinson in New Orleans for a year, and he teamed up with Lou Hudson in Atlanta, but his teams never were that good. He was the show, and all the attention he got bothered the older players. Like with Truck, who led the league in rebounding one year. He'd get a rebound and fire the outlet pass, then race down court to get involved in the fast break. But before he could get to midcourt Pete had already launched the shot. That's how he irritated his teammates. If you do all the work to get the rebound but never get to shoot, there's going to be jealousy.

Pete was wild in those days, too. He drank too much in New Orleans, a real hell-raiser. He came over from Atlanta and had all that money and partied too much. He was always picking up tabs in bars. One New Year's Eve he walked into a bar in Houston, and put down four or five $100 bills and bought drinks for everybody in the place. He couldn't hold his alcohol, though. Five beers and he would be swinging from the chandeliers. Pete had phenomenal individual success as a basketball player and was so well-loved in college, but as a pro his teams struggled and people got on him. People came out to see him perform, but criticism of him, whether from his teammates, the fans or the media, hurt him. There was something missing in his life.

I remember one night we were staying at some hotel in Cherry Hill, New Jersey, for a game the next night in Philadelphia. We both had a few drinks and I was helping him to his room. His mom had died recently, committing suicide, and he was feeling sorry for himself. He went through a lot of turmoil over that, and you could sense the despair he was feeling. I shoved him in his room that night and he got mad at me. We got in a fight and started rasslin' around in his room. We were on the 20th floor and there were glass windows covering one whole wall. We banged into the window as we were tearing around the room and I thought, oh my gosh, I can see the headlines now: Pistol Pete and Hot Rod Fall Out of Hotel Window. I finally twisted his arm behind his back and got him to calm down.

Then we sat down and talked. I talked to him like a father, telling him, "You know what? There's a lot of kids out there who idolize you. They think you're the greatest thing ever. Your mom died, I understand that. It's terrible, but you've got to get on with it. You're young, you're a great basketball player, you've got the whole country looking at you." He was immature about the whole thing, very immature.

A lot like Rod Hundley.

I don't think I changed him, but he got changed around. Pete went from one extreme to the other. Later in life he took great care of himself, really got his life straightened out. He just flip-flopped from one extreme to the other. Don Sparks, the Jazz trainer, was a good friend to him, too. He would go to dinner with him, talk to him about his problems and be a good listener, like his dad.

About eight years after Pete retired, the Jazz were in Philadelphia for a game one January day in 1988. We were at the baggage claim area of the airport when Frank Layden got paged to the phone. Frank took the call and came back to me with a blank look on his face. "Pete Maravich is dead," he said. You talk about shock. Pete was 40 years old. He was speaking to a church group in Pasadena, California, that day. He went out and worked out with these kids and somebody asked him, "You OK, Pete?" He said, "I feel great," and just fell over dead.

Before Pete died, he had really turned his life around. He was a born-again Christian, preaching, going around to church groups and talking about his life, how he changed. Even his diet, the food he ate, was a big change. He quit eating meat, started drinking goat's milk and things like that. When we traveled to a city, he would find a market and pick out his fruit and vegetables. It was a wonderful story the way he turned around, became a family man.

The Jazz retired his number in Utah during the 1985-86 season, and they had a program back at the Superdome after he died to retire his number there. Archie Manning, who quarterbacked the New Orleans Saints, had his No. 8 retired and Pete's No. 7 hangs next to it, the only two numbers hanging in the Superdome. I should have emceed Pete's ceremony in New Orleans but Barry Mendelson insisted on doing it. The people there hated Mendelson and booed him out of the building. Pete's wife was there with their kids and it was kind of embarrassing. These young little kids knew they were there for a ceremony honoring their dad and were wondering why everyone was booing. Then I went up to the microphone and got the crowd turned around. I talked about Pete and the New Orleans days with the Jazz and the people soon were cheering for him.

To this day, one of my most cherished possessions is a bottle of champagne Pete gave me in 1977. He won the NBA scoring title that year and to celebrate, on the last day of the season he gave everyone in the organization a bottle of champagne. Teammates, coaches—everyone. And it was the good stuff, too, a 1969 vintage of Dom Perignon. That's the way Pete was. He bought the best. I've had that unopened bottle for more than 20 years now and it's sitting on a shelf like a trophy, a reminder of just how special Pete Maravich was.

Chapter Eighteen

PIONEERS

I lived in an apartment on Rue Chartres in the French Quarter when I got to New Orleans, but later I bought a duplex in Metairie, a suburb close to town. One Saturday morning in 1979 I was dead asleep when I heard a knock on the door. It was about 8 a.m. and there was a man I had never seen before standing on my porch. He said, "Are you going with them?" And I said, "Am I going with who?" He had a newspaper with him and showed me the headline: "Jazz Moving to Salt Lake City."

I grabbed the paper and read the story. It didn't say much other than the team was moving. Salt Lake City? Give me a break. I couldn't believe it. I returned his paper and he asked me again if I was going with them. I said I guess so, I've got to work. It turned out he wanted to buy my duplex, that's why he wondered if I was going with the team to Utah. I told him he could call back in a couple hours because I had to make some phone calls to find out what was going on. So I got on the phone and sure enough, we were moving to Utah. The Jazz had packed up all their office furniture and equipment in the middle of the night because they had bills on everything. They snuck out of town and shipped everything to Salt Lake City. The guy came back a couple hours later and we worked out the price. I sold him my house just like that.

Everybody hated to see the Jazz leave New Orleans, the whole NBA. Players hated to give up the night life there. Everyone loved that city, including me. I was popular in New Orleans and it was my kind of city. I'd walk down the street and people would say, "Hot

Rod, where you at?" That's what they all said down there, "Where you at?" and I'd say "I'm right here. Where you at?" It was a New Orleans thing. When I heard we were moving I was disappointed. I had this town working for me and now I had to go to Salt Lake City and start over. No one knew me in Utah. I had to sell myself all over again, but the transition went a lot smoother than I could have imagined.

Frank Layden was in charge of things now and he told me to hurry up and get to Utah to start doing P.R. work, selling this team to the city. I checked into the Salt Lake Hilton on a Sunday night, not really sure what to expect from Utah. I said to the guy at the front desk, "I don't suppose I can get a beer in this town at this hour?" He told me the bar on the 10th floor was open so I went up there and the place was packed.

Flying into Salt Lake City earlier in the day, the weather was gorgeous. It was a beautiful summer day and the mountains still had snow on them. Summers in Utah are like Phoenix in September and October. It was dry like Phoenix. I remember thinking a man could get healthy living here. The people were nice and I was very much impressed by the basketball knowledge of the people. They knew who I was and made me feel right at home. Everyone wanted to talk basketball and they talked intelligently about it. I learned to love Salt Lake City and it didn't take long at all. I didn't want to leave New Orleans, but after I got to Utah I made a quick transition; I was glad we made the move. I've always liked the West better than the East from my days in L.A. and Phoenix. The East is too congested and the cities are overpopulated. Out here the streets are wide and clean. It's wide open and the climate is so much better.

Frank Layden had been hired as general manager about a month after the team announced its plans to move to Utah, so already they were making good decisions. They hired a basketball man to make basketball decisions. Frank coached all his life on various levels and he was an assistant coach with the Atlanta Hawks so he knew the NBA. His first move was hiring Tom Nissalke to coach the team. Nissalke was another guy experienced in the pro game, having coached in the ABA and the NBA, so we were also making moves that made basketball sense.

Then the Jazz got Dave Checketts involved. He was a great businessman and quickly started turning around the problems that plagued the team in New Orleans. It helped too that we were the only game in town on the major league level. In New Orleans we shared the spotlight with the Saints and we shared it equally: We were both awful. Archie Manning was the quarterback and every time you looked up he was on his lying on back, hammered to the ground by some huge defensive lineman. He was a team player, though. He always took the blame for losing even though he was the only guy on the team who could play. People used to go to the Saints games with brown paper sacks over their heads, they were that bad. And the Jazz never were much better.

With Layden and Nissalke, they started by building almost an entirely new roster. Pete Maravich and James Hardy were the only players to survive the move. Spencer Haywood was traded for Adrian Dantley, Rich Kelley was traded for Bernard King, and Ben Poquette, Allan Bristow and Duck Williams were signed as free agents. Paul Dawkins, a 10th-round draft choice, made the team. Shortly after the season started they traded for Ron Boone and brought in Tom Boswell, Mack Calvin and Terry Furlow as free agents.

Don Sparks, the original trainer for the Jazz, moved with the team to Utah and remained until he retired in 1994. He was a colorful character, an old Texan with lots of sayings, most of them crude. When he'd go out on the court to treat an injured player, he loved to pull out a penlight, shine it in one ear and hold his hand by the other. If the light didn't shine in one ear and out the other, Sparky would say, "You're OK. Get up and play."

It took time for the Jazz to catch on in Utah. The team struggled early, going 2-19 to start the season. I think most people were turned off at the start not so much by the losing, but because of what happened with the Utah Stars of the American Basketball Association. Fans were afraid to invest in season tickets because they thought they might get stuck if the team folded. I think in the back of their minds they remembered the Stars going bankrupt and disbanding 16 games into their last season even though they had success on the court, winning an ABA championship. Fans feared the Jazz weren't going to make it here, that they would only last a year or two and they would be stuck if they bought tickets. So there was a negative attitude to overcome. As general manger, Frank Layden did more than help put the team together, he really worked to sell this team to the city. Frank and I did a lot of speaking engagements, promoting the team, and Frank especially did a good job of resurrecting interest in professional basketball here, letting people know that we were here and we weren't going anywhere. This is your team, he told the people of Utah, you're in the big time now.

The starting lineup for the first game in Utah Jazz history was Pete Maravich and Duck Williams at guard, Adrian Dantley and Bernard King at forward, and James Hardy at center. Hardy is the only one of those five guys who was in the starting lineup for the last game of the season. He started at forward for that game along with Tom Boswell. Ben Poquette started at center and the guards were Ron Boone and Mack Calvin.

Pete Maravich was the biggest name the Jazz had going for them, but the people of Utah never got to see him play much. He wasn't nearly the player he was in New Orleans because of his knee injury, and in Utah, Nissalke put him on the bench. Pete never fully recovered from knee surgery, never coming close to being the player he was in New Orleans. Nissalke didn't help Maravich at all. Pete had a bad knee and Nissalke didn't want to play him, so we had a problem there. He was trying to rebuild and he wouldn't play Pete. He was trying to win. He thought the right way to go was to play the young kids because Pete was on his last legs. Nissalke did the same thing to Rick Barry when Rick was on his last legs in Houston, like he wanted to show them. Pete was a liability defensively. Still, he was better than what they had out there. The team went 24-58 that year and missed the playoffs by 14 games.

Pete played 17 games but he sat out nearly twice as many before the Jazz waived him in the middle of the year. He averaged 17 points in Utah and the Celtics ended up picking him up for the end of the season. That was his last year in the NBA playing 10 years in the league: four for the Atlanta Hawks, five for the Jazz in New Orleans, then the final year split between Utah and Boston. So he played 5 1/2 years for the Jazz but only a half year in Utah—and he never really got to play here, even though people were coming to see him. The average home attendance that year was 7,821. We drew better on the road than we did here, by about 2,500 fans a game.

The Jazz picked up Adrian Dantley from Los Angeles before that first season in Utah and it was a good move, but Maravich was the only other name player on the team. We had Bernard King, but he drank too much. On buses he couldn't even sit up in his seat. He played 19 games and averaged nine points, but he was injured a lot and drank heavily. Everything was wrong, and then he got arrested and was charged with five sex-related offenses plus possession of cocaine. That blew up and we had to get rid of him. He eventually pleaded guilty to a reduced sex charge and was sentenced to two years probation, and he checked into an alcohol rehab program. But what a great talent. Ironically, a city like Salt Lake is where he got in trouble, then he goes to New York of all places and straightens out his life. He went on to win a Comeback Player of the Year award.

In Dantley, Maravich and King, we had three guys who combined for more than 58,000 points in their career. That's more than Karl Malone, John Stockton and Jeff Hornacek combined for, but there was no comparison. King only played 19 games for the Jazz and Maravich only played 17 games in Utah. Dantley was the only one who emerged as a key player for the Jazz in their early years in Utah.

We had two first-round draft choices in 1980, our second year in Utah. We used the first to get Darrell Griffith from Louisville and the other, the 19th pick overall, was used to draft John Duren out of Georgetown. Duren was an enjoyable guy to be around, a 6-foot-2 guard, but he wasn't as good as he thought he was. He didn't seem to work that hard, a borderline guy to make the team. He played two years in Utah, another in Indiana and was out of the league.

As good as Darrell Griffith was, he wasn't a great, great player. We took him with the No. 2 pick that year—Golden State took Joe Barry Carroll with the No. 1 pick—and Boston took Kevin McHale at No. 3. McHale was the player we should have drafted but we couldn't afford to. We were coming to Utah and trying to get noticed and Darrell was the college Player of the Year. He won a national championship at Louisville, he was the most valuable player of the NCAA tournament and in several all-star tournaments. We were in a position where we had to take the No. 1 college player. Darrell was a great guy, a class act, and a pretty good player, but he wasn't a franchise player. He was a great 3-point shooter but he didn't have very good hands. He would just lose control of the ball. Kevin McHale was a franchise player. Had we taken McHale, I think we would have been a better team. The Celtics took him after we passed him over and he went on to a great career in Boston. But Darrell was good for Utah; everyone loved him. He was really a nice kid, a well-mannered gentleman. He fit in with the community and I think the people here appreciated him.

Ron Boone, my longtime broadcast partner, was traded to the Jazz early in our first season in Utah. He was already a hero in the state from his playing days here in the ABA. He played five years with the Utah Stars and helped them win a championship in 1971. He was a solid player and he always played hard. He wasn't a superstar but he averaged 18 points a game in eight ABA seasons and 14 a game in the NBA. All together he played 13 years and never missed a game. For a 6-2 guard he was tough. He didn't back down from anybody. He competed hard and was an excellent shooter. When I was broadcasting for New Orleans he had a 25-point game for Kansas City and I had him on the postgame show. I didn't know him at all then. Little could we have guessed then that we would be working together one day.

Booner has always been a great athlete, adept at any game he cared to play. He's a fine golfer, a tremendous softball player, and the basketball speaks for itself so that's three sports he excelled in right there. He's not a bad pool player, either, and he plays tennis. He's like Rick Barry. He can pick up any sport and hold his own. He's just a good athlete.

Booner's biggest claim to fame was playing in 1,041 consecutive professional basketball games which, if you combined the ABA and NBA, is the most ever. A.C. Green broke Randy Smith's NBA record in 1998 but he was still more than 100 behind Boone when he did. That's incredible. Being an ex-player I can relate and understand. You would think somewhere along the line with all of these games you would get sick, get injured, have a problem with the altitude or have transportation problems, something that would keep you out of a game.

Cal Ripken broke Lou Gehrig's baseball record for consecutive games played, but he traveled first class his whole career and had the greatest conditions in the world. Lou Gehrig was on a train, living in flophouse hotels on the road. Back in those days they probably had three guys in a room. When you look at the conditions Gehrig had to endure, I don't agree with Ripken getting the record. He should get an asterisk like Roger Maris did when he broke Babe Ruth's single-season home run record. No one would beat that record of Lou Gehrig's if they had to play under those conditions.

And to some degree that's what Ron Boone faced. It wasn't as severe—he never had to go by train—but he should be recognized for the same reason. The conditions he played under are nothing like today. The travel was all by commercial flights then, where everything today is by charter. Instead of walking through airports, making connections and following the airlines' schedules, their bus takes them directly from the hotel or the arena to the plane and they're off to the next city. After a game you're wound up and you're not going to get to sleep until after 1 a.m. even if you wanted to. So if you had a 5 a.m. or 6 a.m. wake-up call the next morning to catch your flight to the next city, then took the better part of the day to get there, you never got a solid night's sleep. Now teams can fly straight to the next city after a game. They usually get to their hotel rooms by 1 a.m. or 2 a.m., when they probably would be falling asleep anyway, but now they can sleep through without the early wake-up call. Instead of traveling all the next day and trying to play a game that night, they are well rested. As a player you get to the next city, you get your rest, there's no hassle going through the airport, getting through security, waiting on delayed flights, waiting at baggage claim. That makes a huge difference, yet Ron Boone set his record in what could be called the old days of the NBA.

Adrian Dantley talked to me about that after the Jazz had traded him to Detroit. The Pistons were pioneers when it came to owning their own plane. That was before the Jazz started using chartered flights and commercial travel was all Dantley had known. He said, "Hot Rod, I'll play another five years because of the private plane. You can't believe how great this is." He ended up breaking his leg and that shortened his career, but he still played in the NBA until he was 35, then went to Italy and played for a year.

In 1982 we had the No. 3 pick and took Dominique Wilkins. The Jazz knew he would be a great player but they couldn't afford to sign him. The franchise was hurting for money so they traded their draft rights to Atlanta for John Drew, Freeman Williams and a ton of cash. A lot of people like to point to that as one of the worst trades in NBA history because Wilkins went on to score more than 26,000 points for his career and Drew had drug problems. In reality, it wasn't a bad deal. For one thing, the Jazz needed the cash to stay afloat, and signing Wilkins would have sunk the franchise. And for another thing, Dominique Wilkins was overrated. He's one of the top 10 scorers in NBA history, but he couldn't make the 50 Greatest Players list. He's not a franchise player because he was very selfish and never passed the ball. He had great talent and spectacular moves, but I think he was omitted from the list of great players because he was so selfish. He passed the ball defensively— he only passed it when he couldn't get a shot. It was a waste of talent for a guy with that much ability. He jumped so high when he dunked, he could go backwards with his elbows through the rim and all sorts of spectacular stuff. So why couldn't he rebound the ball if he had such leaping ability?

The key to the Dominique Wilkins deal, besides the cash that kept the team afloat, was John Drew. He was a great offensive basketball player, a lot like Eddie Johnson. He could come off the bench and really light it up. He was a fast shooter with a quick release. He and Dantley gave you a nice pair of offensive weapons. Drew had a good heart and was a sweetheart of a guy. He and I both wore size 13 shoes so he would always give me a pair of his shoes. When he played for the Atlanta Hawks and the Jazz were in New Orleans, he always asked me to say hello to his mother on the air because she lived in New Orleans.

He played 11 years in the NBA, averaging more than 20 points a game for his career, and he played in two All-Star games. He was still averaging 16 points a game when the Jazz cut him early in the 1984-85 season. It was such a sad case because he was so talented and such a good person. I really liked John and I think Frank Layden did too.

It's a crying shame he got his life so messed up with drugs. He was into drugs in Atlanta and that's why they got rid of him. I never tried drugs and never would but they must be a powerful, powerful force because Drew and a lot of other guys have been destroyed because of them. Once he got into it he couldn't get out. He tried; he went through rehabilitation programs. He was really close to Don Sparks. Don took care of him the best he could. Drew would call him in the middle of the night and Sparky would talk him through his ordeal, calm him down when he was on drugs. Sparky was like a father to him. He took him by the hand and walked him through the tulips.

During the exhibition season one year, John Drew gave a talk to a bunch of kids about staying away from drugs. He was just so sincere, speaking from experience. He did a wonderful job with these kids, telling the story about how he had cleaned himself up— but he hadn't. It was a sad thing. It wasn't too long after that he was back in rehab. He made a lot of money in his career and could have been set for life, but he lost everything. He cashed in his pension early because he owed money. He pops up at a Jazz game every once in a while.

That's the way it was for the Jazz in those days. They were taking chances on guys and filling out their roster with other teams' castoffs. Tom Boswell played for us that first year in Utah when

Tom Nissalke was coach, then came back in '83 when Frank Layden coached and Phil Johnson was Frank's assistant. We cut him after 38 games and he called Phil Johnson a racist. That's ridiculous. In all the years he has been in the league, Phil never had a problem with anyone, so a comment like that says more about Tom Boswell than it does Phil Johnson.

James Hardy out of San Francisco was the first-round pick our last year in New Orleans. He was very talented but a sleepy-type guy. You had to jab him with a metal poker to get him to play. I was taping the coach's show with Tom Nissalke one night before a game and I asked him about Hardy. Tom said Hardy was one of the guys who was going to be out of here if he didn't start playing. He needed to get his butt in gear. We taped the show on a cassette recorder and after the interview, Tom called Hardy over. He said "Hey, James, listen to Hot Rod's tape," then had me play the interview for him.

Allan Bristow, who went on to coach at Charlotte and was general manager at Denver, also was on that Jazz team. He got in a fight with Larry Bird one night at the Salt Palace in Bird's second season in the league. It was just one of those scrambles where they both went down for the ball and came up swinging. Bird was standing over Bristow as he tried to get up so Bristow tackled him. Bird punched back and it was broken up quickly, but they both got kicked out of the game. This was late in the third quarter and Bird had been playing great. He already had 25 points and 12 rebounds, but now he had to sit out the rest of the game. Afterward Tom Nissalke, said, "Yeah, but we lost Allan Bristow," who, of course, was just an average player.

Johnny Most, the legendary voice of the Celtics, went crazy. He was a big homer broadcaster. I always kidded him that he read his commercials while the other team had the ball. He was a good friend and fun to talk to about basketball. He could sit in a coffee shop and talk about basketball all day. He loved the Celtics, he loved the NBA and he was a great broadcaster, but he was a big homer. He called Bristow a hamburger player, saying he should be thrown out of the league for messing with Larry Bird, just going on and on. I gave a normal call of what happened. It was to Utah's advantage that they both got kicked out and I said that. Bird was a great, great player and Bristow was an average player, but it was one of those skirmishes where both players were at fault.

The next morning, Tom Barberi, a radio host in Salt Lake City, played Johnny Most's description of the fight all the way through to the two players getting kicked out, and then he played mine behind it. Now you talk about two different versions of the same thing. Johnny Most was going crazy. I explained it just the way it was, being very frank about it, and Johnny went crazy.

Ben Poquette out of Central Michigan was our forward then. I called him "Gentle Ben." Nissalke didn't like that. He said, "Don't call him 'Gentle Ben.' I want the SOB to rip somebody's head off." Twenty games into the season, Atlanta traded Terry Furlow to us. He was a star at Michigan State and a first-round draft choice by Philadelphia in 1976. He was a good-looking kid, 6-foot-5 and built something like Clyde Drexler, the same type of body. But he was a messed-up kid, into drugs and all that. He was a great talent but could never get it going. We were his fourth team in four years and shortly after the season he was killed when his car rolled over on an exit ramp back home in Ohio.

The Jazz were constantly looking for players in those days and sometimes the gambles paid off big. Frank Layden was in Billings, Montana, for a speaking engagement when he spotted Rickey Green and Jeff Wilkins playing there for a team in the Continental Basketball Association. Frank signed them both on the spot and Green went on to play in an NBA All-Star game three years later, the first CBA player ever to become an All-Star. Wilkins played nearly six seasons for us.

Wilkins scored 35 one night in Kansas City and all the guys in the locker room afterward were calling him "The Franchise," so that's what I started calling him on the air. "Franchise to the hoop..." In six years with the Jazz he averaged eight points a game. We traded him to San Antonio late in the 1984-85 season, and he was out of the league by the end of the season. But he was forever known in Utah as "The Franchise."

Rickey Green was another story. I called him "The Fastest of Them All." You'll never catch him. He could flat-out run. He had a wiry body, a little guy who could play forever. He played until he was 37 and gave us eight good seasons. He eventually lost his starting job to John Stockton and couldn't accept being a backup. He wanted out of here because he wanted to start. That was the wrong attitude. He could have played forever backing Stockton up, playing 15, 20 minutes a game. It would have been a perfect situation for him but he didn't want to do it.

The draft was 10 rounds long in those days and good thing for the Jazz it was. In 1982, the same year they drafted Dominique

Wilkins in the first round, they took a gamble in the fourth round on a 7-foot-4 center from UCLA who never played. The only scouting tape the Jazz could find on Mark Eaton was of him taking off and putting on his warmup jacket and doing layup drills before games. But as Layden always said, you can't teach height. The first time I saw Mark I thought, man is he BIG!

I never thought he would make it, though. He was too slow and he couldn't score. I give him a lot of credit for the career he had. He made himself into a decent basketball player just by hard work. He was a very intelligent guy, smart enough to play within himself. He knew what he could do and he worked at it. I give Phil Johnson, the Jazz assistant coach, a lot of credit. He spent hours with Mark that no one knows about. They would go to the gym, just the two of them. They worked on footwork, a little hook shot, how to keep the ball up high after getting a rebound, making the outlet pass ... they worked on it all. Mark got to be very good at rebounding and making the outlet pass, getting the ball to Stockton ahead of the defense to trigger a fast break. It was very impressive what he did in his career. He won the NBA Defensive Player of the Year award twice. He only scored about 5,000 career points but that wasn't what he was here for. People never realized how good he was until after he retired. Then you saw all those people running in for layups against the Jazz. Our players got so accustomed to Mark saving them by picking up their man. In a half-court game they would just let them go because Mark was going to block anything they put up. Now all of the sudden Mark wasn't there and guys were making those shots. His value wasn't appreciated until after he was gone. Fans used to get on him but these same people applaud him now.

Mark had some unbelievable nights. In 1985 he blocked 14 shots in a game against Portland, and in 1989 he had 14 blocks against San Antonio. He had as many as six blocks in a single quarter five times in his career, including twice in one game. He blocked everybody's shot, I don't care who you were. And he made everybody alter their shot, too, including Michael Jordan. Jordan would run right at him and Mark just stood there with his hands up so Jordan had to change his shot. He would move the ball around, put it up higher than he normally would. If you make Jordan change his shot, you're a pretty good defensive player.

Scott Layden, the Jazz vice president of basketball operations and son of Frank, said Eaton brought credibility to the franchise, and he was right. You can score all you want but if you don't stop people you're not going to win much. You always had a chance with Mark on the floor. When the Jazz played the Lakers they could contend with Kareem Abdul-Jabbar because of Mark's size and his ability to rebound the ball. And it wasn't just blocking shots, it was his ability to change them. That's where defensive players make a big mistake, by trying to block everything. Just make a guy change a shot and he'll miss it. You're making a guy do something he doesn't want to do. That's what Eaton did. You might get a shot off but he made you rush it. He made you shoot it a little higher, he made you lean away. All those things that reduce your odds, he created defensively. So your chances changed from "excellent" to "maybe." That's the difference he made.

It's nice that the Jazz retired his number. A lot of people might look back and wonder why. He averaged nothing offensively, but he was twice named Defensive Player of the Year. No one else on our team ever did that.

By 1984 we had shocked the world by winning our division and making the playoffs for the first time in franchise history. We had Rickey Green and Darrell Griffith in the backcourt, Adrian Dantley and Thurl Bailey at forward and Mark Eaton giving us a defensive presence at center.

Thurl was the seventh player taken in the 1983 draft. He won a national championship at North Carolina State the year before and had some good years with the Jazz. You can't knock his overall play. He was a consistent, professional player and everyone liked him. He was a musician and sang the national anthem a few times. He formed "The Jazz Brothers" with Karl Malone, Darrell Griffith, Rickey Green and Carry Scurry, and recorded a couple of songs in Provo.

One summer Thurl and I were riding to Evanston, Wyoming, with Malone and Dave Wilson from the Jazz P.R. office, who was in charge of putting on Junior Jazz basketball clinics. Wilson was driving us all to Evanston and he got pulled over for speeding just as we pulled into Wyoming. Dave was all flustered, probably never had a speeding ticket in his life. The motorcycle trooper walked up to the side of the van with his sunglasses on, motorcycle helmet, starched shirt, the whole bit. He looked in the window and we automatically felt like criminals. Dave thought he was going to talk his way out of it, though. It said "Junior Jazz" on the side of the van and Dave said, "I've got Karl Malone and Thurl Bailey and Hot Rod

Hundley of the Jazz in here." But the officer wasn't impressed. He said in a stern, deep voice, "We'll get the autographs later. Right now let's take care of this ticket." We all just broke out laughing.

Shawn Bradley was in the Junior Jazz program when he was in high school and worked out with those guys. The players would have a game of their own for the kids and Shawn got out there with them. He was impressive. I don't know if Shawn is hungry enough be a basketball player, though. He needs somebody to kick his ass on the court. He's too soft. I don't know if that's growing up in Utah or what, but he doesn't have that killer instinct. He's got the talent and he's 7-6 but his weight hurts him. In this league you can't finesse anybody underneath. Kareem Abdul-Jabbar could, but he was sneaky-strong too. Very few centers can succeed if they don't have the weight. They get moved around and that's what happens to Shawn. They move him right out of there. But if you're 7-foot-6 and can play a little basketball there will always be a job for you. And you will always make good money.

Thurl Baily spent most of his time in Utah coming off the bench. Even when we had Marcus Iavaroni, who only scored three or four points a game for us, Thurl came off the bench. Iavaroni started at small forward and then a few minutes into the game, Thurl would come in. He averaged about 19 points a game off the bench. Some people have that mentality to be the sixth man. Kevin McHale was a great sixth man for many years. John Havlicek probably was the best of all time at that. Havlicek was the best player on the team but he was coming off the bench. He liked to watch the first few minutes and then come into the game. Bill Walton was another sixth man for Boston who did a great job coming off the bench. And those three guys—McHale, Havlicek and Walton—were all on the NBA's 50 Greatest Players list. Bryon Russell is an example today of a guy who plays better off the bench. Everybody would probably like to be a starter. There are egos involved. You associate starting with the five best players, but it's not always true. It doesn't really matter who starts. You're going to play the same number of minutes anyway if you're a good player.

Billy Paultz, "The Whopper," was another character. He never saw a beer he didn't like, or a hamburger. He was the kind of guy you'd say ate himself out of the league except he played 15 years in pro basketball, six in the ABA and nine and NBA. He was a very likable guy and always found a job. He would battle anybody. He was a competitor and he knew how to irritate the opposing centers. He'd make them lose their concentration. Billy didn't have a world of talent and was always so big and heavy, so overweight, but he was smart and knew the game. And he was always well-liked.

He averaged 16 points and 11 rebounds a game in his ABA days but by time we got him he was at the end of his career. He only averaged 1.3 points and 1.5 rebounds for the Jazz, but he will forever go down in Utah folklore for taking a punch from Hakeem Olajuwon in a playoff game to help spark a Jazz rally.

There's a rule of thumb in the NBA that it takes a new team five years to make it as a franchise and establish itself. For the Jazz, their five years in New Orleans were essentially wasted. The team had to start over once it got to Utah. But sure enough, five years after the team arrived in Salt Lake City, they made the playoffs. And they haven't missed out on the postseason since.

Chapter Nineteen

TONIGHT'S TOP STORY: BYU SIGNS A SWIMMER

When Salt Lake City television station KSL carried the Jazz games in the mid-1980s, I did live one-minute spots from the Salt Palace for the 6 o'clock newscasts, usually grabbing a player warming up for the game for a quick interview. Then after wrapping up the post-game show I'd race to the studios three blocks away and get there just in time for the sports report on the 10 o'clock news. KSL paid me $75 for each one-minute segment, so I was picking up $150 a game. Paul James was the sports director then and he wasn't much of an NBA fan. The Jazz were still fairly new so they took a back seat to college sports, particularly Brigham Young University—which Paul happened to be broadcasting. I would get on the set just as Dick Nourse, the news anchor, was turning the show over to Paul. Dick would say something like, "Hey, the Jazz got a big win tonight" and Paul would pick it up. And every single time, Paul would put us down to about fifth in his lineup of sports stories. The Jazz could have just beaten the Celtics or the Lakers, and Paul still wouldn't lead with it. I called it "BYU Syndrome." Nourse would say to me, "We have the Jazz-Celtics and Larry Bird scored 40, but he's not going to lead with it?"

We half expected Paul to say, "Oh no, BYU signed a swimmer today."

Dick would just look at me and shake his head. And when I was getting ready to do my Jazz report, Paul would say, "Hurry up, I've got to get to the high school basketball scores." The Jazz could have just beaten the Chicago Bulls and Michael Jordan, and he would still do that. I had the story the audience wanted to hear but he would bury me in the program. I didn't care. I still got paid, but that was really funny to me.

Paul James once asked me what was the most points ever scored by a guard in a playoff game and I told him about 45. He asked me who scored them and I told him John Havlicek. Then he asked me how I knew that off the top of my head.

"Because I was guarding him," I said.

It was never just me broadcasting Jazz games. I worked with so many color analysts over the years. Red Robbins worked with me in New Orleans and so did David Fredman, who is now an assistant coach with the Jazz. Dave and I are the last remaining original employees of the New Orleans Jazz still with the team. Frank Layden, Carl Arky, Jim Nantz, Craig Bolerjack, Zelmo Beaty, Dave Blackwell and Ron Boone all worked with me in Utah. One year in Salt Lake we used celebrity guest analysts on the road. Rich Kelley, the former Jazzman, worked the games in Sacramento and Oakland, and a couple former teammates of mine with the Lakers, Rudy LaRusso and Slick Leonard, also did some games that year.

Boone played until he was 34, which was remarkable considering he never missed a game in his career. Then he returned to Utah nine years later as my analyst on the Jazz broadcasts. He always wanted to come back and live in Salt Lake and he quickly built up a loyal following. People remembered him from his ABA days with the Stars, especially for their championship season, in addition to playing for the Jazz.

Like me, Boone had no experience as a broadcaster before he got this job. We both played the game, however, so that helped us grow into it. He has a hard time sometimes getting in and out with his comments, though, and it's very frustrating for him. I know where he's coming from. He loves to watch basketball on TV. If he has a day off and there's a game on television, whether it was college or the NBA, I guarantee you he's watching it. And he follows what the color analysts are doing in those games, trying to learn from them. They're basically having conversations with the play-by-play guys because it's television, and it frustrates Booner that we're not doing that on our Jazz broadcasts. It's hard for him to accept because he sees other guys doing it. But when we're on the air together we're doing simulcasts—radio and television together. Because of radio, a color analyst has to inject quickly and move on, which is different from the way he hears other guys do it. He gets frustrated because I'm always cutting him off, and I understand that.

Booner doesn't talk real fast like I do. He takes a lot of time analyzing and sometimes I have to jump in and cut him off because the ball is in play and I've got a radio audience I have to think of. And my producer in the truck is in my ear to get a spot in. Booner wants to talk and I have to inject those other things. People on the street come up to me sometimes and ask me why I cut off Booner, and that's why. My play-by-play style is for radio and his color style is for television and that doesn't always mesh. But Booner brings a lot of insight to the broadcast, and he has held the job longer than anyone before him.

There aren't many teams left that do simulcasts but I think they make the TV broadcasts more interesting. Because I keep up with the play-by-play I keep up with the excitement. I think the national broadcasts of our games are boring because all those guys do is sit there and talk back and forth. The last national play-by-play guy who did it right was Brent Musburger. He did a hyper, upbeat broadcast. He was enthusiastic about it. These guys today sit there like they're watching tiddlywinks. They all do that and it's terrible. I can't watch it. They're network-programmed robots. Don't be hyper, don't step on anyone's toes, they tell their broadcasters. Don Criqui made a statement once that a player had white man's disease, that he couldn't jump. It wasn't that bad, but they were going to fire him. It was a sensitive issue and the networks didn't want that.

Broadcasting an NBA game is the best job in the world but it is not just walking in there and sitting down because you played. This is a tough thing to do if you're going to do it right. Ex-players have a lot to offer in terms of insight, in terms of explaining things you have to have been through to really understand. On the other hand, some of the best analysts I worked with never played basketball, but they were successful because they were broadcasting professionals. They studied broadcasting in college and they worked their way up in the business.

Guys like Frank Layden, Zelmo Beaty and Ron Boone understand the game better than someone who went to broadcasting school, but the professionals I have worked with, guys like Jim Nantz, Carl Arky and Craig Bolerjack, understood the television business better. Zelmo and Booner had never done this in their life while Nantz and Bolerjack had dedicated their lives to it. It's not that easy. I think it was easier for me because I had the personality to do it. I couldn't wait to get in front of a camera when I played. I even auditioned once for the lead role in a television show, "No Time for Sergeants." I didn't get the part but some people thought I could have had an acting career if I would have pursued it more. But for a lot of new broadcasters, they're not comfortable in front of a camera. You put a microphone in their hands for the first time and they get nervous. It's hard to be yourself the first time you're looking into a camera but it came easy for me. It was my nature to ham it up so I was never nervous. I could walk right in and be myself. When I worked games with Chick Hearn he would say, "Jerry West is three out of six. Hot Rod, what's his percentage?" And I would play off that. "Chick, I'm from West Virginia. Give me a minute to look that up." Then I would say, "It's 50 percent," and Chick would be right back into the play-by-play. You have to think on your feet.

Ted Green did a story on me for *The National* newspaper in 1991 and talked to some Jazz players about me. Two or three of the guys thought I was too hard on them. Ted said that was the greatest compliment in the world, to have the play-by-play man who represents a team not be afraid to say when someone makes a bad play. Sure I want the Jazz to win and I try to bring an enthusiasm to the game, but you have to have credibility, too. If some of the fans think I'm too pro-Jazz and some of the players think I'm too anti-Jazz, I'm probably right where I need to be. I played the game on every level—playground, junior high, high school, college and the pros. I know what I'm talking about, so I have a tremendous advantage. I've been in this league all my life. You may disagree with something I say, but there's always a basis for my opinion.

I worked hard to learn the broadcasting business. I wish I had the opportunity to go to school or be tutored but I worked on my own to improve. I listened to tapes of broadcasters I admired, like Chick Hearn and Bill King, and I tried to emulate them. Whenever kids ask me for advice I tell them to get a tape recorder and go to a game—any game, it doesn't have to be the NBA—and go sit on the top row away from everyone else and do the play-by-play of the game into the tape recorder. Go home and listen to the tape, then listen to a tape of me or someone else and see how they compare. Pick out something you can work on, then go do it again. You can't get better if you don't work at it, but if you're willing to work, that's how you learn. Those are the things I did.

Chapter Twenty

FAMILY FEUD

There's something about a guy from Notre Dame. Look at all great Fighting Irish players who have had success in the NBA—Kelly Tripucka, Orlando Woolridge, Adrian Dantley, Bill Laimbeer, Austin Carr—all of them had an attitude. They're all holier-than-thou for some reason. I don't know if that's a trait they picked up at Notre Dame, or if Notre Dame just appeals to guys who already had the attitude, but if you look at guys who went to Notre Dame, they're a different breed. They have an air about them. Rick Barry never went there but he should have. He would have fit in nicely with those other guys. Austin Carr is probably the nicest of the bunch, but they've all got an attitude. Probably the only exception is LaPhonso Ellis. Joe Theisman, who quarterbacked at Notre Dame, was the same way, and even Digger Phelps got that way after he coached there. I think it's really hard for NBA coaches to deal with Notre Dame guys.

The Jazz had two of them, Dantley and Tripucka. They both played for Frank Layden, and Frank had problems with them both. The Jazz in fact traded Dantley to Detroit for Tripucka, Kent Benson and a couple of draft picks in 1986. Tripucka played two seasons in Utah but never was a good fit. He didn't want to come here and seemed unhappy. I'd interview him after games when he played here and he'd refer to the team as "they" and "them," like he wasn't a part of it. He had a lot of ties in Detroit. He was a 20-point scorer for the Pistons but was strictly an offensive player. Tripucka always felt he deserved more playing time than Frank gave him. He was a full-time player in Detroit but only got about 22 minutes a game with the Jazz. Tripucka wasn't the best shooter in the world, but he could score. He was a fair player, but he shot too much. He wasn't a complete player, so Frank didn't play him as much as Tripucka liked, and that was always a source of friction between the two of them.

Before Tripucka, though, was Dantley, and Adrian was an even bigger headache for Frank. Dantley was the Jazz's best player from the day they got him in a trade with the Lakers for Spencer Haywood. In fact, he was one of the top five players to ever to wear a Jazz uniform. Dantley and Karl Malone were the two best forwards, and Pete Maravich and John Stockton were the best guards ever. Add Mark Eaton at center and that's a pretty damn good basketball team. Without question, by position those were our best players.

Dantley was as good a low-post player as I've ever seen at his height. He was 6-foot-4 and you couldn't stop him, his moves were that good. Big guys would hang over him and they still couldn't block his shot. You'd jump and he would just shoot over you. Malone is a great post-up player but he's five inches taller than Dantley. Bernard King was good with his back to the basket too, but he was three inches taller than Dantley. Adrian had long arms and could flip the ball over or around defenders with a nice shooting touch. He had that instinct, he knew what to do and you couldn't stop him. He knew how to use his body. He would lean into you to get you away from him, then shoot right in your face. With most shooters, the mistake they make in the low block is they turn away from the defender. Now you're giving the defensive guy running room to block your shot. Dantley would go right into you to get you going back, leaning into you and shooting. He had that knack.

You couldn't wait for him because he could quick-shoot, too. He would catch it and flip it if he caught you off balance or leaning. He had patience. He would pump-fake and get you to commit, then he would go when you're coming down. He was very patient about what he did. And he knew who was guarding him all the time. There were different things he could do against different guys and he adjusted his moves to the defender on him.

Pete Maravich was an All-Star in New Orleans but Dantley was the first Jazz player in Utah to make an All-Star team. But he was as selfish as he was talented. I'm not sure he was good for our basketball team. You're not going to win with him out there playing 45 minutes. Maybe if he was with a greater team he would have fit in more, like he did with Detroit, where he could fit into a system. But here he was the whole show like Maravich was in New Orleans.

Frank Layden didn't like Dantley's attitude and Dantley didn't like Frank. Dantley would verbally abuse Frank, say nasty things about him. I don't think he respected Frank as a coach. He would talk back and chatter around the locker room. Frank was overweight then and he didn't try to dazzle anyone with his wardrobe. He'd joke about it, too, saying he was the youngest of nine kids and wore hand-me-downs —from his eight older sisters. Frank was jovial and always made jokes when we were getting beat and Dantley didn't like that. But Dantley played selfishly and Frank didn't like that. Dantley would get a rebound and throw the outlet pass to Rickey Green, then run like hell to get a fast break going. He wanted to score. He *loved* to score. I'm sure he kept score in his head. After a game if you gave him a stat sheet that showed he had 50 points, he'd grumble that he really had 51, that they shorted him a point. At halftime of games in the Salt Palace they passed out stat sheets in the crowd and Dantley would ask fans in back of the Jazz bench for a look. He knew Frank didn't want players looking at stat sheets, caring about individual numbers, so Adrian had to be discreet. He would set the stat sheet on the water cooler as he got a drink and kind of glance at it with one eye, watching for Frank out of the other eye.

Adrian always ran the fast break, busting his tail to get every point he could, because stats mattered to him. And he expected to get the ball at the other end. If he was open but the point guard threw the ball to the other side, Adrian would just stop at the baseline, put his hands on his hips and roll his eyes at the crowd. His disgust was obvious to the fans. "How could he not throw me the ball?" his face would ask. Meantime, while Dantley was pouting under the Jazz basket, the other team would be pushing the ball up court in the other direction.

Dantley always worked hard to get open and he expected the ball once he did. Whether he was out on a fast break or working for position in the low post, he expected the ball. Sometimes he would be in the low post with great position, the defender on his back, and Darrell Griffith would have the ball out on the perimeter looking in. Dantley would be begging for the ball and Griff would look in to him, and look and look and look, then jump up and shoot a 3-pointer instead. Adrian would just look up in the air and roll his eyes in disgust. He wouldn't even go for the rebound, he was so disgusted Griffith didn't pass him the ball. So Dantley would be mad at Griff for not throwing him the ball and Frank would be mad at Dantley for not going after the rebound. Frank would jump up and grab somebody off the bench and shout, "Get in there for Dantley." That happened so many times. You could understand why Frank was upset. Dantley wasn't playing team basketball. It looks bad to the paying customers. But on the other hand there's Adrian. He's the star player and the coach is taking him out. Dantley wondered what Frank was doing. The guy he's putting in isn't any good. So those things just fueled the feud between the two.

Adrian had all sorts of tricks to make sure he was the one who got to shoot. If he was double-teamed and had to give up the ball to Griff or Rickey Green or whoever was open, he would throw a high pass so the defense would have time to catch up. That way they had to give the ball back to him. Or if he was leading a two-on-one fast break and the defender came to him, leaving the other guy wide open, Dantley would throw the ball a little behind his teammate so he would have to stop to get the ball. That allowed the defender to get over, so Adrian got the ball back. A lot of guys had that knack. I played with a guy named Dick Barnett who had it mastered. He'd throw the ball in back of me on the break, right in the position where I'd have to throw it back to him and he'd get the two points. Then he'd say, "My fault, baby. Nice pass back to me." And that's Dantley. Adrian had that knack.

The feud between Adrian and Frank reached a boiling point on March 7, 1986. The Jazz were in Phoenix that night, the third game of a four-game road trip. They trailed the Suns by 10 going into the fourth quarter but Dantley put on a spectacular performance to win the game. He scored 19 points in the final period, making all eight of his shots from the floor, and finished with 36 points for the game. The Jazz led 104-103 with 9 seconds left and Karl Malone went to the free throw line with two shots to build the lead. He missed them both, though. It was his rookie season and he struggled with his free throw shooting all year. He was shooting just 47 percent at the time, and Frank tore into him something fierce.

Frank had worked on Karl's technique and his concentration. He encouraged him and coddled him. None of that worked, so now Frank decided he was going to *demand* Karl start making free throws. The Jazz got the ball back with a couple seconds left and they still led by one, and the Suns immediately fouled Karl again.

They called a 20-second timeout before Karl went to the line and Frank yelled some more. Karl then went to the line and missed again, but this time he made his second shot to put the Jazz up 105-103.The Suns called another timeout to set up their last play, which failed, and the Jazz won by two.

After the game, a great comeback victory on the road which featured a sensational fourth-quarter performance by Dantley, Frank was talking to the team in the locker room.The players all sat around the room looking at Frank, except for Dantley, who was dressing with his back to Frank. Frank says, "Hey, I'm talking," but Dantley kept undressing with his back to Frank, muttering, "Yeah, yeah, yeah." He also told Frank to leave Karl alone, to stop yelling at him about the free throws.

Frank went bananas. He turned to Don Sparks, the trainer, and said, "Sparky, give him his plane ticket and get his ass out of here." He sent Dantley back to Salt Lake while the rest of the team went on to Portland for the last game of the road trip the next night. Adrian didn't say a word. He just took his plane ticket and went home.The Jazz went to Portland and got clobbered by 14, then returned to Salt Lake to see if Frank and Adrian could patch things up. Frank said it wasn't the one incident in Phoenix that caused him to send Dantley home for "disciplinary reasons," but an accumulation of things since the All-Star break. Frank's problems with Dantley went even deeper than that, though. Frank also was the team's general manager, which meant he had to negotiate contracts with the players.The season before, Dantley held out all of training camp plus the first six games of the regular season trying to get a new contract. Frank was adamant that the Jazz didn't negotiate with Dantley while he was holding out because he was under contract. When ownership went ahead and gave Dantley a new deal, Frank felt that undercut his authority.

Frank never actually suspended Dantley and he rejoined the team for practice the next day, but Frank fined him 30 dimes—which reporters around town interpreted as a Biblical reference to the 30 pieces of silver Judas Iscariot got for being a traitor. What infuriated Dantley the most was that the Jazz sent him home for "disciplinary reasons." He felt that was what teams said when a player was caught with drugs. He felt slandered by it because he never touched drugs. He thought that hurt his reputation around the league and in the community, and he and his agent, David Falk, demanded a retraction from the Jazz.The Jazz were surprised by

Dantley's belligerence since Frank had shown a willingness to put the matter behind them and accept Dantley back on the team. Besides, how do you retract an action? If you say he wasn't sent home for disciplinary reasons, then why was he sent home? The Jazz only issued a statement saying they would issue no more statements on the matter.

That night in Phoenix was the beginning of the end, although Dantley went out in a blaze of glory. Over the next 15 games he averaged more than 34 points, topping 40 points three times and winning an NBA Player of the Week award along the way. He led the Jazz in scoring all 15 games and never scored less than 25. He sat out the final game of the season with an injury, missed the playoffs and never put on a Jazz uniform again. That summer he was traded to Detroit for Tripucka.

Dantley had a Hall of Fame career, scoring more than 23,000 points in 15 NBA seasons, and his best years were in Utah. That's why he deserves to have his number retired by the Jazz. He is the only Jazz player since the franchise has been in Utah to lead the league in scoring. He scored 13,000 points here, more than anyone in franchise history until Malone and John Stockton passed him. He also averaged six rebounds a game, shot 56 percent and had more than 500 steals in Utah. And he could play defense when he had to.

But he had that Notre Dame attitude, and maybe that's why the Jazz never retired his number. Darrell Griffith averaged 16 points a game and never played in an All-Star game but the Jazz retired his number. That's not a knock on Griffith because he deserved it, but Dantley averaged 29 points a game for the Jazz and he made the All-Star team all six seasons he was in Utah.

Another factor might be the wins. Dantley was the whole show here and the Jazz had some success with him, but they were never going to be contenders as long as he dominated the team. In that last great stretch of his, those final 15 games he played in a Jazz uniform when he averaged more than 34 points a game, the Jazz only went 8-7. He went out in a blaze of glory, but he never brought the team with him.

Chapter Twenty-one

HOLDING ON

The Jazz made the playoffs for the first time in 1984 when Adrian Dantley and Darrell Griffith led the way. The following summer they drafted John Stockton and a year after that they selected Karl Malone. The Jazz finally were arriving as a franchise, but Sam Battistone still struggled financially. Even in our first playoff year we averaged less than 10,000 fans a game. We were televising 15 games a season then compared to the 55-plus we do now, in addition to upwards of 20 playoff games. KSL picked the games that got televised because it was a network station and had difficulty pre-empting shows, so they had to fit the games in where they could. Now the Jazz own their own TV station.

Even after we started having some success, we had to take some gambles on the roster. When you're a young team like we were, you take other teams' castoffs trying to find a way. The Jazz have cleaned up their whole act since then. Now there's a whole system in the NBA. You go back and check a kid's life, his background, his friends, how well he did in school. Everything is checked out. But look at the guys we had filling out our roster in the early years, guys like Tom Boswell, Carey Scurry and Darryl Dawkins. These were all bad actors.

Dawkins only played four games in a Jazz uniform but what a piece of work this guy was. He said he wasn't from the planet Earth. When I did games for CBS, I went to his house to tape an interview. He said he was from the planet Lovetron. He had a round bed with mirrors on the ceiling. He was nuts. We were excited to get him in

Utah, willing to take a shot because he was so talented, but it never worked out. In the short time he was with the Jazz he ran up bills at a clothing store and charged it all to the Jazz, then skipped town. He never came back. He played four games and disappeared. He was like a big kid.

In the same deal that brought Dawkins to the Jazz for all of four games, the Jazz also got Mel Turpin—Dinner Bell Mel. His car was programmed so it was impossible to go past a Wendy's or a McDonald's without turning into the drive-thru to get a cheeseburger. You talk about eating your way out of the NBA. He was a great, great talent and at 6-11 he had great size, but after three average seasons in Cleveland, one in Utah, another in Washington, that was it. He could never get in shape to take advantage of all that talent he had.

Another character was Carey Scurry. Now there was a talent, but that guy wasn't real smart. He had unbelievable ability. It was scary how good he could have been but he wasn't a very bright kid. One time in Houston, Scurry and Mel Turpin got off the bus on the way to practice and they went after it. I mean they were trying to kill each other. Those guys were crazy, and Jerry Sloan jumped in there to break it up and took a couple blows himself. The Jazz kept Scurry around for two years because he had phenomenal athleticism, but they never could find a way to tap into it.

Bart Kofoed was a no-talent kid out of Kearny State College in Nebraska but a hard worker. He got in a fight with Bobby Hansen on New Year's Eve in 1988 and that blew up on the Jazz. Hansen was a good kid. He was a good shooter and he worked his tail off. He missed 16 games with a broken cheekbone from that fight with Kofoed, and the Jazz waived Kofoed four days later.

The Jazz tried some local heroes over the years, too. I saw Pace Mannion play at the University of Utah his sophomore year. Tom Chambers and Danny Vranes were on that team but I was really impressed with Mannion. He was only a sophomore and really played well. He showed a lot of talent and I thought he was going to be a player, but he never made it. He came in like he owned the place, strutting around like he was a veteran, a big star. He had a bad attitude. He was one of those clubhouse lawyers who couldn't play. He hung around with Dantley but wasn't liked by anybody.

Fred Roberts out of Brigham Young University played two years for us, then we traded him to Boston in 1986 for a third-round draft choice and "future considerations"—which turned out to be a couple of exhibition games. The Celtics didn't play their preseason games just for the practice then, there was big money to be made. A lot of teams had to schedule games wherever they could, but the Celtics could be pretty choosy—and they commanded a pretty hefty fee from teams that wanted to play them in the preseason.

So the Jazz traded Roberts for two exhibition games and played one of them in Provo, Utah—at BYU—the following year. The Celtics had Danny Ainge, Greg Kite and Roberts in those days, and they all played at BYU so the game was a big draw in Provo. Almost 23,000 people showed up. It was the final exhibition before the season started, so both teams played their front-line players much of the night.

Marcus Iavaroni got in a scuffle with Larry Bird during the game going for a loose ball. It wasn't much of a fight, just some pushing and shoving, but it pissed Bird off. And he remembered. Six weeks later we were in Boston for our one trip of the season there, and the first eight or nine times Bird touched the ball, he shot over Iavaroni. He never passed the ball, he just threw Iavaroni in the hoop. He scored Boston's first 12 points of the game, and Frank had to take Iavaroni out. Iavaroni only played 11 minutes that night and Bird scored 38.

By then the Jazz were making the playoffs every year and had started selling out the Salt Palace regularly. That's what winning does for you. By the process of getting better, I knew we would catch on. You can apply all the gimmicks in the world, and we tried them all in New Orleans. We did every promotion in the book, but there's nothing that beats winning for selling tickets. Utah is basketball country, very much like the state of Indiana. They had the Utah Stars, BYU, and the University of Utah basketball has always been hot out here. Utah State and Weber State have been successful and the fans have always liked basketball in this state.

I wasn't surprised we were successful, but I was surprised to see us build our own building, getting nearly 20,000 a night. I thought we would be in the Salt Palace forever. If we start winning 20 games again—and losing 50 or 60, attendance is going to fall off, but not to what it once was. Pro basketball has sold itself. I think you will always see at least 12,000 to 13,000 at games even in the bad times, and with any kind of success, the Jazz will continue packing the Delta Center. With the growth of television it's becoming the No. 1 spectator sport in the world. And with all the kids playing the game, I think it will always do well.

Sam Battistone never saw that prosperity, though. He sold half the team to Larry Miller in 1985, and on the eve of selling to buyers in Minneapolis the following year, Miller bought the other half of the team to keep it in Utah. Investors in Minnesota wanted to buy the Jazz and move the team and Battistone felt he had to get out. Miller stepped in, though, and matched the offer. I think if Battistone could have lasted one more year financially he would have been over the hump. Larry Miller had unbelievable timing in buying this team. It was just instant success. By then the league had all those great players—Magic Johnson, Larry Bird, Michael Jordan, Charles Barkley—and the Jazz had Karl Malone and John Stockton. The NBA was rocking and rolling, just growing like a wildfire, but Sam couldn't afford to hold on.

Chapter Twenty-two

GREATEST POINT GUARD EVER

Frank Layden always said John Stockton had three things going for him: He's Irish, he's Catholic and his dad owns a bar. It was a funny line Frank used at speaking engagements, but there's more to it. There's something about the way Stockton plays basketball that stems from the way he was raised. His old man's bar, Jack and Dan's in Spokane, Washington, has grown to almost legendary status in Utah. Everyone has heard of the place even though it's 800 miles away. It's a neighborhood bar with a satellite dish so they can watch the Jazz. Seattle is the closest NBA city but they love the Jazz up there because of John. But there aren't any pictures of John on the walls of the bar. Jack Stockton won't allow it. His partner tried to put one up once. He put up a poster of John early in his career, probably the first time he was on one. Jack later came in, saw the poster and pulled it right off the wall. We didn't have any pictures of John up there before he became a basketball star, Jack Stockton said, so why are we doing it now?

There's something in that, in his dad's reaction, that helped make John what he is on the basketball court. If you think about it, that's a reflection of why John is who he is. Pulling that poster off the wall, that's his family, that's his dad doing that. John grew up learning there are more important things in life. Competing and winning are important, but don't blow your own horn. I read all this between the lines through his mom and dad. And his brother, Steve, who looks just like him, is the same way. I told Steve, if John ever got hurt we'd throw Steve in his uniform and scare the other team. Steve works for Anheuser-Busch so I'm a big fan of his, too.

John's dad is a great guy who loves to drink beer and talk about the NBA, and his mother is a wonderful woman. But they never, ever say a word about John, at least not whenever I've been around. Except for one time when there was a group of people gathered and they waited until no one else was around to pull me aside. They said they wanted to talk to me. I was guarded, not really sure what they wanted. They said, "We want you to know we appreciate all the nice things you say about John." And I said, "What do you mean? I'm just telling it like it is." What else am I going to say? He's the greatest point guard to ever play the game.

Dave Blackwell, a former sportswriter in town and now a broadcaster, always jokes that I would adopt Stockton if I could. And he's right. If I had a son I'd want him to be just like John. He's a family man all the way, he's not into all this ballyhoo. His kids are always running around the locker room or playing on the court after games. I think I'm a bigger fan of his than his mom and dad. I think he's the greatest, the best ever. I've never seen a guy play with the heart he has and the competitiveness, and to have achieved what he has. I mean, look at the assist record. By the end of the '98 season he had 12,713 career assists. Magic Johnson is second with 10,141. You talk about shattering the record, he just keeps adding to it. He has the all-time steals record, too, and he's scored over 15,000 points. Not bad for a kid from Gonzaga University.

John is about winning. He's a fierce competitor, a fighter. He plays hurt, a throwback to the old days. He's so much like Jerry West in his approach to basketball it amazes me. John doesn't like to talk about injuries, he just goes out and does the job whether he's hurt or not. He does everything to win. Play defense, play offense, get involved. The worst thing you could do when you were playing against Jerry West was embarrass him, and it's the same thing with Stockton. If you make either one of them look bad you're going to eat it. Either one of those guys, they're coming right back at you. If you knock John down and take the ball away from him, or drive over him, the next time he gets the ball he's flying right at you. Now it gets personal. That's part of his competitiveness, part of who he is. It's not about making a name for himself, it's about trying to win. That's the way he was brought up.

How many guys could have come back from a knee operation like he did? He had knee surgery before the start of the 1997-98 season and doctors predicted he would be out eight to 12 weeks.

Eight weeks to the day he was back in the scrap against Indiana, getting kicked on the floor by 6-10 Dale Davis and getting his nose bloodied by 7-4 Rik Smits.

Jerry West shot the ball more than Stockton, and if John has a weakness it's that he doesn't shoot the ball enough. He's a great shooter. Not just a good shooter, a great one. He might be the best shooter on this team, even better than Jeff Hornacek. He can flat out shoot the basketball and he doesn't take enough shots. He never averaged as many as 12 shots a game for a season. For his career he averages about nine shots a game and he's a 52 percent shooter. But that's the way he is. He doesn't care about scoring. He wants to get everybody involved. And he's the master at doing it early. He wants to make sure all four guys on the court with him take shots before he takes one, unless he's absolutely taking a layup or a five-foot jump shot where he's wide open.

He also sets the best picks of anybody in the whole NBA. Karl Malone is 6-foot-9, 256 pounds, and Stockton sets screens on the guys guarding Karl, who are usually just as big as Karl. He's holding off giants. Anthony Mason. David Robinson. Moses Malone. Dale Davis. John puts his face right in there and holds his ground. He takes a beating. Big guys can't stand this little 6-1 guy sticking it to them. They knock him on his ass, kick him, whatever, and he jumps right back up. He's a tough cat. He's the NBA's all-time leader in assists, the all-time leader in steals, he's a great shooter and he sets the best screens in the league. He does it all. That's why it was a terrible, terrible oversight that he was left off the All-Star team following his knee surgery.

Bob Cousy loves Stockton. He and John have a lot in common. They have the same approach toward the game. As a point guard, Stockton overall is the best I've ever seen. Cousy was better running the fast break but Stockton is better in a halfcourt game. Cousy was the best middle man on the fast break I've ever seen. I put John second. Sometimes John makes the pass a little bit too early. He'll throw it out in the open court. You don't throw the ball to big guys like Malone when they're 25 feet from the basket. Wait till they get where they can put it on the floor once and lay it in, or catch it and go right on in. John does a remarkable job, but Cousy just had that uncanny ability to find the right guy at the right time on the run.

John might make the wrong decision on the fast break because he wants to get a particular guy involved, he wants to get that guy on the board. Maybe I'm wrong, but that seems to be his mentality. Cousy got it to the guy who would get the bucket every time but John is so unselfish that if he has two choices, sometimes he'll give it to a guy who shouldn't have it. John will do that to make sure everyone gets involved. There are many times he should give it to Karl but he gives it to someone else to get him some points, to get him in the game, which is good. But what if the other guy misses the shot or mishandles it or something? You know Karl is going to finish the play. I know the way John thinks might be a part of why he makes the questionable choice sometimes.

John isn't nearly as flashy as Cousy was. The thing about Cousy is you tended to watch him instead of guard him. You got hung up watching him doing what he's doing instead of trying to stop him. Bob and I got to be pretty good friends. I played against him all six years I was in the NBA and got him to come out for my celebrity golf tournament. I introduced him at a banquet a few years ago and said, "I guarded this guy for six years and this is the closest I've ever been to him."

"He uses that line twice a year," Cousy says today. "When you get a good line, stick with it."

I ran the fast break quite well myself when I played, but deciding who to pass to on the Lakers was a no-brainer. With Elgin Baylor running the court on one side of me and Jerry West on the other, how could I go wrong? They're both in the Hall of Fame. I had no decision to make, I just threw it to either one of them and we scored.

Stockton is such a smart player, it's just like having another coach out on the floor. Jerry Sloan says he gets criticized sometimes for not calling enough timeouts. The opponents might run off 10 straight points on the Jazz yet Sloan might sometimes hesitate to call a timeout. When a team calls a timeout and the players huddle up around the coach, what usually happens is the coach talks to the point guard and tells him what he wants. Sloan says, "Why should I take a timeout? I've got a guy on the floor who's smarter than I am. He knows what to do."

On the team plane, players ride in the front and the coaches sit in the very back. Almost always on the way home after a game or on the way to another city, Karl and John will walk to the back of the plane and talk to Jerry and Phil Johnson. I don't think they talk a lot about basketball. They talk about other things. They're the only two players who do that. John and Karl have all the respect in the world for Sloan.

Anywhere the Jazz go, when they get off a bus there's always a crowd. Fans go after all the players but particularly Stockton and Malone. This one guy outside the team hotel in Portland had a picture of John and said, "Hey, John, remember me? I knew you from blah, blah, blah. Could I get you to sign this?" John never stopped walking and told the guy no. The instant John turned him down, the guy turned his attention to another player. He went up to someone else and said, "Hey, remember me? I knew you from blah, blah, blah." John had never seen this guy in his life and he's trying to trap him into signing an autograph that he was probably going to sell. It's easy to knock players for not signing autographs, but they run into so many insincere people you can see why they don't like to sign. John signs a ton of autographs, but he does them on his terms. Sometimes I'll see him walking and signing along the way but as soon as he gets to where he's going, that's it. If he ever stops it's all over, so he keeps moving.

One night at the Sports Arena in Los Angeles, we were waiting on the bus for Karl after a game with the Clippers. John and Karl are always the last ones on the bus because they both ice their knees and ankles after games, and they both have the most interview requests. If John is on the bus first he'll yell out, "Let's go, we don't need the Mailman. Let him find his own way back. He can afford his own plane ticket home." Then as soon as Karl walks on the bus, Stockton says, "Hey, Karl, all the guys wanted to leave but I made sure we waited for you."

One night outside the Sports Arena there was a big crowd behind a fence. So while we waited for Karl, John got off the bus and went over and started signing all these autographs. He had a restraining wall so they couldn't get to him, so he was comfortable. They passed him things which he would sign and pass back. As soon as Karl was ready, John stopped and got back on the bus. If John had signed 25 autographs that night, 25 people went away happy but whoever was the 26th in line probably went around telling people what a jerk John Stockton was for refusing to sign an autograph. That's the way people are. You can't win.

John reads a lot on road trips and loves to do crossword puzzles. He stays to himself and likes his privacy. He loves to golf but he won't play in celebrity golf tournaments. When I had mine he said, "I don't play in celebrity tournaments, but if I ever do, I'll play in yours." That was his way of saying no in a nice way. He would go out and play golf with me if it was just us, but he wouldn't play in a celebrity tournament. He's very loyal to me, though, and Karl is too. They are probably the two best superstars in the NBA as far as doing radio and television interviews after games, not just for me but for the other team's broadcasters as well.

It's funny when you think of the kind of celebrity Stockton is now and compare it to the day he was drafted. There was a big gathering at the Salt Palace that day for the annual draft party and when the Jazz announced they were taking a 6-1 guard from Gonzaga, everyone booed. No one had ever heard of John Stockton. I never heard of him. Well, everyone has heard of him now. On draft day in 1992 we traded Blue Edwards and Eric Murdock to Milwaukee for Jay Humphries and Larry Krystkowiak. There were several thousand fans at the Delta Center for that draft day party and they booed when I announced the trade. When things quieted I went back up to the microphone and, "You know, the last time I heard you boo a transaction by the Utah Jazz was when we drafted a kid by the name of John Stockton." They got quiet as a mouse. Tim Howells, the Jazz general manager, was sitting up on the stage and he flashed a thumbs up when I sat down.

Stockton has had an amazing career and is still going strong. He was 36 years old when he led the Jazz into the 1998 NBA Finals and I can't think of anyone who was nearly as effective at that age. I hate to see the day when he puts that uniform away, but I think he should retire before he loses it. I like to see great players retire while they're still on top. People tend to remember you the way you went out, not necessarily for the great years. That's what I admired about Jerry West. He could still average over 20 points a game when he quit, but he couldn't do all the things he used to do. So he walked away. Some guys fake-and-go their whole career and see nothing but a clear path to the basket. Then one day they fake-and-go but the defender is still in front of them. That's when you know it's time to get out. I hope John and Karl both see that. They don't need to hang on, they don't need the money. They still can play, but they can't go on forever. They both have so much pride, they probably will see the end before the rest of us do.

Karl has said if the day comes when he goes for a loose ball and can't get there, he's going to keep on running, right off the court and out the door. I hope he does go out while he can still play. And I hope Stockton does too. Karl is going to last longer than John because of his body. Karl can take a beating. John is smaller. He's every bit as much of a competitor as Karl, but John is starting to slow. Karl is playing his best ever and John is starting to slip a little, and he's also had knee surgery. But Karl? He won the MVP award in 1997 at age 33, and he was even better the next year. He's the only basketball player I've ever seen in my life who was still getting better at that age. At age 34, he was playing better than he ever has. Michael Jordan was still a great player at that age but there's no way he was better than he was earlier in his career. For Karl a lot of it has to do with his workouts. He's always strong and in good condition. He really takes care of himself. He doesn't smoke or drink. He eats well and gets his sleep.

It wouldn't surprise me to see them both go on for several more years, especially Karl. Someday, though, they will see something the rest of us can't, and that will be it.

Chapter Twenty-three

A MAILMAN COMES
TO SALT LAKE CITY

T he year after we drafted John Stockton and the selection
was booed, we drafted Karl Malone and everyone cheered.
It was 1985 and by then we were getting several thousand
people at the Salt Palace just to watch the draft. A stage was set up
and all of the Jazz coaches and front office members were up there
working the draft. There was a big screen set up above the stage for
the fans to watch things unfold on television, and I was serving as
emcee. We had the 13th pick overall and about an hour into the
draft it was getting close to our turn. Malone was still available and
the fans knew it. There was a buzz in the crowd. The Jazz didn't
even scout Malone that much because they never thought he'd be
available. Now he was slipping and they were wondering what all
those other teams knew that the Jazz didn't.

We were sweating it out up on the stage just like the fans
were out in the crowd. Washington had the pick ahead of us and
when their turn came, the place got dead quiet. The commissioner
came up on the TV screen and announced the Washington Bullets
would take Kenny Green of Wake Forest. You've never heard anyone cheer so loud because of another team's draft pick. The place
went absolutely nuts because everyone realized the Jazz were going to get Malone. The Salt Palace erupted with chants of "The Mailman! The Mailman."

I introduced Frank Layden so he could announce the Jazz selection to the crowd a minute or so before the commissioner announced it on television. Frank walked up to the podium and ev-

eryone was yelling for Karl Malone. Frank finally gets the crowd quiet and says, "The Utah Jazz, selecting in the first round at position No. 13, are very happy to announce to the NBA and the people of Utah ... that a Mailman is coming to Salt Lake City!!!!! The Utah Jazz select Karl Malone!!" The crowd erupted and it was a madhouse in there. Just a year earlier with the Jazz picking at 16, they announced they were taking a guard from Gonzaga and everyone booed because they had never heard of him. But they knew who Malone was, and we can thank Washington for passing on him. Kenny Green went to Washington, played 20 games and was traded to Philadelphia for Leon Wood, who is a referee in the NBA now. Green played 40 games in Philadelphia and was out of the league.

The other interesting sidelight of that year's draft was that the Jazz finished tied with San Antonio in the standings for the 1984-85 season. Both teams finished 41-41 so they had a coin flip to determine the 13th and 14th pick in the draft. The Jazz got Malone with the 13th pick, and San Antonio took Alfredrick Hughes from Loyola of Chicago with the 14th pick. Hughes was a ballyhooed showman, a Fancy Dan who took all kinds of crazy shots. He only lasted a year, but thanks to the luck of a coin toss, the Jazz ended up with Karl Malone.

He came to town a few weeks later and was there for Pioneer Days, which is a big holiday in Utah that just happens to fall on Malone's birthday, July 24. He rode in the parade on the Jazz float with Frank and me. That was the first time I met Karl. He was a country boy, big as an ox. The fans were excited to have him and he was excited about playing here.

He built a nice rapport with Frank right from the start and really respected him. The amazing thing about Karl that first year was that Adrian Dantley was the post-up player on the team. We ran a high-post offense with Karl, who was 6-9, at the top of the key and Dantley, who was 6-4 inside. Karl fed Dantley as much as Rickey Green or John Stockton did. I thought then that Karl was the best passer on the team, I was so impressed. I was amazed at how good a passer he was as a power forward, and a rookie one at that. And he has continued to improve as a passer. He has gotten fancier with it. The passes are a lot tougher for him now that he's the one down on the low blocks. He's great at finding the cutters through the double-teams where it's hard to see. He throws the passes now behind the back or over the shoulder, and he does it better than anybody his size. He gets a little careless every now and then but that's a tough pass from the low block.

He may be the best true power forward ever to play the game. Larry Bird might have played that position, but he wasn't a power player. He was more of a point-forward, the quarterback of the team. In Boston, everything went through Larry Bird just like in Utah everything went through Malone, but they were much different players.

Karl has gotten better every year and still hasn't peaked. He won the Most Valuable Player Award in the 1996-97 season when he was 33 years old, and I think he was a better basketball player the following year, the best year he's ever had. He was better at age 34 than he ever has been in his life. He's smarter, he doesn't force issues, he has great patience. He doesn't have to work as hard to produce more, which makes him stronger late in games. He doesn't take bad shots. He reads the defense and he gets everybody involved like John does. His outside shot has really improved and so have his free throws. He didn't have any confidence from the free throw line as a rookie. Frank got on him once in Phoenix, yelling, "We're paying you big bucks to make these free throws, now get up there and make them!" Karl went out and made them, and he got better at it every year.

Karl got a lot stronger over the years, too. As big as he was as a rookie, his body changed dramatically. He's sculpted now. He works out every day he's not playing basketball. When he's on the road, every city he goes to he looks for a place to work out. He's lifting weights for his upper body one day and the next day he'll do legs or something else. That guy takes better care of himself than anyone I've ever seen. He works out religiously in the off-season, too. He's proud of that and he doesn't understand why these other guys like Greg Ostertag don't. Get on the same program, become a player. With the money that's out there, it's amazing more guys don't have that same attitude.

When Karl started making money he was like a kid with a new toy. He had a truck with his name all over it and he's still got a lot of that in him with his motorcycles. There's nothing wrong with that. I've still got it in me. You should try to stay a kid all your life. Enjoy life. Don't let yourself grow old and act like an old man. That will never happen to Karl. He likes new things and he can afford them. He has his toys and they're very expensive toys. He has his Harleys, and I have my Harlee, too. Harlee is my two-year-old golden retriever. He doesn't care what time I get home or where I've been, he's always happy to see me. And he doesn't care if the Jazz win or lose. He helps me keep the game at the arena. It's nice to come home to a happy face after a bad game to remind you it's just a game.

Karl's family does the same thing for him. His kids don't care if he had a bad game, they're just happy to see daddy. In the 1997 playoffs against the Lakers, Karl had the worst game of his life. He was 2-for-20 from the field and the Jazz lost by 20. After the game he's talking about it to his wife on the phone and it didn't matter to her. It reminded Karl what's important in his life and helped him put that game behind him. He came out the next game, scored 42 points and went 18-for-18 from the free throw line to set an NBA playoff record.

Karl's toys help him stay fresh as a basketball player because they let him get away from the game. He loves to hunt and fish, anything outdoors and away from basketball. Except golf. He has absolutely no desire to hit a golf ball. His definition of golf is "the biggest waste of cow pasture there is." Maybe because he has so many outside interests he always has two or three outdoors magazines with him on road trips, reading about camping and things most guys in professional basketball don't read about. He is an excellent interview. He speaks his mind, he's funny and he talks. He doesn't give you one-word answers. I think the whole league likes to talk to him because he will talk back.

Those were two lucky tricks, having Stockton and Malone fall into our laps. You get those two guys and your franchise is made for 15 years. You can put anyone out there with them and you're not going to lose too many games, they're both such fierce competitors. Without question they are the best twosome in basketball I've ever seen in my life—and I've played with Jerry West and Elgin Baylor. West and Baylor were great, great Hall of Fame players but they never thrived off one another like Stockton and Malone do. It's like John and Karl have one brain between the two of them. They just look at each other and know what the other guy is thinking and doing. The beauty of it is the other team knows what's coming and they can't stop it. Karl and John have so many options and they do it so quickly, you can't react to it. Boom! It's done. Before you react they've got the ball in the hoop.

His timing with Stockton on the pick-and-roll is absolutely perfect. What determines whether that play is successful or not is the timing of the pass, what instant you get the ball to the shooter. All it takes is a split second to break up the play or a split second to break loose. That's why Stockton and Malone are so good at it. Look at how they dismantled the Los Angeles Lakers in the 1998 Western Conference finals. They ran the pick and roll over and over and over, for four straight games, and the Lakers never figured it out. Malone and Stockton ran the same play a hundred different ways and swept the Lakers because of it.

They've scored more than 43,000 points between the two of them, and they did it all with the Jazz. Add up Karl's assists with John's and you've got more than 16,000, and add up John's rebounds with Karl's and you've got more than 14,000. And they've got more than 4,000 steals between them. It's unbelievable what they've done. You look at all the other great tandems, like West and Baylor, Michael Jordan and Scottie Pippen, Bob Cousy and Bill Russell, and they never fed off each other the way Stockton and Malone do. Then you look at other highly touted twosomes like Houston's Twin Towers of Hakeem Olajuwon and Ralph Sampson, or Washington forwards Chris Webber and Juwan Howard, and they never lived up to their billing.

Like Stockton, Malone has tremendous respect for Jerry Sloan, and that's a big reason they have been so successful. Karl will get in foul trouble sometimes and he knows Jerry is going to take him out of the game, so he'll motion for Jerry to leave him on the floor, that he's got it under control. But Jerry just turns his back to Karl and sends someone else in. Karl might be upset when he walks to the bench, but once he gets a second to think about it he realizes, "If I was the coach I'd take me out too." You've got to in those situations. But then if it's later in the game and Karl has five fouls and there's seven minutes left in the game, I'll say on the air, "You might be wondering why Karl's in the game, but we're not saving him for the prom, baby. It's now or never." It's a coach's judgment, and Karl has a lot of faith in Jerry, just like Jerry has a lot of trust in Karl.

Throughout their careers you almost never saw Karl and John out of the game at the same time. I learned that from my brief coaching stint with the Lakers. Every time Fred Schaus got kicked out he would tell me as he left the court, "Don't rest West and Baylor at the same time." I thought, "Same time? I'm not going to rest them at all. I want to win." Lucky for them I wasn't their coach all the time because I would have played them 48 minutes every night. But Fred's point always stuck with me. He never rested his stars at the same time. West and Baylor could go a whole year without talking to each other because they were never on the bench at the same time. And I told that to Jerry Sloan once, that either West or Baylor were always on the court for the Lakers, and Karl or John should always be on the court for the Jazz. And Jerry did that. He never rested them at the same time, at least not until Stockton underwent knee surgery.

I don't understand why the Bulls didn't do that with Jordan and Pippen. When do you make a run at the Bulls? When Jordan and Pippen are sitting on the bench together. People who don't follow the Jazz regularly wonder why Stockton always comes out of the game so predictably, six or seven minutes into the game. He doesn't need a rest yet but it gives the Jazz two things. First, it allows Howard Eisley to play with the first string so that makes Eisley better. And second, when Karl is ready for a rest to start the second quarter, John can come back in fresh and play with the second unit, making them more productive. That rotation has really worked well for Jerry.

Malone and Stockton are the greatest tandem of our time. I've never seen anything like it in my life. And they both play to win. Karl says the only thing he keeps playing for after all these years is that ring. He has come so close and when you think of all the last-second shots over the years in the conference finals and the NBA Finals, it had to have been discouraging, but he kept coming back. He never gave up. He never quit. Malone and Stockton, those are different people, and so is Sloan. Those guys are definitely three of a kind.

Chapter Twenty-four

BEST TRADE EVER

As excited as the Jazz were when they drafted John Stockton, it took a couple years before they realized what they had. By then Karl Malone was well on his way to becoming a superstar. The nucleus was in place. Then it was a matter of finding the pieces to put around it. The first big trade we made came in 1990 when Scott Layden, the Jazz personnel director, horned in on a deal between Washington and Sacramento and made it a three-way trade. We sent Bobby Hansen and Eric Leckner to Sacramento and got Jeff Malone from Washington.

Eric Leckner was tall but he had no heart for the game, no work ethic. He was a lot like Greg Ostertag. He had talent but he just didn't have the desire. Leckner has never done anything for anybody in this league, just a complete failure as an NBA player. He's still hanging around, though. If you're close to 7 feet tall and can get up and down the court without falling down, you can always find a job in this league.

Look at Danny Schayes, our first-round draft choice in 1981. His father, Dolph, is a Hall of Famer who played 16 years in the NBA. Danny has been a sub all his life, a role player, but he lasted 17 years. He's basically the type of player you keep in case somebody gets hurt. There's nothing wrong with that. He enjoys the game and has gotten smarter with experience. He's the kind of guy who will never hurt you and he'll always have a job.

So we give up Hansen and Leckner for Jeff Malone, and giving up Leckner didn't cost us anything. Jeff Malone probably helped us more than Bobby Hansen could. He gave us another offensive weapon to go with Karl Malone and John Stockton. We were immediately better in a lot of ways, but it was only a fair trade. Jeff Malone had better offensive skills but Bobby Hansen was a better defender. Bobby was a hard-working guy, a real tough guy who would play hurt. He was a pretty good jump shooter if he got an open look and he could hit the 3-pointer, but he didn't have the skills of a great player.

Jeff Malone wasn't the answer, though. He was a great shooter from 15 feet in but if he wasn't scoring, he wasn't helping you. He was smart enough to put the ball in Stockton's hands, however, because if he got open he knew the ball was coming back. Nothing kills a great shooter more than when he makes the perfect move without the ball, really works to get around a screen to get open, and then you don't get him the ball. Next time down, if the same guy's got the ball, a shooter's not going to make that move again because the playmaker didn't get him the ball. He's not going to waste all that energy if you're not even going to throw him the ball. That's why everybody likes Stockton. If you make that move, the ball is there and at the right time. So Jeff always worked hard on offense when Stockton was on the court with him.

Jeff was always fading when he shot the ball but he had great control of the shot. Great shooters can do that, shoot off-balance, going toward the hoop, falling backwards, falling left, falling right. He practiced that stuff. A 15-footer was just like a layup for him. Anything from the foul line in was a great shot, and he was great along the baseline too. He could even drift behind the plane of the backboard and make that shot. A lot of guys have to be in front of the hoop looking right down the barrel, but Jeff could shoot just as well from the baseline. He didn't have the shooting depth, however. He couldn't shoot the 3-pointer.

The one thing about Jeff Malone was that you could expect him to miss some games every year. It was probably in his contract. He just wasn't going to play 82 games. He just sat out games, saying his back was hurting or something. He was that kind of a guy. He didn't have that Stockton-Malone attitude about playing, he just floated through games. I don't think it bothered him whether he played or not.

Mike Brown played for the Jazz then, and he had one nice playoff series against Phoenix in 1991. He averaged 9.6 points and 7.3 rebounds through the playoffs, and he had sense enough to do it when his contract was up. He parlayed that series into a multi-year contract, but he never came close to those numbers again. I started calling him "The Brown Bear," and he even marketed T-shirts with that on it. He was a likable guy with fan appeal, an intelligent guy who made the most of what talent he had. Really his only talents were being big and being strong. He wasn't a bad shooter from five feet in. I called him the Brown Bear, but really he was a bull in a china shop. That's the best way to describe his game. He was big enough he could play. Guys who have big bodies like he does could play 10 years in this league, which he did. There's always someone who will pick you up. When you retire, no one will ever know who you played for, but you can go in there and make yourself a living. This was about the time Mark Eaton's injuries were catching up to him and the Jazz were desperate for a center. Mike wasn't a true center but he was all they had, so they threw him out there. At 6-foot-10 Mike wasn't anything more than a stopgap.

Blue Edwards was our first-round draft choice in 1989. He had a lot of natural ability but never played the way he should. He had the talent to play the game and he didn't use it. Here's a guy who could jump so high he dunked the ball with ease, but he could never get a rebound. On offense he would just wander around and shoot the ball, a selfish player. He has been able to last in this league because he could score, but he could have been a lot better player than he was. He couldn't rebound, he couldn't defend that well and he was selfish offensively. I don't know if he was taught this way but in his mind, if you don't score you're not doing anything and if you do score that's enough. He didn't seem to have the confidence in himself to accept constructive criticism. He has always had a problem with coaches—a great natural talent but he never played up to his capabilities. He was very popular here, though. I think his nickname made him more popular than anything, that and his ability to dunk. People loved yelling out, "Bluuuuuuuuuuuue." Same with the Big Dawg, Antoine Carr. Fans loved to bark for him. They both have that fan appeal.

David Benoit was another wasted talent. He was the kind of player who was going to give you one out of four games, scoring 20 points one night and nothing the other three. If he would only tell you which one he was going to play, you could sit him down the other three. The Jazz discovered him in their summer camp and worked hard to develop him. He had great ability, could jump out of the building and could shoot it from deep, but he never lived up to his potential. He was a very quiet person and played his games the same way. He had a world of talent but just didn't have that killer instinct.

Thurl Bailey was reaching the end of the line so early in the 1991-92 season they traded him to Minnesota for Tyrone Corbin. With Jeff Malone and those other guys now surrounding Stockton and Karl Malone, the Jazz made it to the Western Conference finals for the first time ever that year. They beat the Los Angeles Clippers in the first round of the 1992 playoffs, which was delayed by rioting in L.A. The verdict in the Rodney King trial came out between Games 3 and 4, and all hell broke loose. The Sports Arena, where the Clippers played, was turned into a National Guard command post, with tanks in the parking lot. When they got around to playing Game 4 several days later, they had to play it out in Anaheim. That was a scary few days, riding in a police motorcade everywhere the team went.

The Jazz then went on to beat Seattle 4-1 in the second round, but Portland was too tough for them in the conference finals.

That summer they traded Blue Edwards and Eric Murdock to Milwaukee for Jay Humphries and Larry Krystkowiak. They hoped Krystkowiak could take minutes away from Malone and counted on Humphries easing Stockton's workload. Jay was a good backup player. It was probably his best suit. You've got to be a different mentality to back up, and he had that.

With the success from the previous year, plus the addition of those new guys, expectations were higher than ever. So when Seattle beat the Jazz three games to two in the first round of the 1993 playoffs, the Jazz kept looking for other pieces to the puzzle. Mark Eaton was a big question mark going into the 1993-94 season because of injuries and Mike Brown wasn't the answer at center, so the Jazz traded Brown to Minnesota for Felton Spencer that summer.

Every year Felton was among the leaders in fouls-per-minute. I always wondered how long it would take him to foul out if coaches left him in the game. But he got his money's worth when he fouled. If you ever wanted to give a foul, to stroke a guy because he was hot and you wanted to take him out of his rhythm, I'd have Felton do it because he'd put the guy in the third row. If the defense is letting some guy come down the lane, you've got to close the door on him. Stroke him one time and he probably won't do it any more. And if Felton strokes him, I guarantee you he won't do it any more.

He fouls about as hard as anybody. He doesn't do it maliciously, he's not trying to hurt anybody, he's just a hard-nosed player. I don't think he realizes how hard he is fouling people.

He was another big body, a little better shooter than Mike Brown. He was one of the all-time great guys, good natured and fun loving. You do the best you can with the ability you've got, and if you don't have it, you work hard and hang in there. He was the sixth player taken in the draft even though he averaged just nine points and five rebounds for his college career. He never was a great player but he has hung in there, so I give him credit for that.

Moments before the NBA's trading deadline hit that season, on February 24, 1994, the Jazz finally found the player they had been searching for all this time. They sent Jeff Malone to Philadelphia for Jeff Hornacek, and it was the greatest trade this franchise has ever made. The trade made the Jazz so much better and really, the whole deal was Eric Leckner and Bobby Hansen for Jeff Hornacek, and we got to use Jeff Malone for three years along the way. With Hornacek the Jazz have made it to the conference finals four times in five years, as well as advancing twice to the NBA Finals.

Hornacek has a much deeper shooting range than Jeff Malone had and he can help you in a lot of ways even when he's not shooting. He doesn't have to have the ball to help you. He's a great passer, and great in the half-court offense. He's very unselfish. He's a pretty good defender, better than the other Jeff. He's fundamentally sound defensively—he never crosses his feet, he slides defensively, stays between his man and the basket. His only problem defensively is that he isn't that strong. When he has to guard Michael Jordan, it's very hard for him because Jordan will back him down. Jordan will beat anybody, but people who have that physique—6-6 and strong—it's a problem for Horny if they try to take him inside. But out front from 20 feet out, he can guard you. A quick guy might get around him and beat him, but he knows how to play perfect position. He always keeps his man away from the basket on the backside.

Hornacek has been well-coached. His dad was a high school coach. He doesn't make many mistakes fundamentally. He has learned how to shoot the ball with the right spin, how to release it correctly. He can use either hand. Hornacek is a competitor like Stockton. He's a smart player and they make a great backcourt.

He's not going to beat you isolated one-on-one but you've got to guard him because he's a born shooter. They have to run screens for him to get him open, but if you give him one instant you're too late. If you're not there defensively, he's going to burn you.

Going to the hoop he has great control and he has the ability to flip that quick shot. He's like a pitcher in baseball that sets a guy up with a fast ball, then strikes him out with a change-up. He catches you leaning then quick-shoots over you. Or like when a pitcher will come in with a slow curve, then the next time comes back with that slow arm motion but sneaks a fastball by you, that's Hornacek. When you pull that hand down he goes up, and when you've got the hand up there to block it he hangs until you put the hand down. Or you could compare him to a boxer who fakes with his right to get your arms going one way, then bam, he jabs you with the left. He sets you up. Hornacek knows how to get you to commit defensively. If you go up, he never releases the shot until your arm comes down. And if you don't go up he has a quick release to get the shot off over you. He knows how to adjust his release to get it over a shot-blocker. He can shoot the ball very effectively with a high arc or a slight trajectory.

And he's got that shot off the glass, slightly off target so you can't block it, then with just enough English for it to spin into the basket. He's the best I've ever seen on those English shots, with great touch going right at the hoop. That's the toughest shot to make in basketball, driving straight at the basket full speed and shooting overhand from four or five feet away. When you go overhand like that you have a tendency to throw it too hard. It's much easier using an underhand scoop when you're going hard toward the basket but he goes overhand to keep if from getting blocked. And he slips it in just dead center with a perfect touch. I call it his bar-of-soap shot the way he squeezes the ball out of his hands. He's the master of that and he can do it from any angle.

On this franchise he should get more shots. He doesn't get as much help as I think he should have, or else he's not trying to use the help. Sometimes he goes to the locker room at halftime with one or two shot attempts. The guy should be getting seven or eight shot attempts a half, 15 to 18 shots every night. Sloan says he wants Jeff to shoot the ball, but they don't seem to get him enough shots. Part of the problem is that teams know he can't beat them driving to the basket so they get right up on him, right in his face, because they respect his great 3-point shooting. He doesn't have a lot of speed to beat you off the dribble unless he gets help, a screen to help him get a step on the defender. That makes it hard for him to get open. He likes to shoot as much as anyone but it doesn't seem to bother him when he's not getting shots. He doesn't pout.

What I like about Jeff is that when he gets mad he gets mad at himself, not his coach or his teammates. When he misses a couple shots he normally makes, or he throws a bad pass, he gets disgusted. You can see the fire but it's directed toward himself, not anybody else. That's a healthy attitude. That's the kind of guy I like.

I'm a big fan of Jeff Hornacek's. He's got a lot of Stockton and Malone in him, a real competitive spirit. He plays to win. That's a nice trio to have on your team, a nice nucleus. John Stockton, Karl Malone and Jeff Hornacek are without question the three best players on the team.

Jeff has a lot of Stockton in him off the court, too. He reads a lot, does crossword puzzles, he's not a drinker. He's also a family man. A lot of the guys on the team are, but Stockton and Hornacek both really like to do things with their kids and stay home with their families.

I think he could coach in the NBA if he wanted to. He could break in as an assistant somewhere and end up being a great coach. He's got a coach's mentality. He understands the game, is very knowledgeable. I think he would be tough enough on the players so they couldn't run over him, but I think guys would enjoy playing for him.

Chapter Twenty-five

FINALLY

There's no way to explain what the Utah Jazz experienced in the wee hours of May 30, 1997. More than 15,000 feverish fans gathered at 3 a.m. for a spontaneous party at a Salt Lake City airport. Five hours earlier, John Stockton hit the shot in Houston that sent the Jazz to the NBA Finals for the first time ever and no one in town could go to sleep. So they all went to the airport and met the team's chartered plane when it landed. It was the middle of the night and fans had been celebrating for hours. They just couldn't contain their exuberance. They wanted to be a part of it, to share it with someone.

You have to understand how long the wait had been to understand why so many people gathered at 3 o'clock in the morning to greet the team. The players were all festive on the plane ride home but they had no idea what was waiting for them when they landed. They could barely get out of the parking lot as thousands of fans lined the streets for several blocks, even young kids. It was an amazing thing to experience and shows just how much the Jazz meant to the state of Utah. It had been 23 years since the franchise was born in New Orleans, and 18 years after the team moved to Utah, that the Jazz finally reached the NBA Finals. Finally. And everyone wanted a piece of it.

Ever since the 1988 playoffs, when the Jazz pushed the Los Angeles Lakers to seven games, every move the team has made was aimed at putting a contending team around Karl Malone and John Stockton. Hopes got higher and higher every year, but there were plenty of disappointments along the way. Once Jeff Hornacek arrived in Utah, though, it was just a matter of time. He had been a consistent outside scoring threat, a good 3-point shooter and a great free throw shooter, but the most telling sign of what he did for this team was in their road record. The Jazz never had a winning record on the road before he joined the team but they've been winning every year since. In the 1995-96 season, the Jazz won 15 in a row on the road, challenging the all-time NBA record of 16 and forever establishing the mind-set that this team could win on the road. That's a big part of the Jazz making it to the Western Conference finals four times in five seasons since he teamed up with Stockton and Malone.

Stockton, Malone and Hornacek are who they are, so if you fill in the holes around them you've got a great team. That's where Bryon Russell, Shandon Anderson and Howard Eisley fit in. All three of those guys really stepped up in the 1996-97 season and helped lead the team to the NBA Finals for the first time.

Russell probably was the most improved player on the team. In the 1995-'96 season, he was the 12th man most of the year, but he got a big break in the playoffs. We played Portland in the first round and were down after three quarters of Game 1. Bryon came off the bench and scored 12 points in the fourth quarter to help them win, then stayed in the rotation after that. Against Seattle in the conference finals, we lost in seven games but Bryon had an unbelievable series. The Jazz were down 0-2 when Bryon broke out for 24 points and 10 rebounds in Game 3. Over the final five games of that series he averaged 14.7 points. Because of what happened in those playoffs, he earned a starting job in the 1996-97 season and really became a player in this league. But with that came a big new contract at the end of the year, and complacency set in. At the start of the 1997-98 season he wasn't as good of a player as he was a year earlier. Your attitude changes a little bit when you get the money for the first time. You get in that comfort zone. The same goes with Greg Ostertag. He looked like maybe he was going to start improving. Then he got a contract and he hasn't played since.

Bryon finally got back to that level by the end of the '98 season and was a big reason the Jazz made it to the Finals two years in a row.

Shandon Anderson was a nice surprise his rookie year. You've got to have good backups to win because five guys can't do it no matter how good they are. It's too long of a season. You'll wear everybody out so you've got to have players who can give you a lift off the bench, especially on a veteran team like the Jazz. They need young, energetic guys backing them up. Shandon doesn't have the shooting skills to be a two-guard, which hurts him, but I like him. He's a player. He's limited by his skills but he can run, he can jump, he's quick, he plays defense and he moves. Best of all he's got a great attitude. He doesn't shoot like Hornacek, but he puts the other things, the tangibles and the intangibles, together and makes himself a player. He's a really good post-up player, taking advantage of his size and strength.

Bryon and Shandon play a very similar game but Bryon has better skills. He is a little better shooter. They both play a little out of control at times defensively. Bryon has improved in that category just from experience, and I think Shandon will, too. That just comes from being a player. You get smarter. It's just like Karl Malone, your game gets better each year if you're given a chance, if you can get off the bench.

Howard Eisley is in that same mold, giving John Stockton the rest he needed. He did a nice job filling in when Stockton got hurt early in the 1998 season, but he was a big part of what the Jazz did the year before, too. He didn't just buy time while Stockton rested, he came in and produced. There are a lot of role players in the league whose job is to just buy time, like Jim McIlvaine in Seattle. The Sonics know he won't get a lot of playing time and gets in foul trouble, but he keeps other guys out of foul trouble so he is effective that way. The Jazz have to have someone buying time behind Stockton so John can get his rest. They've always been able to buy minutes with Eisley, but for two years he has done a lot more than that. It wasn't just a case of him holding onto the lead John gave him but actually adding to it. At times he has even outplayed John.

I like Howard Eisley. He's a nice kid, a quiet kid. You never even know he's around, but on the floor he's got a real competitive fire. He'll get after anyone. He has done a remarkable job coming in from the Continental Basketball Association, getting a chance and playing behind the best point guard of all time. He was cut by three teams—including the Jazz—before he finally got a second chance in Utah to prove himself. He got very few minutes but did his job. Then when Stockton had knee surgery and Howard had to step into the starting role, he was absolutely marvelous the way he handled it. And when John came back, Howard returned to his backup role and continued to do a good job.

Antoine Carr has had his moments for the Jazz. He is a good outside shooter and on defense he can swat a shot right out of the air. It's a pretty thing to watch and it gets all of his teammates excited about playing defense. He could have been a superstar in this league, though. He has great athletic ability, but he's never been in shape. He shows up at the start of the season out of shape and that leads to injuries, and when he comes back from injuries, he's out of shape again. For that matter he's never in shape even when he's in shape. If he could have ever found a way to stay in shape and control his weight, he would have been an All-Star.

Chris Morris is another interesting player. If you take all the great plays Chris has made in his career you could put together an incredible highlight reel. They called Dominique Wilkins "The Human Highlight Film," but you could put together a highlight film of Morris that matched anything Wilkins did. Just take all the great moves, the great shots twisting and leaning, the great passes, right hand, left hand, no-look, and put them on one tape. If that's all you ever saw of Chris Morris you'd think he was the greatest player who ever lived, he has so many great athletic moves. But with all of the flying shots he has taken over the years you could also put together a film on how not to play the game. He scares me and I'm just the broadcaster. Imagine if you were his coach. He could scare a coach to death if he had to play the last five minutes of a close game. But if you're coaching against him and he's going good, he'll scare you to death too with his ability.

Chris might have been the most talented player on this team and the fans loved him, but he just doesn't seem to care sometimes. He has unbelievable talent hidden in that body. It was like he has that "I don't give a damn" attitude. You just couldn't keep him under control. Sometimes you wonder if he's not smarter than he's given credit for. I think he's just a free spirit. He's going to play his way and nobody's going to change him. When the Jazz signed him as a free agent, it was the kind of move you gamble on. Maybe a different coach and a different atmosphere can bring it out of the guy. Like the trade that fell through with Orlando. He probably could have gone down there and started for Chuck Daly. But he's got to be flying up and down the court to be successful. That's his style, but that's not our style of play so he's not the right piece to the puzzle. After the trade to Orlando in the '98 season fell through, he sat on the bench for a couple games and sulked. But then he got in against Phoenix a week later and played great. He played 25 minutes, scored 20 points, he rebounded and got steals, and he did it all under control. That's a luxury you have with a deep team. You play him a couple minutes and if things are haywire you just sit him back down. You're not going to get hurt. But if he comes out hot, you keep him in there and ride him as far as you can go.

After that game I asked him why he thought he didn't play. I knew why and he answered it hemming and hawing. He said, "Well, I play Eastern style." He's a wide open player, and in the West they're more conservative. What he was trying to say was that he liked to toss up left-handed running hook shots from 20 feet out when he's right-handed and the score was tied with a minute to go. He is what he is. He's like a racehorse. If he's going good, you take him to the Kentucky Derby. If he's not, you keep him in the barn. Maybe we'll use you the next game. It's kind of a shame. When he's going good I really enjoy watching him play. He can pass, he can handle the ball, he's got great moves. But he'll drive a coach crazy. When he comes on the court there's no such thing as a play. It's "Give me the ball and get out of the way."

The only time that style of play really helped the Jazz was when they were in a rut. He was the kind of guy who could get something going. If you've got five guys who can't get going, that's when you give Chris a call. Maybe he can pick up everybody. Instead of going back with your starters when you're down 15, maybe he can bring us back. If he's hitting his shots, making those flyers or an exciting no-look pass, that pumps up the other guys. It gets everybody involved, back on track, and now he has done his job. That's the way the Jazz tried to use him. That's kind of a left-handed compliment, but it is a compliment. He does have that ability and if he's hot he can get you back in the game. If he could play 20 or 25 minutes a game and play within himself, play the team game, he could have really helped this team. We needed that guy, we needed shooters.

Greg Ostertag has great skills but is not in the right frame of mind for NBA basketball. He wants to high-five a guy who blocks his shot and say, "Hey, nice block," instead of turning around and punching him in the mouth. He doesn't have that killer instinct. He doesn't compete and he's not in shape. He's got a lot of baby fat. If he followed Karl Malone's work ethic it would be unbelievable what he could do, if he would just put the effort out. I think he's a wasted talent. He's not stupid and he's still young enough that he could change it around if somebody could get to him. But I don't think they can. What's missing with him is something you don't teach. It's inside, it's in your heart; it's instinct to play hard every second, to not let anybody embarrass you. It's like he doesn't even care, he just kind of floats. There's something that's ingrained in you. Maybe it's the way he was brought up, who knows? Different players react differently. You see a talented guy like Chris Morris who doesn't really produce to his ability with all the skills he has. You see a guy like Ostertag and you think about how good he could be and you'll never see it. Compare him to a guy like Jim McIlvaine at Seattle. That guy doesn't have any talent but he wants to play so badly he gets out there and busts his butt. Then you've got Ostertag who has all the talent but he doesn't have what McIlvaine has. If you put the two together you'd have a great player, but the way things are, you don't have anything.

Greg Foster has to be a tough guy to coach because he has a little bit of redneck in him. He'll talk back when he shouldn't and tick off Sloan. Like most guys he doesn't want to come out of the game and he'll get that attitude. But he can flat out shoot the ball. He's an in-between player. He's not skilled enough to be a forward and put the ball on the floor, and he's not big enough to be a great center. At 6-11 he's forced to play center for the Jazz because they don't have anyone else, but he plays more like a small forward. He's most effective shooting out on the perimeter. But he's a role player and he's done a nice job here.

Adam Keefe is a studious guy, a Stanford graduate, and he has his own ideas about things, too. He can have a bit of an attitude and be a tough guy to coach at times but I like his hustle and his effort. He's a role player, but a team player. He's not looking to score a bunch of points, he plays for the team, and he plays hard. When it comes to offensive rebounds he has a nose for the ball. I attribute that to playing volleyball at Stanford and on the beach. Playing in that sand, he has become a quick jumper. He doesn't jump high but he jumps quick. He'll jump three times while other guys are jumping once. He might miss the rebound the first time but he gets right back up there. Or he can tip the ball away from the traffic, then go grab it. Either that or he gets to it before the other guy even gets off the ground. He doesn't quit on a rebound and that comes from volleyball. He's aggressive and he has improved his shooting slightly. He's still not a good outside shooter but he's better than he was. He's smart enough to work on it, especially his free-throw shooting. He was a terrible free-throw shooter and now he's up over 80 percent. He's a great finisher too. He gets away with dunks over great shot-blockers because of that quickness. Other guys his size would get that shot blocked, but because he jumps so quickly he's got it in the hole before the defender can react. He moves well without the ball and he's not a bad defender against certain people. He is a step slow but there are people he can guard because he works hard at it.

Jerry Sloan has paid his dues as a coach. He scouted for the Chicago Bulls and the Jazz, and he served as an assistant coach for both teams. He has improved tremendously as a coach from his days coaching the Bulls. With the Jazz he was a very loyal assistant coach to Frank Layden—so loyal he gained 30 pounds one year running around with Frank. Those were the days when Frank weighed about 280. If Frank wanted to go somewhere to eat after a game, Jerry went with him because Frank was the boss. Jerry gained weight like crazy. I told him one time that he was really bulking up and he said it was from going out with Frank after games. That's the worst time to eat, late at night when you don't digest the food before you go to bed. But that was a point of loyalty. A lot of coaches go their own way but Jerry knew Frank wanted him with him. Jerry was always there for him.

He coaches a lot like he was as a player, hard-nosed, very defensive-minded. But the players love him, at least the main guys. Stockton, Malone and Hornacek really like him and those are the guys you want to like you. Morris might not like him and Foster has had his moments with him. He stands up for his players. He defends them and never criticized them in public.

Phil Johnson is the perfect assistant for Jerry Sloan. Jerry is very fortunate to have him. They really work well together and they're great friends off the court. Whenever Jerry is about to get thrown out, Phil always grabs him and steps between Jerry and the official, trying to keep him in the game. There's no jealousy there. Jerry will listen to Phil and Phil listens to Jerry. They've been a great combination. Phil was an assistant coach in Chicago when Jerry played there so they've known each other for almost 30 years. Phil won Coach of the Year honors in 1975 with Kansas City so Jerry has the ultimate respect for him, but he also knows Phil isn't trying to steal his job. In this league a lot of assistants are behind the coach's back trying to steal the job. But Jerry knows Phil would never do that to him so he's not afraid to take a back seat to Phil when Phil has a good idea. Sometimes it's Phil who stops practice to make a point to the team and Jerry just sits quietly on the sidelines, thankful to have an assistant like Phil who brings so much to the team.

Gordon Chiesa, the second assistant, does a nice job too. He's not in the same mold with Jerry and Phil, but he makes big contributions. He's a quiet guy who does a lot of the pencil work. He compiles the scouting reports on other teams and does a nice job of breaking down the opponent. He can tell you about any player in the country, whether he's in college or the pros. He also spends a lot of time after practice working with the shooters, and organizing drills for the players before games. Kenny Natt does a lot of that, too. He played for the Jazz in the 1980s and they paid him the ultimate compliment by bringing him back as a coach in 1996. He's a good guy and the other coaches like him.

Stability of ownership has been a big part of the team's success, too. They've only had two owners going into their 25th year, Sam Battistone and Larry Miller. They're exact opposites but both were good for the franchise. Sam kept the team going as long as he could. He was a very popular owner but he couldn't hold on long enough. When Sam was going to sell the team to a group in Minnesota before they got the Timberwolves, Larry stepped in and kept the team in Utah. Larry is a workaholic; all he does is work. That's his entertainment. He's a great businessman with great timing, but he's still got that kid in him. He shoots around with the team in pre-game warmups, the only owner in the NBA who does that. Larry was an athlete himself so he's like a kid with a new toy, and that's great. I've noticed a change for the better in him and better for his health. He doesn't blow off steam like he used to. With all the pressures he has from his businesses, he doesn't need to worry about whether we win or lose a game. This is supposed to be enjoyment, entertainment. He has learned how to be a fan, to come to the games to be entertained and not take it home with him.

I used to get that way as a broadcaster. It would just kill me when we got beat. I gradually started accepting it as a game. Sure I wanted us to win every game, but it's not going to happen so you've got to give credit to the other team. It's not always a matter of us losing, sometimes it's the other team winning. No point in getting wrapped up in something you can't control. It's the 12 players who control it and they want to win. They might try harder some nights than others but they don't want to lose any games. There have been close games that go to the wire and we lose, but I've been entertained. It's learning how to accept those nights and enjoy them as fun NBA games instead of letting the fact that we lost tear you up. You can be sad that we lost, but happy that you saw a great game.

From top to bottom, the Jazz are recognized as one of the better franchises in sports. They play by the rules. If they put a guy on the injured list, he's injured. You go back to the Rony Seikaly deal. He had an ankle injury the Jazz didn't know about and he refused to report, so the deal with Orlando was voided. Someone, whether it was the team or the agent or the player himself, was trying to hide the injury from the Jazz. Some teams do that. The Suns sent Neal Walk to the Jazz in New Orleans and he was hurt. The Jazz play it straight and they've shown it through the years, at least since they moved to Salt Lake.

It all came together in the 1996-97 season. You could tell early on there was something special about this team. Experience and depth, and a very, very mature Stockton and Malone. The Bulls came into the Delta Center early in the season with a 12-0 record and played well, but the Jazz beat them. This is such a psychological game and beating the Bulls did wonders for the Jazz. Two games later the Jazz had that great comeback against Denver, trailing by 36 points just before halftime then steam-rolling them in the second half, outscoring the Nuggets 71-33 over the final two quarters. The Jazz won by four points in the greatest recorded comeback in NBA history. That taught them to keep the faith because if they could come back in that game they could beat anybody.

The problem with getting that sort of confidence, though, is that you think you can turn it on whenever you want. When we're playing at home they have a tendency to let up because they know they can come back. Meanwhile that clock's running and all of the sudden you're out of time. We have had difficulty at times putting teams away for some reason. When you get teams down you need to step on them. We let them come back. If the great Lakers teams of the '80s ever got you down by 20, you were never going to get closer than 15 the rest of the game. They didn't let up when they got the big lead and they kept you down. They weren't going to let you make a run so they would have to pull the game out at the end and beat you by a point or two. They we're going to finish you off. The Bulls team that won 72 games did that. That's what great teams do. Paul Westhead, when he coached the Lakers with Magic Johnson and Kareem Abdul-Jabbar, would quote Shakespeare's Macbeth, saying, "If it were done when 'tis done, then 'twere well it were done quickly." Westhead was a Shakespearean scholar and he used that line in a timeout once. Magic said, "I know what you mean, coach. Get it in to the big guy," meaning Jabbar. But we haven't always done that.

By the end of the '97 season, though, the Jazz were rolling over everyone. The month of March was one of the best in franchise history. They went 14-1 and 11 of those games were on the road. You talk about March Madness, this was an incredible month for the franchise. They had the longest road trip in team history in the middle of the month, a seven-game Eastern swing, but the Jazz just got better and better. On an Eastern trip earlier in the season they went just 1-4. It was the lowest point of the season, but they stayed upbeat.

That first trip in January started out in Chicago where they got beat pretty bad, and they even got whipped by the expansion Toronto Raptors. They limped into Philadelphia on the tail end of the trip, just trying to avoid getting swept on the trip. The 76ers weren't very good, winning only 22 games that year, but they pushed the Jazz into overtime. The Jazz escaped with a one-point victory, though, and came home to lick their wounds.

They eked out a victory over Phoenix, then went back on the road to Vancouver and thumped them pretty good. Now they were winning again. It was only a modest three-game winning streak, but you could see they were headed in the right direction. Give Jerry Sloan a lot of credit for that. As a player he never stopped competing and he's the same way as a coach. He tells players there are going to be some bad times but they have to fight through them and things will work out. And that's what happened. The stars especially kept fighting. When they went out on that extended road trip in March they won six of seven. Malone averaged 31 points a game for the month and won the NBA Player of the Month award, and Jerry Sloan was named Coach of the Month for March. They closed out the month with nine straight wins, and they won their first six games in April to give them their second 15-game winning streak of the season. They lost only once in April, then closed out the season with four straight victories to roll into the playoffs.

Not only did the Jazz have great momentum, winning 19 of 20, they also got a great draw in the playoffs. We played the Clippers in the first round and they were 10 games below .500 that season. They were no threat and the Jazz got their first sweep in playoff history, as they should have. There were no surprises in that series. It helps any time you can put away a team early. Some people point to the layoff you have waiting for the next series to start when you sweep somebody, arguing you can get stale. But I think because of the time of year, it has been a long season and rest is the most important thing. The quicker you finish off a team, that's to your advantage, especially if the team you're going to play has to go the full five or seven games.

While the Jazz swept the Clippers 3-0, the Lakers were extended to four games before beating Portland 3-1. That gave the Jazz five days off before facing the Lakers, who only had one day off. The Jazz might have been a bit rusty, but the Lakers were tired and the Jazz won the first game of that series by 16 points. That put the Lakers back on their heels and the Jazz beat them 4-1 in the series. Houston, meanwhile, needed seven games to beat Seattle in the second round, the Jazz had six more days off before facing the Rockets in the conference finals. The Jazz won the first game of that series by 15 points, so it's a big advantage to put teams away early. Not only do you get extra rest, you get to watch the end of that other series and look at both teams. That helps you prepare for the next round because teams usually make a few minor changes in the playoffs.

Perhaps most important that year, we avoided Seattle. I think we still would have beaten the Sonics, but it would have been a war. Houston beat them in the conference semifinals, though, and the Rockets were a better matchup for us. Seattle plays us better because they are really physical defensively. They just manhandle Stockton. They know John has the ball all the time, so they try to take it out of his hands. They double-team him, they bump him, just get very physical with him. They show you different defenses.

But instead of facing Gary Payton, who is much bigger and a great defender, the Jazz drew Houston and Matt Maloney. Stockton eats Maloney's lunch. Payton makes Stockton work his tail off at both ends of the court, but Stockton has time to rest when he's playing against Matt Maloney. When I saw we were playing Houston I said it was over. No way could Maloney play Stockton. John has always had big games against Houston. Like in the game that sent us to the NBA Finals, he took the game over in the fourth quarter.

There was a game at Houston midway through the season when the Jazz were down by four with about 24 seconds left but Stockton hit a 3-pointer to help them force overtime, and the Jazz won by five. John knows he can score against Houston when he has to. He can get a shot whenever he wants to. Maloney played better against Stockton in the 1998 playoffs, but in '97 he was no match. That was the whole difference in the conference finals. They had no one to play Stockton, where Seattle would have made it awfully tough on John. And they had Shawn Kemp then, too. He could at times get Karl in foul trouble. So we dodged a bullet because we didn't have to play Seattle. We got the right team. That's not to take away from the Jazz because I think they would have beaten either one of them, but it would have been a lot harder beating Seattle than beating Houston.

The key matchups in our favor throughout the playoffs was at point guard. The Clippers didn't have a top point guard. Nick Van Exel of the Lakers was erratic and feuding with his coach when the Jazz faced them, and Maloney didn't have a chance. The toughest matchup was at center, with Shaquille O'Neal of the Lakers followed by Hakeem Olajuwon of the Rockets. Greg Ostertag did OK against those guys, but the biggest difference Greg made was being a defensive presence against the other four guys on the court. Forget about Olajuwon because Greg wasn't going to stop him. Where he made a difference was when he could stop the other guys. When he could stop Clyde Drexler from getting on top of the basket, when he could get in the way of the guys who like driving to the basket, he was effective. When he could switch over and help, when he clogged up the middle, that made a big difference. That's why the Celtics won so many championships when they had Bill Russell in the middle. You didn't dare go in there because he was going to hand it right back to you. A big guy in there changes the whole complexion of the game not just for the opposing center but for the other four guys as well. That's where Ostertag was valuable to the team in the playoffs.

That's the same reason Mark Eaton was so valuable to the team for so many years. He made you change your shot coming into the lane. We don't have anybody like that on this team other than Ostertag once in a while when he wants to play. He can make all the difference in the world. Greg Foster can't do it because he's not big enough. Antoine Carr is a great shot-blocker in close to the hoop, but he's only 6-9 and he's not quick enough to help on other guys the way a 7-footer could. You can move Karl Malone to center but defensively he has to worry about getting in foul trouble. If you lose him to foul trouble you lose a big chunk of your offense, and

the Jazz can't afford to put him in that position. That's why Greg
Ostertag was so important.

Right around mid-season in 1997 when Karl Malone got on a
roll, there was an inkling he might have a shot at winning the league's
Most Valuable Player award. "Karl for MVP" signs started showing
up at the Delta Center and the pressure started. Personally, I think
Karl wanted to win the MVP award. He was proud of it, to prove
who he was. It brought recognition to the state of Utah, to the
team and to Karl. It was great for the Jazz, it was great for the state.
We get recognition through Karl Malone.

By getting named MVP a couple weeks before the series with
Chicago started, though, I thought Karl carried a tremendous bur-
den into the Finals. He deserved the award, but they should have
held off announcing it until after the playoffs. He received the award
just before Game 1 of the conference finals with the Rockets, but
then he had to go against Michael Jordan, the greatest player in the
world. By time the Jazz finally got to the Finals, Karl had the weight
of the world on his shoulders because he had the MVP trophy instead of Jordan. In all of his interviews, Karl said he was focused on
the playoffs, on playing for a championship, but it had to be in the
back of his mind that he was going against Jordan and if he didn't
produce people were going to say he didn't deserve the MVP award.

It's hard to comprehend just how much pressure that put on
Karl, but I thought he handled it well. That's a terrible position to
be in. I think the NBA makes a mistake announcing the MVP award
while the playoffs are still going on. I understand why they do it, to
get the publicity that it generates for the playoffs. They want to get
all the ballyhoo they can. But that's an injustice, in our case to Malone
and the Jazz. The votes can be in but it shouldn't be announced
until after the championship game. Karl had that off his back in
1998, though. His approach in the NBA Finals was different because he didn't have the same pressure.

With just a couple minor breaks, the Jazz could have won a
championship in 1997. They lost to the Bulls four games to two,
but in three of those losses the margin of defeat was razor-thin. In
Game 1 the score was tied with 9.2 seconds left and Karl went to
the line for two free throws. He missed them both and that set up
a final shot for the Bulls to win it, which Michael Jordan did with a
19-foot jumper at the buzzer. There wasn't as much pressure on
Jordan when he took that shot because if he missed they still would
have gone to overtime. But if Malone had made even one of those

free throws, then Chicago would have been down by a point and they would have lost if Jordan missed. That shot becomes a little tougher to make when you're one down than when the score's tied. If Karl makes both of those free throws, or even one of two, that might have changed the whole series around.

The Bulls won easily in Game 2, the only real lopsided game of the series. Back home for the next three games, the Jazz won the first two to even the series at two games apiece, and we had them beat in Game 5 before letting it slip away. The Jazz rolled to a 13-point lead in the first quarter and still led by five going into the fourth quarter, but the Bulls pulled out a two-point victory. If we would have won that damn thing, we would have gone back to Chicago up 3-2 and we might have won one of the two there. We lost the series 4-2, but we could have won five out of the six games. It just wasn't to be. That's where experience comes in. The margin of victory was so slim for the Bulls that there were any number of things that could have swung the series in our favor. The Bulls had been through it four times before, though, and everything was new for the Jazz.

After the experience gained from playing in the NBA Finals for the first time in 1997, I always felt if they could ever get back, the Jazz would win it all. I thought the toughest part of the 1997-98 season would be winning the Western Conference. Once they got that far, I thought they were going to win it all. I thought the experience from the year before would be the difference.

Michael Jordan, however, had other ideas.

Chapter Twenty-six

BEST OF THE BEST: I'VE SEEN THEM ALL

When the NBA celebrated its 50th anniversary by bringing together the 50 greatest players of all time, there were plenty of debates over who should have been on the list. And if you get that many arguments over the top 50, you can imagine how difficult it is to come up with just one player, the single best. Or even a best five. I have my thoughts, though. Of the 50 Greatest Players in NBA History, I've seen every one of them play. There's only one guy on the list whom I haven't either been a teammate with, played against or seen as a broadcaster throughout his career. That's George Mikan—and he was my coach my rookie year. He played more in practice that year than the guys on the team. So I've seen 'em all. For the greatest player of all time, I have two—Michael Jordan in the air and Larry Bird on the floor. Bird couldn't run or jump, but he still did everything on the court. And he won. Jordan is the most prolific scorer in NBA history and a perennial All-Defense selection, and he won too.

My list of the five greatest, regardless of position, are Jordan, Bird, Magic Johnson, Oscar Robertson and Jerry West. Four of them are guards and Bird was a point-forward, but those are the five best players ever in my eyes. If you think there's a problem without a center on that team, I'll coach them and take on anyone. I'll be the sixth man, too, a player-coach. We'll go small and kick everyone's butt. Magic has the hook shot so he can play center, I'll put Jordan at small forward and Bird at power forward, and let West and Robertson play the backcourt. You'd better be very careful with the ball when West and Jordan are guarding you. Those are two of the best defensive players of all time. I'm 3-0 coaching and I think I might keep my record intact with this group.

Since I've been a part of the NBA for five decades, from the '50s through the '90s, I've compiled a list of whom I consider the five greatest players of each decade, regardless of position. That's why my teams from the 1950s, '60s and '70s are top-heavy with two centers each. The teams for the '80s and '90s are balanced with two guards, two forwards and one center. I also have cast my vote for the five greatest teams of all-time, as well was the five greatest showmen.

The 1950s

The players:	Bill Russell, Celtics
	Bob Cousy, Celtics
	George Mikan, Lakers
	Bob Pettit, Hawks
	Paul Arizin, Warriors
Sixth man:	Dolph Schayes
The coach:	John Kundla, Lakers
The team:	Minneapolis Lakers

There isn't a person alive who wouldn't pick those first four guys—Bill Russell, Bob Cousy, George Mikan and Bob Pettit—as the greatest players of the 1950s. Mikan and Russell both played center, but you can't leave either one off. Mikan was the most dominating player in the league the first part of the decade and Russell was so dominating by the end of the decade, they both have to be on the team. There is a famous picture of Mikan posing in front of the marquee at Madison Square Garden that promotes that night's game with "GEO MIKAN vs. KNICKS" in bold letters. It wasn't the Minneapolis Lakers on the marquee, it was just Mikan, he was that big. I knew all about him as a kid and then I ended up playing for him my rookie year. He led the Lakers to four championships in the 50s, but Russell entered the league in the 1956-57 season and won a championship his first season.

If Mikan was the first big gate attraction in the NBA, Cousy was the second. He was the guy people came to see when I first came into the league. Pete Maravich was a draw at the gate like that years later, followed by guys like Julius Erving and Michael Jordan. If you could only see one player you came to see Cousy, he had that appeal. He was a showman and a ballhandler, a great passer and a great dribbler. He was a winner, too, playing on six championship teams. He was the best I've ever seen on the fast break, just a master at making the right decision, the right pass. He had the behind-the-back dribble and was the best I've ever seen at the wrap-around, passing the ball around his body in full stride and dishing it off to a shooter. And he did it without traveling. He wasn't a good shooter; he played 13 years and never shot over 39 percent for a season, but nobody shot well back then. He would make them in the clutch, though, and he could shoot free throws, too—80 percent for his career. He was 6-foot-1 but had long arms and great hands. He was a smart player and a leader on the court. He was my idol growing up—I remember when I was in school watching him score 50 points in a playoff game that went four overtimes. He only had 10 field goals, scoring 30 of his points at the free throw line in 32 attempts. I couldn't stop watching him—even when I had to play against him. He was captivating. You tended to watch him instead of defending him. You just marveled at the way he could handle the basketball.

Bill Russell was a big draw, too. He came to Boston six years after Cousy and that's when the Celtics started winning. Cousy lived off him. Not only was Russell the best defensive center of all time, the Celtics now had the great rebounder who could get the ball and get it out to Cousy to start a fast break. The year before Russell arrived, the Celtics gave up almost as many points as they scored themselves. In his first season in Boston they scored as much but gave up five fewer points a game. That's what defense and rebounding does for a team. They didn't keep track of blocked shots when he played but he could have averaged 10 a game. He was 6-9 with cat-like quickness and a great nose for the ball. If he didn't block the shot he made you change it. I remember driving against the Celtics once. I got by Cousy and was coming down the lane. Russell jumps over and yells, "Don't even think about it, Rod."

I said, "I'm not," and kept on going, dribbling back out to the top of the key.

To be very honest, I think it would be very hard for him or anybody to dominate the game today with 29 teams, not like Bill Russell did then. There were only eight teams when he came into the league in 1956 and 14 when he retired in 1969. But there's no doubt Bill Russell dominated the game defensively in the '50s and '60s. He was all about winning. He never ranked as high in popularity as some of the other great players, though. If you look at the popularity of individual Celtic players, it's Larry Bird, Bob Cousy and John Havlicek in that order. They're the three most popular players who ever played in Boston. Why wouldn't Russell be up there? The fact those three guys are white and Russell is black had to have something to do with it. Russell always thought of Boston as a racist city.

Bob Pettit was another great competitor, probably the best forward in basketball in the '50s. Elgin Baylor became the best but he didn't arrive in the league until 1958. Pettit was 6-9 and he played long. He kept the ball up high where the shorter players couldn't get at it. So many big guys want to bring it down where the little guys can knock it way. He would rebound it and go right back up with it, keeping the ball up high the whole time. He was an excellent jump shooter from 18 feet in and could dribble well enough to drive. He would take the one bounce and get a lot of mileage going to the hoop. Pettit was very team oriented too, a great competitor.

He could hold his own with the other stars, winning Most Valuable Player of the All-Star game three times.

The fifth spot was a tough call. Dolph Schayes deserves consideration. Maurice Stokes was a great player too. George Yardley of Detroit led the league in scoring one season but he never made the list of greatest players of all time. Johnny Kerr never missed a game and won a championship with Schayes in 1955. Bill Sharman, Cousy's running mate in Boston, was a great player too. But Paul Arizin led the league in scoring twice and finished second twice. He even took two years off for military service but managed to get back on top of his game, so he gets a slight edge over Schayes.

Arizin was always sniffling and fighting for his breath on the court. He was only 6-4 but played forward. He was a great jump shooter and a smart player; you couldn't stop him. He played on his tippy-toes, which gave him a quick first step. He was very competitive, too. No doubt about it, he was a good player.

Schayes was a good two-handed set shooter. He was 6-8 and played 16 years in the league. They didn't have the 3-point shot back then but he would shoot from out behind where the arc is today. Syracuse ran a play where they would swing the ball around and set up a three-man screen, three guys standing side by side. Schayes would fake in, then come around behind the screen from about 30 feet out to shoot a set shot. And you know what? Teams would fight to get over the screens and try to block it, that's how good he was on the two-handed set-shot. He had the greatest form, too. He always looked pretty when he shot. His feet were together and in his follow-through his hands flew up and glided through the air. He ran like a gazelle, too. He always had great form. He was great with his left hand, too. He was right handed and broke his right hand one year and had to play with a cast. To keep playing, he had to learn to shoot with his left hand and he became a good left-handed shooter. So by time his right hand healed he could shoot with either hand. The one thing I didn't like about him was that every time he drove to the basket, if you knocked the ball out of his hands or if he threw the ball up and missed he'd go "uggghhh!" He did that every time and they'd put him on the foul line. He would just drive in, throw it up and yell, and they'd call a foul. He was a master at that, intimidating the refs.

Vern Mikkelson was another great player from this era. He was a blue-collar player and strong as an ox. He fouled out of 127 games, more than anyone else in NBA history. How's that for getting your name in the record books? He averaged 15 to 18 points a game, he rebounded and hustled. He played hard and he dove on the floor for loose balls. Guys did that back then. They don't now. He had an odd move, though, when he got the ball in the low block with his back to the basket. He'd fake by throwing one arm up in the air. He wouldn't even ball-fake. He'd hold the ball with one hand, throw his other hand up in the air, then turn and shoot. That's the way he played, and the guy got elected to the Hall of Fame with that move. Unbelievable.

As a team, the Minneapolis Lakers won four of their five titles in the '50s with John Kundla coaching them. No one else came close to that, although the Celtics started their amazing run of championships in 1957. Coaching wasn't nearly as sophisticated then as it is now. There wasn't a coaching staff with scouts and video coordinators. There was just the coach, so the game wasn't nearly as technical. You have to say coaches are better today because they have access to so much more information and a staff that can break it down for them. But in his day, Kundla obviously was the best coach because he won championships. He had great players, but he won. You can't win without great players, but some coaches have great players and still don't win. He was G.M. of the Lakers my rookie year, but I knew who he was from his coaching days. He was a legend. And when George Mikan was fired midway through my rookie year, Kundla returned to coaching, giving me a chance to play for him. He was very serious. He was all business, and it paid off for him with his election into the Hall of Fame.

The 1960s

The players: Jerry West, Lakers
                    Oscar Robertson, Royals
                    Elgin Baylor, Lakers
                    Bill Russell, Celtics
                    Wilt Chamberlain, Warriors, 76ers

Sixth man: John Havlicek, Celtics
The coach: Red Auerbach, Celtics
The team: The Boston Celtics

Elgin Baylor made it to the NBA Finals eight times as a player but he never won a title, losing seven times to Boston and once to New York. It's too bad because he was such a great player and he had such a great career. He was an All-Star nine times in the '60s and averaged 34 points or more for a season three times, but he could never get that title.

Jerry West and Oscar Robertson were two of the five greatest players of all time and they came into the league together in 1960 after leading the U.S. Men's Basketball Team to an Olympic gold medal. They were two of the greatest guards of all time, so versatile and tremendous both offensively and defensively. The only other time two of the all-time greats came in together was in 1979 when Larry Bird and Magic Johnson arrived.

The big debate of the 1960s, though, wasn't about the guards. It was over who was the better center, Bill Russell or Wilt Chamberlain. They were not the same kind of player, so it's hard to compare. Russell was 6-9 and defensive minded; Wilt was 7-1 and offensive minded. Russell relied on quickness as his greatest asset, while Chamberlain relied on brute strength. Wilt was the strongest player ever to play the game. Wilt had skinny legs like mine, but from the waist up he was built like Karl Malone, only bigger.

If you go strictly by statistics, it was Chamberlain over Russell by a landslide. He averaged 30 points a game for his career and once averaged 50 points for a season. And no one has come close to the 100-point game he had against the New York Knicks in 1962. He led the league in rebounding 11 times, twice averaging 27 a game for a season. And when he was criticized for being too much of a scorer, he went out the next season and averaged 8.6 assists. In 1960 he was both Rookie of the Year and Most Valuable Player of the league. He wasn't the defensive player Russell was, but he was a good defender. Mostly, though, he was an offensive force. He finished with 31,000 points in his career and there's no question in my mind if he had wanted to play 20 years like Kareem Abdul-Jabbar did—which Wilt could have easily—he could have scored 50,000 points for his career. It's amazing he could score all those points, though, because he may have been the worst free-throw shooter in NBA history. He missed more than 5,800 free throws for his career, shooting just .511 from the line. And he only had one shot from the field, a fall-away bank shot from the left side. He always had to bank it, and it was always from the left side. But it was a great shot. He could dunk, of course, and they called him The Dipper because he would dipsy-doodle to the basket and let the ball roll in off his fingertips. But other than that, the only real shot he had was that fade-away banker.

Wilt never came out of the game, either, playing all 48 minutes almost every night. One year he averaged 48.5 minutes a game for the season because of overtimes, an all-time record. For his career he averaged almost 46 minutes a game. Maybe even more amazing is the fact he never fouled out of a single game his entire career.

If you go by winning, though, it's Russell over Chamberlain in a landslide. Russell won 11 championships in 13 years, including nine in the 1960s. His statistical numbers don't stand out because he wasn't a great scorer and because they didn't record blocked shots back then. If they counted blocks, he probably could have averaged a triple-double for several years in a row. He averaged 15 points a game for his career, but that wasn't what he was about. He could score in the clutch, and make his free throws too, but he might have been the greatest shot-blocker of all time. He's nowhere in the record book because no one started counting until four years after he retired. He was a great rebounder like Chamberlain, averaging 22.5 rebounds a game for his career and leading the league five times. He was a poor free-throw shooter like Chamberlain, only making 56 percent for his career, but he was good in the clutch.

It was the winning, though, that made Russell great. He'd walk into a restaurant after a game with Philadelphia and someone would ask, "How many did Wilt get on you?" and he'd break out in a smile and say "50." Then they'd ask him who won and he'd say, "We did!" and start cackling. Russell would get 15 points, 30 rebounds and block 10 shots, and the Celtics would win the game. Russell never took the matchup with Wilt as a personal battle. He didn't have an ego about Wilt outscoring him, he only cared about winning the game. So instead of spending the whole game just trying to stop Chamberlain, Bill would be helping out on the other guys. If someone was driving the lane, Bill would leave Wilt and step over.

Wilt was too strong for him. He was much taller and had a bigger body. If Russell tried to stop him it would be a losing battle because Wilt would get his points anyway. But even if Wilt had a big game, Russell made sure none of Wilt's teammates did much.

Russell didn't have to worry about scoring because he was surrounded by good players, an unbelievable supporting cast with guys like Cousy, Sam Jones, John Havlicek, Tom Heinsohn and K.C. Jones. Whenever people argued Russell was better than Wilt because he won all those championships, that bothered Wilt because he felt Russell had a better cast to play with. Wilt used to complain about that, saying, "How come when Boston loses a game they don't say it was Russell's fault, but when we lose it's always ol' Wilty's fault?" He was bugged by that. Russell got in his craw.

But Wilt was surrounded by good players too. The Philadelphia 76ers won the title in 1967, the only year in the '60s that Boston didn't win, and they won 68 games that year. There were guys like Hal Greer, Chet Walker, Billy Cunningham, Wali Jones, Luke Jackson and Larry Costello on that team with Chamberlain and many people consider it one of the greatest teams of all time. There was a lot of talent alongside Wilt.

After Russell retired, especially when he was working on CBS, he would always get asked to name his best five ever. He'd say Jerry West, Oscar Robertson, Elgin Baylor and Bob Pettit, and that's all he'd name, four players. And they'd say, "Well, who's the center?" Russell just laughed as if to say, "Who they hell you think is the center? Me." He knew he belonged on that list so he wouldn't even bother saying it. He would just pick four guys. When I played, the guys on our team all thought that Russell was the best player in the league. If you switch teams, putting Russell on Philadelphia and Chamberlain on Boston, Russell would have still won. Philadelphia would have had all those championships instead of Boston. That's why I vote for Russell over Chamberlain.

Havlicek once received the best compliment I've ever heard. Russell told me right to my face the best player he ever played with was John. Of all those great Celtics, he said Havlicek was the best. Russell never played with Larry Bird, but he played with an awful lot of the great ones, so that was a nice compliment for Havlicek to be singled out. The great thing about Havlicek was that he could play every position. The coach could send him in the game for anyone on the court, whoever needed to come out.

Red Auerbach loved the game and was a fiery coach. He had the referees in the palm of his hand. He worked the refs better than anyone I've ever seen. He was a great bench coach, too. He had a great feel for playing the right people at the right time. Coaching is all about how you treat players and how they treat you. He demanded a lot out of his players, but he also earned their respect. To this day the guys who played for him talk about him with respect. They always gave him their best. He was a good strategist, and he knew how to manipulate the lineup to get the most out of everyone. He was a great judge of talent, obviously.

Because they won every year, they always had the last pick of the first round, but they still came up with great players. Sam Jones was the last pick of the first round in 1957 and John Havlicek was the last pick of the first round in 1962. They were both among the 50 greatest, and they weren't picked right off the bat, so Auerbach snapped them up. He also pulled off the greatest trade of all time, sending Ed Macauley and Cliff Hagan to the St. Louis Hawks for Bill Russell. The Hawks drafted Russell but he never played for them. Boston wasn't the friendliest city for black athletes, but St. Louis was even tougher then. Macauley played for St. Louis University and Hagan was a great white player, so they made the trade, and Russell went on to win 11 world championships for the Celtics.

The 1970s

The Players:	Walt Frazier, Knicks
	Rick Barry, Warriors
	Elvin Hayes, Rockets, Bullets
	Wes Unseld, Bullets
	Kareem Abdul-Jabbar, Bucks, Lakers
Sixth man:	Bill Walton, Trail Blazers
The coach:	Red Holzman, Knicks
The team:	New York Knicks

We're going big on this team, the toughest one of them all to pick. There were a lot of guys who deserved to be on this team but when you're only picking five, this is what I come up with. With a front line of Kareem Abdul-Jabbar, Wes Unseld and Elvin Hayes, you have a huge lineup, but it's hard to leave any one of them off. And there were a lot of other big players left out. Willis Reed was a tough player and won a couple of championships with Walt Frazier, and he didn't make the cut. That's how good this team was. Moses Malone started his ABA career in 1974 and his NBA career in 1976, and he was left out too. Dave Cowens was a great forward.

Hayes and Unseld teamed up together for nine years on the Baltimore-Capital-Washington Bullets. Hayes had a great turnaround jump shot. It was similar to the one Karl Malone shoots today from 15 feet out, but Elvin's was all in one motion. When Karl has his back to the basket that far out, he turns and squares up, then shoots. Elvin would turn around, bounced it and bam! He'd shoot that quick. He was a great scorer and rebounder, just a terrific player. He played for the great Houston team in college and had some great battles with Jabbar in college and the pros.

Wes Unseld is one of my all-time favorite players. I loved the way he played. He was all about winning. You talk about a competitor, he always had that game face on, always scowling. He was tough but he never said much, he just played. Wes was a master at rebounding and the outlet pass. He was 6-7, which wasn't very tall for a center, but he had a big body. He had big legs, a big trunk and a big rear end. He could really block you out. No one has ever played center at 6-7 as well as he did. Like Wilt Chamberlain did nine years earlier, Unseld won Rookie of the Year and Most Valuable Player the same season, 1969. He won a championship with Hayes in 1978 and a rebounding title in 1975. Not only is he the Bullets' all-time rebounding leader, he's the franchise's all-time assist leader, too.

Abdul-Jabbar was equally dominant over two decades, playing 20 years and scoring more than 38,000 career points. In the 1970s he won one NBA title, four MVP awards, two scoring titles and a rebounding crown. In the 1980s he won five NBA titles and one MVP award. You could even count the 1960s when he won everything there is to win in New York City in high school and three national championships at UCLA, in addition to two College Player of the Year awards. What else was there for him to do? He had the greatest hook shot for a center of all time, the sky hook. Chamberlain always criticized him for his rebounding, saying a Labrador could get more rebounds. But Kareem got some rebounds, averaging 11.2 for his career. If he had to get them he got them, but he had to do so much at the other end of the floor he might not have been that aggressive on the defensive rebounding. When you name the three best centers of all time, he has to be there with Wilt and Bill Russell.

He mentioned me in his book because his mother thought I was the best announcer working college basketball games when he was in school. He asked me once to say hello to her on TV so I did.

If Rick Barry wasn't one of the five greatest players of all time, he certainly was in the top 10. Without question he belongs there, yet he rarely gets mentioned. It was his attitude that worked against him. He treated people rudely. You had to go where he wanted to go and you had to do things the way he wanted to do them. You had to do it his way. He always tried to suggest things and that irritated people. I liked the guy but I could see why other people didn't. We'd play a lot of gin rummy together and when I won he'd throw the cards against the wall and call me a lucky SOB. I think sometimes he tried too hard to be nice but didn't know how to pull it off. He doesn't know how to be a nice guy and that's a shame.

Here's a great example. The first year we worked together broadcasting games at CBS, when Game 7 of the playoffs was over he caught a flight home that night and I stayed over until the following morning. When I checked out of my hotel there was a letter waiting for me from Rick, telling me how much he enjoyed working with me and that he looked forward to working together again the next year. I was touched. It was a real nice letter and such a classy thing of him to do. No one does that. Then he adds, "P.S. You asshole, I'm still a better gin rummy player." He was joking of course and I took it the right way. But the P.S., where he was just joking around, is the type of thing some people would take the wrong way.

When it came to playing basketball, though, there's no denying he was a great talent. The first time I ever saw him play I went to a Lakers game when I was working for Converse and Jerry West was talking about him. He told me then I was about to see one of the greatest players ever to play this game, and he was right. That's something Jerry told me three times in my life when I was about to see someone for the first time. He'd call them one of the greatest players ever and he was right every time. The first was Oscar

Hot Rod Hundley: "You Gotta Love It, Baby!"

Robertson when I had to play against him in his first pro game and another was when I went to a college game with Jerry and we saw Bill Walton play at UCLA. Jerry told me that Walton was the best college basketball player in the world, and he was, the best college player I've ever seen. And the third was Rick Barry that night in L.A.

Rick was a great shooter and a great passer. He ran like a deer and he knew how to draw fouls. He could handle the middle on the fast break, too, better than any big guy other than Magic Johnson. He could fake and drive, and was one of the greatest free-throw shooters of all time shooting them underhanded. He shot .900 from the line for his career, which is second all-time to Mark Price. Rick wasn't considered that good defensively, but he could steal the ball. He had a great nose for the passing lane and knew how to play a guy so he could get the steal. He had more than 1,100 steals for his career and they didn't even keep track of them the first four years he played. He led the league with 228 in 1975, the year the War-riors won a championship. He had incredible shooting range too. He averaged more than 23 points a game for his career and that was without the 3-point line. They didn't have that until his last season in the league, 1979-80. Even at age 36, he made 73 3-point-ers that season, shooting 33 percent from behind the arc. He did have a hot head, though, always complaining to the referees. Al-ways.

Walt Frazier was one of the flashiest players in the league, but there was a lot of substance there, too. He was noted off the court for his Bonnie-and-Clyde hats and full-length fur coats. He drove a Rolls-Royce and always double- or triple-parked. He drove me around town in his Rolls once. We'd pull up to the clubs and instead of looking for a parking lot he'd leave it on the street and pay some-one to watch it. He did everything with style on the court, too. He was really good defensively and was a clutch player, too. He had the whole package, a great all-around game. He could pass the ball, dribble it, shoot it, defend and rebound well for his size. He was a smart player. He did it all. He and Jerry West had some great battles. He was a huge favorite as a player and he does a nice job now as a broadcaster. He's a nice man, very genuine. He's not conceited at all for all the fame he has enjoyed. He doesn't go around telling everyone how wonderful he is. He's a very down-to-earth guy. He also had one of the great games of all time no one ever talks about.

In Game 7 of the 1970 Finals against the Los Angeles Lakers, when the Knicks won their first championship ever, everyone remembers Willis Reed hobbling onto the court just before tipoff. Reed had a torn leg muscle and no one knew if he could play, so when he limped out of the locker room while everyone else was warming up he gave them an emotional lift. More than anything, that got inside Wilt Chamberlain's head, which was easy to do. Willis hit his first two shots and that was enough to psych Wilt out. He was playing on one leg and didn't do anything the rest of the game, but he got in Wilt's head. It was Frazier who won the game, though, scoring 36 points and also getting 19 assists and seven rebounds.

Bill Walton was great player, leading the Portland Trail Blazers to a championship in 1977, but he was injured too much to make the top five for the decade. He actually missed more games than he played in this decade. He was the best college player I've ever seen but his body just couldn't hold up. He might have become the best center who ever played if he could have been more durable. He had a love for the game and a very intelligent understanding of it. He was great at both ends of the court. He had it all: shot-blocking, shooting, passing, hustle, a passion for the game. The only thing missing was longevity. He played just 468 games, the equivalent of about five full seasons, over a span of 13 years. Shaquille O'Neal, at age 26, had already played nearly as many games.

If I wanted to add more guards to the '70s team, Jerry West played until 1974 and should be considered. Earl Monroe was a flashy player but when you're only picking five, it's hard to move him up.

Red Holzman was a great coach in the last three minutes of a game. He'd run players in and out like it was a football game. He'd have two offensive players and two defensive players he'd switch every time the clock stopped over the last two or three minutes of the game. If the Knicks had the ball out of bounds he'd put in a couple of shooters, and if the other team had the ball he would put in his best defensive players. He'd flip-flop them at every dead ball, back and forth, the same four guys two at a time. You don't see that a lot any more. He was an ex-player himself with a very astute basketball mind. He ran a figure-8 offense with a lot of ball movement where everyone got their hands on the ball, a lot of weaving in his half-court sets.

If you have players you win, and if you don't, you lose. Red Holzman had Frazier, Reed, Dave DeBusschere and later Earl Monroe, that's why he won. Of course, a lot of coaches who had talent didn't win, so Holzman had to have something to do with their success. They were a smart team. I don't know if it was Red rubbing off on them or if he just inherited a smart basketball team.

Eight different teams won championships in the '70s, with Boston and New York winning twice each, but I think the Knicks teams were a little better.

The 1980s

The Players:	Magic Johnson, Lakers
	Michael Jordan, Bulls
	Julius Erving, 76ers
	Larry Bird, Celtics
	Kareem Abdul-Jabbar, Lakers
Sixth man:	Moses Malone, Rockets, 76ers,
	Bullets, Hawks
Coach:	Pat Riley, Lakers
Team:	Los Angeles Lakers

The two most important years in NBA history might have been 1960 and 1979. Jerry West and Oscar Robertson came into the league together in 1960, heroes of the 1960 Olympics in Rome. They were household names already, so they did a lot for the popularity of the game. Then in 1979, Larry Bird and Magic Johnson came in together and carried the league to a new level. They really made the league go right from the start. Bird won Rookie of the Year and Magic won Most Valuable Player of the NBA Finals that first season. What they did for the NBA was bring the college fans with them to the NBA. It all started in Salt Lake City when they played in the 1979 NCAA championship game at the University of Utah. The whole nation fell in love with them that season and followed them to the pros.

I've never seen anyone who loves to play as much as Magic Johnson. He has a lust for basketball, an absolute love for the game. And he's got that smile that just lights up the room. Tiger Woods has that same smile. I worked as a sideline reporter for CBS during Magic's rookie year, and in the NBA Finals, I would grab a player for a quick word just before tip-off as he heads out on the court. I'd grab Magic and just before they cued me I'd tell him, "Five seconds, Magic, light 'em up, light 'em up." Then the camera would roll and he'd flash that grin that lit up the world. It was such a lovable look, and it was sincere, too, because you knew he loved to play. Even if he wasn't good enough to play in the NBA he would have been at the gym every night playing basketball. He was a 6-9 point guard, but not really. He was great at that position, but he really transcended it. I've always felt guys like Magic, Bird and Jordan didn't really have a position. They just chased the ball. They played anywhere they wanted and everyone else got out of the way. If they wanted to bring the ball down the court, they brought it down. They called Bird a point forward, and Magic had the ball all the time. All three of them had the ball all the time.

Magic won MVP of the NBA Finals his rookie year and Brent Musburger and I were the deciding vote. The Lakers were up three games to two going into Game 6 at Philadelphia. Kareem was hurt, so Magic played center that game and scored 42 points to lead the Lakers to victory. Jamaal Wilkes had 35 points that day and nobody remembers Wilkes was even on the team because of the game Magic had. In the closing minutes they came by to get our ballot for series MVP. They said they needed it because the voting was tied be-tween Magic and Kareem. I looked at Brent and said let's go with Magic and we did. He deserved it. Kareem didn't even play the final game. I emceed the awards banquet where Magic picked up the award and he said he was going to share it with the big fella.

Magic had that flare for showmanship like Cousy and Maravich, but there was substance to his game, too. He was a good shooter and had a nice hook shot. Here's a guy who played point guard and could shoot the hook shot. He could play center. He could play anywhere. He was an excellent shooter because the shots he took were on the run much of the time. He took 15-foot hook shots, too. Those were tough shots.

Magic had a hard time coaching because he wondered why guys wouldn't compete like him. Basketball was so much fun to him, the work was easy. Yet some guys only saw the work and didn't want to do it.

I was amazed Kareem remained competitive all those years, that he still had the desire at age 42 when he retired. I think Magic Johnson had a lot to do with it in his last years. Magic made him young again and kept him competitive. I don't think Kareem would have played more than 14 or 15 years if it wasn't for Magic. I broad-cast the first game Magic ever played, in San Diego against the Clip-pers. Kareem hit a hook shot from 17 feet out, right down the barrel on an out-of-bounds play and the Lakers won 103-102. The buzzer went off and Magic grabbed Kareem and started dancing like they won the world championship. Kareem, who was 32 at the time and entering his 11th season in the league, pointed out to Magic there were 81 more games to go and he needed to pace himself with the excitement. But Magic got him going.

Larry Bird did a lot of the things on the basketball court that Magic Johnson did, but they had different styles. Magic was more of a showman and Bird was more serious on the court. He didn't lollygag with the ball, his attitude was get it done now. As soon as you catch it, do something with it. Bird could have fun on the court, though. Once when the Jazz assigned a rookie to defend him, Bird hit about three shots in a row and looked over at Jerry Sloan, the Jazz coach, as if to say, "You keep this kid on me I'll throw his ass in the hoop." He was a great shooter, all the way out to 3-point range.

Bird was always my favorite player. From a coaching standpoint, Bird would be easier to coach because he does things wherever you need help. Jordan plays the game by himself. He doesn't need any help. Bird was more team-oriented in everything he did, the epitome of what a basketball player should be, just a fundamentally sound team player with exceptional skills. All great players made their teammates better and Jordan did that too, but no one was better at that than Bird. You talk about popular in Boston, he's by far the most popular player who has ever played for the Celtics.

Larry and Magic had the greatest admiration for each other, always talking about the other one with respect. They met each other in the NBA Finals three times in the mid-80s, extending the rivalry between the Lakers and the Celtics that started when I was playing with West and Baylor against Russell and Cousy.

If Magic and Bird brought the NBA to new heights, Michael Jordan kept it there. What can you say about Jordan? I first saw him in 1982 when he was a freshman at North Carolina. Each year, the National Association of Basketball Coaches issues a college Silver Anniversary team that honors five players from 25 years earlier. The award goes to guys who made contributions to the game of basketball and also achieved success in their chosen profession. I received that honor in 1982 and they presented the award at the Final Four. That's where I saw Jordan hit the winning shot for North Carolina in the championship game. I had never heard of Michael Jordan before then.

I've heard of him a few times since. Jordan didn't arrive until the 1984-85 season but he averaged 28 points his rookie year and won three scoring titles before the decade was out. The acrobatics he pulls in the air are unbelievable. He's one of the best showmen of all time, but also one of the most competitive players ever. When he turns it on, he simply refuses to let his team lose, he's such a fierce competitor. He just won't let them lose. The incredible shots he's made, the game-winners, there are just so many of them. He hit the shot to beat the Jazz in Game 1 of the 1997 NBA Finals and he's done it a couple times to Cleveland in the playoffs. He's the MVP of the NBA Finals every year he's been there. He's just a tremendous athlete. He's a competitor. He's a decent golfer and obviously a decent baseball player.

He is who he is. There has never been anybody like him in sports. He's the most popular athlete in the world since Muhammad Ali and Pele. Those three have to be the most popular athletes of all time. Soccer has been the No. 1 sport in the world and boxing speaks for itself, so that shows you how much basketball has grown around the world. The way he handles everything just amazes me. He can't go anywhere because of his popularity—he gets mobbed everywhere he goes. He has to sneak in and out of hotels, and he has to go into a movie after it starts and leave before it ends.

Despite all the demands on him he's very gracious. I went into the visitors' locker room before a game one night when the Bulls were in town. I had a copy of Michael's new book and wanted to get it autographed. He was on the trainer's table getting his ankles taped when I walked in and we made small talk. I handed him the book, which he graciously signed, and we chatted some more. As I got set to leave I glanced inside the book and noticed he signed his name but nothing else. I said, "Michael, do you mind personalizing it?" He said, "It's for you?" He was surprised I wanted his autograph. He thought I was getting it for someone else. So he took the book back and wrote, "Hot Rod, Thanks for everything," above his signature.

The biggest star in the ABA, Julius Erving's best years were split between the two leagues, but he did win a championship with the Philadelphia 76ers in 1983 and was the Most Valuable Player of the NBA in 1981. He was an early model of Michael Jordan, an acrobat on the basketball court. And a great guy, too. Of all the players who ever played in either league, Julius would have to be the ambassador of goodwill for the game of basketball. He handled himself with class, a real gentleman. Michael Jordan has a lot of that in him too. Same thing with hangtime. Jordan and Dr. J. were both unbelievable the way they could float through the air. Julius would float to the basket with the ball stretched out in one hand and seem to hang forever. Jordan could change hands and flip it up, float to the basket from one side, going underneath the hoop and coming out the other to reverse dunk.

Julius did a lot of that too, a master of the reverse dunk. His jump shot was suspect from outside 18 feet. Jordan was a better shooter. Dr. J was a tremendous leaper for someone 6-foot-7 and he had unbelievable quickness for a guy that big. It was impossible for anybody not to enjoy watching him play basketball. He was going to electrify you every time he stepped on the court. You knew he was going to do something, just like Jordan, a tremendous gate attraction.

Utah played the first-ever regulation NBA game outside the United States in 1990 when the Jazz and Phoenix Suns played two games in Tokyo. Dr. J and I put on a basketball clinic there sponsored by Converse and at the end, he and I played a game of H-O-R-S-E for the crowd. I was beating him, H-O-R to H-O-R-S, but that's when he got serious. He took the basketball and stood out of bounds underneath the basket, a good three feet behind the backboard, and jumped out and up and dunked the ball. I was 56 years old at the time but I couldn't even make that shot when I was 20. So he got me on that shot, then did another one like it and that was it. He beat me.

It's hard to leave Moses Malone off this team. He was a blue-collar superstar, a four-time rebounding champion who won two of his three MVP awards in the 80s, as well as a championship with Philadelphia in 1983. He went straight from high school to the pros, playing for the Utah Stars in the ABA. He was a tremendous rebounder and a good scorer, but he lacked the fundamental skills of other superstars. I think he would have picked that up if he had gone to college. He was a great player, though. He was strong and tough, crude but effective, blue collar all the way.

Clearly, this team is the best of the five decades, and you don't have to look any further than a guy who didn't make it. If Moses Malone can't make the cut, it's got to be a great team. Adrian Dantley, a six-time All-Star, led the league in scoring twice and he didn't make the cut either. Karl Malone was a great scorer in the '80s but it was in the '90s that he became a great player.

Pat Riley just walked in on a great situation when he was handed the coaching job with the Lakers, but he did a great job with it. He's a better coach than I ever gave him credit for. He had Magic Johnson, Kareem Abdul-Jabbar and James Worthy, three of the 50 greatest players of all time playing for him, so of course he was going to win. He lucked out and he used to admit it, but as the years went by, he was less humble about it. When you look at the job he did with New York and then Miami, however, he proved he was more than just a coach who got lucky with the Lakers. He's an extremely hard worker and a student of the game. He worked hard as a player, too, hustling for everything to help his team because he was a very average player. He didn't have enough talent to play a lot and that helped him become a great coach. He sat on the bench and learned the game from the sidelines.

Bench players make the best coaches. It's unusual for a great player to become a great coach. Bill Russell wasn't that great of a coach (except when he had himself as a player). Cousy wasn't that great of a coach. Riley was because of his playing background. He spends more time working at it probably than any coach in the business. His practice sessions are long, maybe too long. He tires guys out to the point where they get brain dead, and maybe it wears them down, too. But his teams are always prepared. On game nights he gets his guys out on the court before the other team has even arrived at the arena, and he walks them through plays they're going to see that night. He puts the time in. His work ethic is impeccable. At the same time he draws a lot of attention to himself, and he always goes to teams that have money so he can buy players. He gets his players, but the guy always wins once he gets them.

One of the greatest rivalries of all time was the Lakers and Celtics in the '80s, when they met three times in the NBA Finals. The Celtics won three titles in the decade, but the Lakers won five so they get the nod as the team of the '80s. Not only did they have three great stars in Magic, Abdul-Jabbar and Worthy, they had Byron Scott and A.C. Green.

The 1990s

The players: John Stockton, Jazz
                Michael Jordan, Bulls
                Charles Barkley, 76ers, Suns, Rockets
                Karl Malone, Jazz
                Hakeem Olajuwon, Rockets

Sixth man:	Grant Hill, Pistons
The coach:	Jerry Sloan, Jazz and Phil Jackson, Bulls
The team:	Chicago Bulls

Charles Barkley is a blue-collar player, but a showman, too. His heyday was from 1992 to 1996 when he played for the Phoenix Suns. That's when he was at his best. No doubt he was good in Philadelphia but he wasn't a complete player then, and in Houston he started to fade. He has a body like a steel block, a big trunk and a big rear end. Once he gets position you can't move him out of there because he's so strong. He's quick for a big guy and he can beat you one-on-one. He protects the ball with his body. It's hard to block his shot because he keeps the ball away from you.

Hakeem Olajuwon won two championships in Houston and when he's healthy, he's the best in the game, better than David Robinson and Patrick Ewing, who are overrated. Olajuwon is extremely competitive, one of the best centers of all time. He's a great shot-blocker, not quite in the same league as Bill Russell, but very good. And he had offensive skills to go with his defensive ability. Olajuwon grew up in Nigeria playing soccer, and that's where he learned to use his feet. He's got great footwork he picked up from soccer. He's got great, quick spin moves for a guy with big, shifty feet, and it helps that they let him walk. Olajuwon has an all-around game. He can defend, block shots, rebound and put the ball on the floor.

What else is there to say about Stockton, Malone and Jordan? All three of them have been perennial All-Stars and All-NBA players.

Grant Hill has a terrific all-around game—with one major weakness. He's not a great shooter. He's not a poor shooter, but his perimeter shooting hurts him. He is so quick and jumps so high it's easy for him to get to the basket, but because he's not a great shooter from 15 feet out, defenders can sag off him to try to stop the penetration. If I was guarding him, I'd make him shoot from the outside. If you play him tight he's going to get by you. Aside from that, though, he has the total package. He does everything. He gets triple-doubles galore, he's a great passer, a great ballhandler and a team-oriented player. I like the guy because he does a lot of little things that don't get noticed. He doesn't stand out. He's just another guy out there, then when the game's over you look at the stats and he's got 20 points, 15 rebounds and 10 assists, he stole the ball and you won the game. He's the kind of guy a coach would love to have.

The irony is that his coaches keep getting fired. He played for three coaches in Detroit his first four seasons.

David Robinson is an incredible athlete. He's tall, quick and strong. He has good moves, is a great scorer and he blocks shots, but he seems soft. There's something missing. Shaq O'Neal is strong but overrated. He could end up as one of the greatest of all time, but he's not there yet.

Chicago won six championships with Phil Jackson and he did a great job keeping some unique characters together. But it's the age-old question—is he a great coach or just lucky to have guys like Michael Jordan and Scottie Pippen playing for him? Jerry Sloan wins 50 or 60 games every year, and he does it without Jordan. Like Riley, Sloan was a blue-collar player who worked hard. But unlike Riley, he's not a self-promoter. Sloan doesn't draw attention to himself the way Riley does. Riley goes around in thousand-dollar suits. Jerry had a suit deal once where he got nice clothes, too. I told him he was the only guy I knew who could made a thousand-dollar suit look like it cost $50. He loved that line. He's more comfortable in khaki pants and a baseball cap from some farm implement dealer. He wasn't a great player, but he was a hard-working guy and he brought that with him into coaching. He knows the game in a book sense but he also has a great feel for the game and the players.

He doesn't have players who can go out and get their own shots one-on-one so he runs plays to get good shots for everyone. It might look like the same thing every time but there are a lot of variations off the half-court game. It's more than just Stockton and Malone. Sloan gets everybody involved. Lots of screens, lots of cutters, good ball movement and good shot selection. Sloan is a good teacher, too. Stockton and Hornacek set the best screens of anyone in the league and that was probably Sloan's teaching. He was a guard and because he wasn't a great offensive player he did everything he could to help his teammates who were. It's important to set screens and he taught these guys what that's about. A lot of that has rubbed off on his players.

He looks like he has a world of confidence but inside he's never comfortable, never satisfied. Jerry Sloan doesn't get a lot of recognition because he's not exciting, he's not a personality, just a dead-serious type of guy. He's recognized by his peers, though. He won the *Sporting News* Coach of the Year award in 1998 and that voting was done by the NBA's coaches. He also was the first player in Bulls history to have his number retired, and for 16 years he was the only one. His No. 4 now hangs on a banner in the United Center, along with Jordan's No. 23 and Bob Love's No. 10. The Bulls also gave Jerry a ring with diamonds forming the number "4," which he wears all the time. He's not a guy to draw attention to himself or get caught up in honors, so for him to wear the ring shows you how much that means to him.

The Greatest Teams

1962-63 Boston Celtics (58-22)
Bill Russell, Bob Cousy, John Havlicek, Sam Jones, Tom Heinsohn, Tom Sanders, Frank Ramsey, K. C. Jones, Clyde Lovellette, Jim Loscutoff.

1971-72 Los Angeles Lakers (69-13)
Jerry West, Wilt Chamberlain, Gail Goodrich, Jim McMillian, Happy Hairston, Flynn Robinson, Pat Riley.

1985-86 Boston Celtics (62-20)
Larry Bird, Kevin McHale, Robert Parish, Bill Walton, Dennis Johnson, Danny Ainge, Scott Wedman, Jerry Sichting.

1986-87 Los Angeles Lakers (65-17)
Kareem Abdul-Jabbar, Magic Johnson, James Worthy, Byron Scott, A.C. Green, Michael Cooper, Mychal Thompson, Kurt Rambis.

1995-96 Chicago Bulls (72-10)
Michael Jordan, Scottie Pippen, Dennis Rodman, Toni Kukoc, Ron Harper, Luc Longley, Steve Kerr, Bill Wennington.

The Celtics won the world championship 11 out of the 13 years Bill Russell was there and any one of those teams could be compared with the greatest ever. There were so many of great teams and great players to choose from. The 1962-63 team gets the nod not so much because of their record but because it was the only year Bob Cousy and John Havlicek played together. It was Cousy's last season and Havlicek's rookie year, so neither player was on top of his game, but Russell was, and the team also had Sam Jones, Tom Heinsohn, K.C. Jones and Tom Sanders. If those seven guys were all in their prime together, they might have never lost a game.

Wilt Chamberlain's Laker team with Jerry West and Gail Goodrich in 1971-72 won 33 in a row, the longest winning streak in sports history, and finished 69-13. That was the year Elgin Baylor retired. They were going along OK early in the season, but after nine games they called Elgin in and said they were going to put him on the bench. It was all done in private but he had been a starter all his life. He took that as a sign it was time to retire, so he did. The day he retired, the Lakers started their 33-game winning streak. Jim McMillian, a 6-5 small forward just like Elgin, moved into the starting lineup. He was a very steady player, averaging more than 18 points a game that season. He stepped into the lineup with Happy Hairston at forward, West and Goodrich at guard and Chamberlain at center. They were strong at every position. Pat Riley played on that team and Bill Sharman won coach of the year. Chamberlain and Hairston were the first duo ever to get more than 1,000 rebounds for the same team in the same season, and West and Goodrich both averaged 25 points a game, the best year ever for two guards. West also led the league in assists that year. That was probably the greatest backcourt I've ever seen. West was the best defensive guard of all time, and even though Goodrich wasn't great, he tried. On offense he was a scoring machine, a great shooter right-handed or left-handed. Baylor, by the way, did get a championship ring that year, even though he retired early in the season.

After Russell, Cousy and Havlicek had retired from the Celtics, the next generation of stars produced many great teams, too. In the mid 1980s they had Kevin McHale, Larry Bird and Robert Parish in the front court with Bill Walton coming off the bench. You talk about a great front line, that's hard to top. Then they had Danny Ainge and Dennis Johnson in the backcourt. Ainge says that's the best team of all time, probably because he was on it, but that certainly was one of them.

Then of course there's the Magic Johnson-Kareem Abdul-Jabbar era of the Lakers. They give you five championships teams to choose from. In 1986-87 they won 65 games and went 15-3 in the playoffs. They had Byron Scott, A.C. Green, Mychal Thompson, Michael Cooper and everyman Kurt Rambis on that team.

The 1995-96 Bulls won the most games ever, 72, but it wasn't the best team ever. They were just beating up on a saturated market. We have too many teams in this league. You spread the talent so thin that it's possible to win 72 games. The Bulls were a great team, no question about it, but I think there have been better teams. As great as Jordan is, the Celtics teams with Bird and McHale were better, and the Lakers teams that same time with Magic and Kareem were better. I would say the 1995-96 Bulls team would be third even though they won 72 games. They beat the Lakers' record of 69 wins in a season set in 1971-72, but there were 17 teams in the league then and 29 when the Bulls won 72. The talent was just spread too thin, but ... they had Michael Jordan. Any team with Jordan has to be recognized, that's how great he is. And with Scottie Pippen and Dennis Rodman, that gave them three great stars, which every great team had.

The Knicks had a great team with Bill Bradley, Willis Reed, Dave DeBusschere, Walt Frazier, Dick Barnett and Cazzie Russell. They won it in 1970, and by 1973 they still had most of those guys but had added Earl Monroe, Jerry Lucas and Phil Jackson. But they were a notch below my top five.

Some argue the 1966-67 Philadelphia 76ers team that won 68 games was the best ever. Wilt Chamberlain says it was better than the Lakers teams he played on in the early '70s. They had Wilt up front with Lucious Jackson and Chet Walker, and Billy Cunningham backing them up. Their front court was Hal Greer and Wali Jones.

And the Minneapolis Lakers with George Mikan, Jim Pollard and Vern Mikkelson merits consideration. They all had big names. Slater Martin and Arnie Ferrin played for them too. But it was a different game then. Those guys would have a hard time playing today.

So my five greatest teams of all time cover two eras with the Celtics, two eras with the Lakers and the Michael Jordan era in Chicago. And every one of those teams had three superstars. Russell, Cousy and Havlicek. Chamberlain, West and Goodrich. Bird, McHale and Parish. Johnson, Worthy and Abdul-Jabbar. Jordan, Pippen and Rodman.

The Showmen

The players: Pete Maravich, Hawks, Jazz
Julius Erving, 76ers
Michael Jordan, Bulls
Connie Hawkins, Suns, Lakers, Hawks
Magic Johnson, Lakers

Sixth man: Earl Monroe, Bullets, Knicks

Coach: Butch van Breda Kolff

These are the guys who put on a show every night. Some of them usually won and some didn't, but these guys were always performers. I'll tell you what, if I could have those six players, I would buy the Harlem Globetrotters. I'd borrow the money, do what ever it takes if I could have these six. Magic and Pistol Pete could play guard, Dr. J and Michael could play forward and Connie Hawkins would work at center.

Earl the Pearl could put you on your heels faster than anybody. Running at you on the fast break he'd start shakin' and bakin' and you didn't know what in the hell he was going to do. Most of the time he didn't either, so what chance did the defender have? He'd go five different directions at once. The crowds ate that stuff up. I played with him in a Legends game in 1989 and he was doing that then. He was 44 years old. But he can't crack this starting lineup. That's how good those other guys are.

As a coach, Butch van Breda Kolff was every bit as entertaining as any of these players. He was very hyper and fans loved to watch him run up and down the sidelines. During one game when he coached the Jazz in New Orleans, he split the seat of his pants in the second quarter. When he went into the locker room at halftime, he never bothered to look for safety pins or tape or anything to hold his pants together. He came out for the second half with the split seam still showing. He didn't care. He was too involved in coaching to care what he looked like, and fans loved him for it.

The most revealing aspect of the players on this list of great showmen is how tall they are. Earl Monroe is 6 3 but all of the other guys on the list are quite a bit taller. Maravich was 6-5, Jordan is 6-6, Dr. J is 6-7, Hawkins is 6-8, and Johnson is 6-9. There was a time when the showmen in the game were all little point guards in the Bob Cousy mold. Cousy is 6-1 and typical of what the showman used to be. Today, the showmen are much bigger. To be that tall and palming the ball, dribbling behind their back and playing to the crowds, that more than anything shows how far the game of basketball has progressed in the past 25 years.

Chapter Twenty-seven

"YOU GOTTA LOVE IT, BABY"

I had a courtside seat to so many unforgettable games in my broadcasting career, and John Stockton has accounted for many of them. He has hit some unbelievable shots to win games, and so has Karl Malone. One of Stockton's first big shots came in 1989 at the Salt Palace against the Chicago Bulls. He simply found a way to win that game, a trait we have seen many times throughout his career.

There were about three seconds left and the Jazz had the ball out of bounds in the back court, down by one. The Jazz called a timeout and set up the four-man picket fence, as I call it. Four players lined up across from the inbounder, then Stockton cut around the screens and scissored off to get the inbounds pass. With the clock winding down, he drove all the way down the right side of the court and made a running one-hander ducking around Michael Jordan at the buzzer to win the game. He got Jordan on the run, beat him to the hoop and shot it over him. The ball kind of hit and rolled around and fell in. The Jazz won by a point.

It was an unbelievable finish and Jordan remembered it, too, because the next year when the Bulls were in town for their annual game at the Salt Palace, Jordan hit a jumper at the buzzer to win it for Chicago, then jumped for joy, uncharacteristic for him in the regular season.

There were so many moments just as memorable. Here are some of the ones that stand out the most.

THE SHOT

May 29, 1997
This has to the be most famous—and most replayed—shot in Jazz history, John Stockton's 3-pointer in Houston to send his team to the world championships for the first time.

Even more incredible than the shot were the three minutes leading up to it when he just took that game over. He went crazy, hitting everything. It was like he said, "We're going to the Finals, baby" and he took us there. He was at his ever-lovin' best, scoring 13 points over the final 3:13 of the game to rally the Jazz from 10 points down to win the game. He did it all, getting assists on the two baskets he didn't score in that stretch and playing defense too as he came up with a big steal.

The Jazz closed out the game with a 19-6 flurry, capped by Stockton's long 3-pointer at the buzzer to close out the Western Conference Finals series. I've never in my life seen John so excited or jump so high as he did after making that shot. He has never dunked in his life but he could have done a reverse dunk right there, he was so high in the air.

At the time that was the biggest play in Jazz history but I never gave any thought to how I was going to call it. I probably should have but I just let it flow: "Stockton for 3 ... Stock! Got it! Unbelievable! John Stockton! John Stockton! It's over! The Jazz win it! We're on our way to the world championships in Chicago!"

OLAJUWON'S PUNCH

April 28, 1985
After all these years, this remains one of the most talked about games in Jazz history. The Houston Rockets were heavily favored in this first-round series in the 1985 playoffs. The Jazz were just a .500 team that season and the Rockets, with the Twin Towers of Hakeem Olajuwon and Ralph Sampson, finished 48-34. The Jazz caught the Rockets in the first game of the series, then snuck away with a two-point victory in Game 4 to even the best-of-five series 2-2. In the final game, though, the Jazz starters didn't have anything going. By then the Rockets knew the Jazz offense so well they were getting to spots before the Jazz did. So Frank Layden cleared the bench and told the guys not to run any plays, just go out and play loose and

free. While Adrian Dantley, Darrell Griffith and Rickey Green were sitting on the bench, guys like Jeff Wilkins, Fred Roberts and the Whopper, Billy Paultz, led a rally. The Rockets were getting so frustrated, Olajuwon threw a punch that landed square on Paultz's jaw. Olajuwon just cold-cocked him, standing there next to him and boom! a fist to the face. I don't know how much leverage Olajuwon could have gotten on the punch because he was standing flat-footed, but Paultz bailed out of there like he was dead, like Muhammad Ali hit him with a roundhouse hook. That served as the rallying cry for the Jazz, who finished off the Rockets to win the series with a 104-97 victory in Houston.

THE BRAWL

January 1972

One of my most memorable moments as a broadcaster came when Marquette played South Carolina at Columbia, S.C. in the 1971-'72 season. Marquette had a great team that year. Jim Chones and Bob Lackey were seniors, Allie McGuire was a junior and Maurice Lucas was a sophomore. They had a hell of a team with Al McGuire coaching, and South Carolina was pretty good, too. Frank McGuire was their coach and Tom Riker and Brian Winters played for him. All of those guys played pro ball.

Al and Frank McGuire weren't related but they had a long history together. Al played for Frank at St. John's and then went on to become his coaching rival. Both teams had great records that season and players on both sides knew how much this game meant to their coaches. It was a great game, which Marquette won 72-71, but the fight that broke out early in the second half was even more memorable than the game itself.

About three minutes into the second half, Bob Lackey and Tom Riker fought for a rebound. Lackey elbowed Riker, and Riker retaliated with a punch. In a matter of seconds, brawls had broken out all over the court. Marquette players were in a circle with their backs to each other, swinging at anyone and everyone, even the security guys in the red coats. A South Carolina state trooper went after Lackey, and they started playing the national anthem trying to calm people down. They must have played it for 15 or 20 minutes. I've never seen anything like it in college basketball. They finally got peace restored and played the game, but it was anticlimactic after that.

THE STREAK

January 1974

I worked both ends of UCLA's 88-game winning streak. Notre Dame beat the Bruins in 1971 when Austin Carr went off for 46 points, and UCLA then won 88 in a row before Notre Dame beat them again in 1974. South Bend was kind of a disappointing city the first time I was there. Here's Notre Dame, the biggest thing in college sports in this little old city. There was nothing there, just a school, and not a very big one at that. It was just a little Indiana town with a tiny airport. I got a real kick out of those games there, though, because of the incredible atmosphere in the Athletic and Convocation Center.

There were so many great players in that game the day the streak ended. Bill Walton was a senior for UCLA and Keith Wilkes and Dave Meyers were on that team. John Shumate and Adrian Dantley played for Notre Dame. Adrian was kind of a fat butt then. He wasn't in real good shape, but he ended up one of the best players the school has ever had. In the end, though, it was a guy named Dwight Clay who made the shot from the corner to win the game for the Irish.

Dick Enberg and I worked that game and what I remember more than anything about that day was watching Bill Walton before the game. The Bruins were out on the court warming up before Notre Dame took the floor and you could already feel the buzz in the crowd. Then when the Fighting Irish came running out the whole building erupted. The band started played their famous fight song and all the fans were singing along, "Cheer, cheer for old Notre Dame ..." at a fever pitch. It was unbelievable.

Walton was taking this all in, watching the home crowd react to the fight song, fans screaming and stomping their feet. He wasn't intimidated by it, he was thriving on it. The place was really rockin' now and he comes over to where we were broadcasting and says, "Isn't this the greatest thing in the world? This is what it's all about." He was the visiting player, the home crowd was in a frenzy, and his 88-game winning streak was on the line. And he was having a ball. Pressure? He loved everything about it. He couldn't wait for them to throw that damn ball in the air. I got such a kick out of watching him.

Three years earlier, he and a couple other freshmen were watching Notre Dame beat them on television and they were saying, "We're never going to let this happen to us."

LAKERS AND CELTICS

1969 NBA Finals

More people probably remember those classic series between the Lakers and Celtics in the 1980s, but their rivalry back in the '50s and '60s was something special, too. The Bill Russell and Bob Cousy era for the Celtics and the Elgin Baylor and Jerry West era for the Lakers produced some unbelievable games. I played in three of those series and was a part of two more as a Lakers broadcaster. What I remember most were the celebrations that never happened.

The first year I broadcast for the Lakers we had the series tied 2-2 but lost Game 5 in overtime when Don Nelson hit a shot that bounced around and went in at the end of regulation. We didn't have much left for Game 6 and lost the series, four games to two.

The next year we had a rematch with the Celtics in the Finals and this time we were in control of the series. The Lakers took a 3-2 lead with Game 6 at Boston Garden. If we won the game it would be over, we'd win the championship. Since I also was the traveling secretary in addition to broadcasting the game, it was my job to get the champagne for the celebration if we won. There was a train station underneath the Garden and they had a liquor store down there, so that's where I went to buy the champagne. I got a case or two and brought the bottles back to the locker room and put them on ice after the players went out on the court so they couldn't see them.

It was perfectly chilled after the game—but the Lakers lost and the coach made me take it all back. The bottles had been sitting in ice and now water, though, so some of the labels had washed off. So I lug the champagne back to the liquor store and half the labels were missing. The guy was a basketball fan so he knew who I was and he could understand the whole story, but he was still upset about the labels. He gave me back about half the money. That was embarrassing for me as well as the team.

So now it's back to Los Angeles for Game 7 and another shot at winning the title. This time Jack Kent Cooke had hundreds of balloons put up in the ceiling at the Forum, planning to drop them on the crowd after the Lakers won to kick off the party.

Butch van Breda Kolff was coaching the team then. We were down by about 10 in the second half and Wilt Chamberlain wants out of the game. He says he hurt his leg or something and takes a seat. So Butch sends in Mel Counts to play center and Mel is an instant matchup problem for Boston. He's 7 feet tall, but he can shoot the hell out of the ball from 15 feet out. He had a great jump shot and started firing away. We chipped away at the lead and all of the sudden there's a minute to go and we were only down by one. So Wilt got up and wanted to get back in the game. He said he was ready to play but Butch told him to sit down. He wouldn't put Wilt back in. He said they were going to win or lose the game with "Big Melvin."

Wilt was so mad he ended up getting Butch fired, but Butch wasn't going to back down from anyone. He had a lot of guts. I admired him for that. He always fought for his players, taking on the refs or anyone he needed to. This time he made a coaching decision. They were rolling, so why make a change? You could argue either way: You put in your best player to win the game, or you stay with your hot player. But he made his decision and stuck with it. Jerry West later said he had played for a lot of coaches but none of whom he would rather win for more than Butch van Breda Kolff. In the end, the Celtics won by two and as he was walking off the court Bill Russell said, "Now what are they going to do with those balloons?"

It just seemed like we could never get over the hump beating those guys. I felt so sorry for Jerry West because he had a horrible hamstring injury in that game, and he played his heart out. They were shooting Novocaine into his leg just so he could play. He played all 48 minutes that game and put on a phenomenal performance despite his hamstring, scoring 42 points and also getting 13 rebounds and 12 assists. I was in the locker room with him after the game and walked out with him. By then the Novocaine had worn off and he was in so much pain he could hardly even walk. To get outside from the locker room there was a long staircase he had to climb and he had to take it one step at a time just to get up. It was agony for him. Then when we got to the top and there were people around, he cleared his throat, straightened up and walked to his car without a trace of a limp. He wasn't going to let anyone know he was hurting. He's an amazing guy.

THE EPILOGUE
June 9, 1985

The Los Angeles Lakers lost to the Boston Celtics eight times in the NBA Finals before they finally beat them in a championship series.The Lakers eventually won a couple of championships beating someone else, but it wasn't until 1985—23 years after they first beat us—that L.A. finally knocked off Boston in the NBA Finals.

When the Lakers finally did beat them I was living in Utah watching it on TV and enjoying every minute of it.The Lakers had a three games-to-two lead in the series and were putting them away in Game 6.We were kicking Boston's ass for the first time ever and I was loving it. There was a minute or two left and they were up by about 12 and my phone rang.

I was wondering who could be calling at a time like this and it was Tom Hawkins, who I played with in L.A. He never calls me. He still lived in L.A. and we didn't really keep in touch, but he called to ask if I was watching. I say, "Damn right I'm watching," and he tells me he's got his uniform on! He's so excited the Lakers are finally beating the Celtics he put his old uniform on.That's how much beating Boston meant to us old Lakers.

To this day I have a lot of good friends who used to play for Boston, but collectively, I hate the Celtics, and so does anyone else who ever wore a Lakers uniform against them in the Finals.

THE CELEBRATION

June 1, 1979
I never had luck winning a championship with the Lakers as a player or broadcaster, so I got my first taste of a winner's locker room celebration in 1974 when I worked for CBS. Boston had a 3-2 lead in the series with the Milwaukee Bucks and looked like they were going to win it in Game 6 so I went to Boston's locker room to cover the post-game celebration. But every time it seemed like they had the game put away, Jabbar hit another hook shot and I came back to the court. Milwaukee ended up winning in double-overtime to force a Game 7, which Boston won. Between the two games I must have gone to the Boston locker room five times.

You're never ready for the mayhem, as I found out five years later when I covered the NBA Finals between Seattle and Washington for CBS. I worked the game with Brent Musburger and Bill Russell. Seattle had it all but wrapped up on Washington's floor in Game 5, so they had me get up from the table with about three minutes to go so I could get to the visitors' locker room ahead of the mob.We get things set up in there and I was listening to Brent call the end of the game on my headset, just me and the champagne in this quiet little locker room. After the game ended I heard on my headset the players are on the way. They come busting through that door and it was unbelievable. They're going crazy, the champagne was flying and I was fighting my way through it all getting interviews. I was doing all right on my end, talking to three or four players while I was waiting for Brent to get there to take over with the interviews, then sign us off the air.

But there was a problem. The mayhem was even worse outside the locker room than it was inside. The hallways were so crowded that Brent couldn't get in there. And the network was running out of time because the top of the hour was getting close. If we go over, then we have to carry the entire half hour. That costs the network and all hell breaks loose.

Bob Stenner and Sandy Grossman were the producer and director in the truck and while I'm interviewing Paul Silas, they start talking into my earphone. Just like any other locker room celebration you've ever seen, this place is absolute pandemonium and they're trying to get an urgent message to me. They tell me to nod if I can hear them, so I do. They say, "Brent is on his way but he will never get to that locker room. You have to take us off the air. Do you know what to say?" I nod again while Silas is still talking and they say, "OK, we'll count you down. If Brent comes through that door now you can't hand him the mike because you've got to get us off the air." They tell me as soon as Silas finishes his answer to get rid of him. Then they start the countdown. "29 ... 28 ... Musburger is coming through the door!" they scream. "Don't give him the mike!"

I see him make his way into the locker room and motion to him from below camera level to stay back. He knew what that was about and stopped. So I turn to the camera and say "From the locker room of the world champions of 1979, the Seattle SuperSonics, I'm Rod Hundley for Brent Musburger and Bill Russell. Once again the final score, Seattle 97, Washington 93." ... 10 ... 9 ... "The NBA on CBS is a production of CBS Sports. Goodnight everybody." The next thing I hear is cheering in the truck like I was the one who won the championship. I felt like a big-league broadcaster then.

THE SIDEKICK

January 9, 1970

One of the most memorable moments ever came in one of my first games ever as a play-by-play man. I was an analyst for the Lakers, I was an analyst for the networks and was an analyst for the Suns. But after Bob Vache died I finished out the season doing play-by-play, and it was right about that time that Johnny Kerr got fired as coach of the Suns. So for half a season, Red and I teamed up on the broadcasts. The first game that we did together, the Suns were playing Milwaukee. It was Kareem Abdul-Jabbar's rookie year but he was still known as Lew Alcindor then. There were five seconds left in the game, the score was tied and the Suns got the ball at midcourt. I set the scene on the radio and said, "OK, Reds, what are they going to do?" He said, "How the hell do I know what they're going to do? If I did I wouldn't be sitting here with you."

THE COMEBACK

November 12, 1986

In a game against Dallas at the Salt Palace, the Jazz fell behind by 10 points in the third quarter and still trailed by seven in the final 30 seconds, setting the stage for one of the most amazing comebacks in team history. The Jazz ended up winning by a point and they didn't even need overtime to get there.

Rolando Blackman's basket with 28 seconds left made it 101-94 and sent the fans racing in droves for the exits. Karl Malone got a quick dunk to make it a five-point game but the clock was racing against the Jazz and few people gave it much thought. Even after the Jazz made a stop on defense and got the ball back, and even after Darrell Griffith sank a 3-pointer with seven seconds left to cut the lead to 101-99, the game still seemed out of reach.

The Jazz quickly fouled Blackman to stop the clock and he calmly sank both free throws. Now it was 103-99, and Dallas didn't even bother to play defense. Bobby Hansen scored quickly underneath so now the Mavericks' lead was back to two, but there were only three seconds left.

The Jazz didn't give up. They put full-court pressure on and Sam Perkins made a boneheaded play. He just wound up from out of bounds after Hansen's basket and threw the ball toward midcourt.

He just heaved it up in the air, putting it up for grabs. Rickey Green was standing right at midcourt and he picked it off. He had to jump as high as he could to get it, but he snatched it out of the air. He saw Griffith standing in front of the 3-point line a long way out and fired a two-handed pass from over his head. Rickey got the pass off before he ever hit the ground. Griff was wide open. He got the ball, turned and fired. The ball fell through the net at the buzzer and the Jazz won the game by a point.

What was left of the crowd went crazy, but by then, half of the fans were getting to their cars and turning on their radios for the postgame show. The Jazz scored eight points in the final seven seconds to win the game, and Griffith scored six of them.

I was giving them the final score on the radio and fans couldn't believe we won the game. I'm sure there were a lot of people in shock that we had won the game. And once that sunk in they were kicking themselves for missing it. That had to have been the damnedest comeback of all time.

Dick Motta, who was coaching the Mavericks at the time, said it best. "I've seen a lot of dumb things in my life," he told reporters after the game, "but none this dumb."

THE OTHER COMEBACK

November 27, 1996

The Dallas victory was spectacular because of how quickly the Jazz struck at the end of the game, but a victory 11 years later was just as remarkable because of how deep of a hole the Jazz climbed out of. They were playing the Denver Nuggets at the Delta Center and the Nuggets came out sizzling. They were hitting everything they put up and the Jazz looked shell-shocked. Denver built a 10-point lead in a matter of minutes and soon it was up to 20. Then 30. The Nuggets led by 36 just before halftime and were still up by 34 at the break. Then it was the Jazz's turn.

They never gave up and when Denver's shots stopped falling, the Jazz started making a game of it. There wasn't any one play that turned the game around, the Jazz just gradually started building momentum and they never gave up. It was a huge hole to dig out of but the Jazz kept working all the way to the final buzzer and walked off with a 107-103 victory.

THE REVENGE

January 27, 1990

Karl Malone was mad. It was midway through the 1989-90 season and he was averaging 31 points and 11 rebounds a game. The year before he was All-NBA First Team, yet he wasn't selected for the starting lineup of that year's All-Star game. He found out about two hours before a game with the Knicks that A.C. Green of the Lakers was voted into the starting lineup ahead of him in fan balloting—by only 1,300 votes. Malone was too shocked to react that night and scored 26 points against New York. After stewing about it for a day, though, Malone set out to show what an oversight that was, and it happened to be the Milwaukee Bucks that were in the way. It could have been anybody. They couldn't stop him and he just made 61. He was just ripping everything.

He scored 17 points in the first quarter, 13 in the second and 20 more in the third. He went back in the game for a couple minutes in the fourth quarter and had scored four points when coach Jerry Sloan sent Jose Ortiz in for him. With Ortiz waiting on the sidelines for a dead ball so he could check into the game, Malone reeled off seven more points in a span of 55 seconds. Karl ended up fouling someone on purpose just to stop the clock so he could come out. His entire line that night was magnificent: 21-of-26 from the field, 19-of-23 from the free throw line, and 18 rebounds in only 33 minutes. John Stockton had 16 assists that game and by beating the Bucks 144-96, it was the largest margin of victory in franchise history.

TRIPLE-OVERTIME AGAINST THE BULLS

February 3, 1992

For drama and entertainment, this game was as good as it gets with great plays and grand misses all night. The lead changed hands 18 times in the first quarter alone and the excitement never slowed. Michael Jordan missed a 20-footer that could have ended the game in regulation, and he missed two free throws late in the second overtime. But Jordan also hit a 3-pointer at the end of the first overtime to force the second, and his basket with 4.9 seconds left in the third overtime tied the score.

The Jazz had their shots too, like John Stockton's reverse layup at the end of regulation and his 3-pointer to force the third overtime.

But the lasting memory from this game was Jordan getting thrown out with half a second left in the third overtime. Big deal. They kicked him out of the game with 0:00.5 showing on the clock. Were they trying to make a statement? He was called for fouling Jeff Malone with less than a second left in the third overtime, plus the technical foul for bumping the ref while arguing the call, giving Jeff three free throws, which he sank to give the Jazz the 126-123 victory.

GAME 7 WITH THE LAKERS

May 21, 1988

This is the series where the Jazz arrived as a franchise on a competitive level. The Lakers won their fifth championship of the 1980s this year with Magic Johnson, Kareem Abdul-Jabbar and James Worthy, but the Jazz played with them to the wire in their second round playoff series. Our franchise finally realized, hey, we can beat anybody. Stop talking about being in a small market that nobody cares about. It seems like it's in the back of our minds as a franchise that we thought we were not going to get a call because we were the Utah Jazz. They wanted New York and L.A. in the Finals and all that. I don't believe in that. I think it would be great for basketball for Utah to win the world championship. It would be great for the NBA to get it spread out and have a small market win.

I think as a franchise we finally started to realize that in 1997 when we made it to the NBA Finals against the Chicago Bulls. But it started nine years earlier in that playoff run with the Lakers. Everywhere we go now, I don't care what city it is we're playing in, there are Jazz jerseys up there in the crowd. They're not from Utah. Most of these people, they're jumping on the bandwagon because we got to the Finals. You see it all around the country because everybody loves a winner, they don't care who it is. If we won a world championship you'd see our memorabilia fly out of the store— baseball caps, jackets, everything. And they'd all be saying "That's our team."

When you look at how far the Jazz have come as a franchise, they have a right to be proud—and the people of Utah have every right to be proud of them. I've had the privilege of broadcasting for them for 24 seasons and into their silver anniversary season. I'll be 64 years old when the 1998-99 season tips off and I'd like to keep doing play-by-play for the Jazz at least until I'm 70, at least as long as I'm healthy and can keep up with the game. It has been a great ride, especially in Utah, and it's been fun tagging along the whole way.

The Jazz and the NBA, you gotta love it, baby.

Appendix

ROD HUNDLEY'S CAREER STATISTICS

COLLEGE

Season	School	G	FG	FGA	%	FT	FTA	%	R	RPG	Pts	Avg.
1954-55	West Virginia	30	260	756	.344	191	255	.749	244	8.1	711	23.7
1955-56	West Virginia	30	218	326	.356	218	326	.669	392	13.1	798	26.6
1956-57	West Virginia	29	235	648	.363	201	254	.794	305	10.5	671	23.1
Totals		89	785	2218	.354	610	835	.731	941	10.6	2180	24.5

NBA

Season	Team	G	Min.	FG-FGA	%	FT-FTA	%	R	A	PF	Pts	rpg	apg	ppg
1957-58	Minn.	65	1154	174-558	.318	104-162	.642	186	121	99	452	2.9	1.9	7.0
1958-59	Minn.	71	1664	259-719	.360	164-218	.752	250	205	139	682	3.5	2.9	9.6
1959-60	Minn.	73	2279	365-1019	.358	203-273	.744	390	338	194	933	5.3	4.6	12.8
1960-61	L.A.	79	2179	323-921	.351	223-296	.753	289	350	144	869	3.7	4.4	11.0
1961-62	L.A.	78	1492	173-509	.340	83-127	.654	199	290	129	429	2.6	3.7	5.5
1962-63	L.A.	65	785	88-262	.336	84-119	.706	106	151	81	260	1.6	2.3	4.0
Totals NBA		431	9553	1382-3978	.347	861-1195	.721	1420	1455	786	3625	3.3	3.4	8.4
Playoffs		53	1020	101-316	.320	68-95	.716	149	157	80	270	2.8	3.0	5.1

1960 NBA ALL-STAR GAME

January 22, 1960 at Philadelphia

EAST 125, WEST 115

West All-Stars (115)

	Min	FG	FT	R	A	F	Pts.
Bob Pettit, St. Louis	28	4-15	3-6	14	2	2	11
Jack Twyman, Cin.	28	11-17	5-8	5	1	4	27
Walter Dukes, Detroit	26	2-10	0-1	15	1	3	4
Gene Shue, Detroit	34	6-13	1-2	6	6	0	13
Elgin Baylor, Minn.	38	10-18	5-7	13	3	4	25
Cliff Hagan, St. Louis	21	1-9	0-0	3	2	1	1
Chuck Noble, Detroit	11	0-5	0-0	1	3	1	0
Clyde Lovellette, St. L.	18	6-11	0-0	8	1	1	12
Rod Hundley, Minn.	23	5-12	0-0	3	2	2	10
Dick Garmaker, Minn.	23	5-11	1-2	4	3	1	11
TOTALS		50-121	15-26	72	24	19	115

East All-Stars (125)

	Min	FG	FT	R	A	F	Pts
Dolph Schayes, Syr.	27	8-19	3-3	10	0	3	19
Bill Russell, Boston	27	3-7	0-2	8	3	1	6
Wilt Chamberlain, Phil.	30	9-20	5-7	25	2	1	23
Bob Cousy, Boston	26	1-7	0-0	5	8	2	2
Richie Guerin, N.Y.	22	5-11	2-2	4	4	4	12
George Yardley, Syr.	16	5-9	1-2	3	0	4	11
Tom Gola, Philadelphia	20	5-13	2-3	4	2	3	12
Willie Naulls, N.Y.	26	5-19	3-4	10	0	1	13
Bill Sharman, Boston	16	8-21	1-1	6	2	1	17
Larry Costello, Syr.	20	5-9	0-0	4	2	1	10
Paul Arizin, Philadelphia DNP-Injured							
TOTALS		54-135	17-24	79	23	21	125

Coaches—East, Red Auerbach, Boston; West, Ed Macauley, St. Louis
MVP—Wilt Chamberlain, Philadelphia
Attendance—10,421

1961 NBA ALL-STAR GAME

January 17, 1961 at Syracuse

WEST 153, EAST 131

West All-Stars (153)

	Min	FG	FT	R	A	F	Pts
Elgin Baylor, L.A.	27	3-11	9-10	10	10	4	15
Clyde Lovellette, St. L	31	10-19	1-1	10	3	4	21
Bob Pettit, St. L.	32	13-22	3-7	9	0	2	29
Gene Shue, Det.	23	6-10	3-4	3	6	1	15
Oscar Robertson, Cin.	34	8-13	7-9	9	14	5	23
Wayne Embry, Cin.	8	2-4	0-0	3	0	0	4
Walter Dukes, Det.	17	3-6	2-2	4	1	4	8
Bailey Howell, Det.	16	5-10	3-4	3	3	4	13
Cliff Hagen, St. L.	13	0-2	2-2	2	0	1	2
Jerry West. L.A.	25	2-8	5-6	2	4	3	9
Rod Hundley, L.A.	14	6-10	2-2	0	2	1	14
TOTALS		58-115	37-47	55	37	30	153

East All-Stars (131)

	Min	FG	FT	R	A	F	Pts
Tom Heinsohn, Bos.	19	2-16	0-0	6	1	4	4
Dolph Schayes, Syr.	27	7-15	7-7	6	3	4	21
Wilt Chamberlain, Phil.	38	2-8	8-15	18	5	1	12
Bob Cousy, Boston	33	2-11	0-0	3	8	6	4
Richie Guerin, N.Y.	15	3-8	5-6	0	2	2	11
Paul Arizin, Phil.	17	6-12	5-6	2	1	4	17
Willie Naulls, N.Y.	16	4-6	0-1	6	2	2	8
Larry Costello, Syr.	5	1-2	0-0	0	0	2	2
Bill Russell, Boston	28	9-15	6-8	11	1	2	24
Tom Gola, Philadelphia	25	6-13	2-4	5	3	2	14
Hal Greer, Syracuse	18	7-11	0-0	6	2	2	14
TOTALS		49-117	33-47	63	28	30	131

Coaches—East, Red Auerbach, Boston; West, Paul Seymour, St. Louis
MVP—Oscar Robertson, Cincinnati
Attendance—8,016

Other Titles by Sports Publishing Inc.

The Greatest Moments in Utes Basketball History

The Greatest Moments in Utes Basketball History
by the editors of the Salt Lake City Tribune

In nearly one hundred years of tradition-rich basketball, the University of Utah has had thousands of moments that could be considered "potential candidates" for the top 50 moments being put together by Sports Publishing Inc. and the editors of the *Salt Lake City Tribune* in this new book scheduled for release in November of 1998. Find out which players, teams, and coaches made the cut. Also included will be a special feature section on head coach Rick Majerus, considered by many to be the top collegiate coach in America.

Fall 1998 • 250 pp • 150 photos • ISBN 1-58261-022-3 •$29.95

101 Little Known Facts About Karl Malone

Did you know that NBA Most Valuable Player Karl Malone's first basketball cost $2.98 which his mother obtained with a down payment of $0.75? This and 100 other facts are yours in this trivia-laden book.

1997 • 101 pp • 4 3/8 x 6 softcover • ISBN 57167-150-1 • $6.95

To Order Call 1-800-327-5557